Data Alchemy in the Insurance Industry

Data Alchemy in the Insurance Industry: The Transformative Power of Big Data Analytics

EDITED BY

SANJAY TANEJA

Graphic Era Deemed to be University, India

PAWAN KUMAR

Chandigarh University, India

REEPU

Chandigarh University, India

MOHIT KUKRETI

University of Technology and Applied Sciences-Ibri, Sultanate of Oman

AND

ERCAN ÖZEN

University of Uşak, Turkey

emerald PUBLISHING

United Kingdom – North America – Japan – India – Malaysia – China

Emerald Publishing Limited
Emerald Publishing, Floor 5, Northspring, 21-23 Wellington Street, Leeds LS1 4DL

First edition 2025

British Library Cataloguing in Publication Data
A catalogue record for this book is available from the British Library

ISBN: 978-1-83608-583-6 (Print)
ISBN: 978-1-83608-582-9 (Online)
ISBN: 978-1-83608-584-3 (Epub)

Printed and bound by CPI Group (UK) Ltd, Croydon, CR0 4YY

INVESTOR IN PEOPLE

Contents

About the Editors

Sanjay Taneja is an Associate Professor in Research at Graphic Era University in Dehradun, India, and an Affiliate Professor at Uşak University in Turkey. With a focus on areas such as Banking Regulations, FinTech, Sustainable Finance, and Environmental Finance, he holds a double Master's degree in management with a specialization in green finance and marketing. He completed his PhD in Banking and Finance and his postdoctoral degree on the impact of the European Green Deal on Carbon Emission in Turkey. He has published extensively in Scopus/Web of Science/SCI/ABDC/UGC Care Journals, with over 50 publications, including research papers, e-books, text books, and edited books. He has also published cases in Case Center, ABDC-B, and Scopus journals, and holds several patents. Dr Taneja has a strong academic record, with citations on Google Scholar and Scopus, and a history of participation in conferences and FDPs. He is frequently invited as a speaker and has served as a session chair, resource person, and judge at various conferences. He is known for his dynamic and positive approach, with a commitment to personal and professional growth.

Pawan Kumar has academic experience of 18 years and has done his PhD from Kurukshetra University, Kurukshetra. He has published more than 30 papers in national and international journals and has presented 35 papers in national and international seminars and conferences. He is also a Guest Editor in three journals (special issue of) indexed in Scopus. Furthermore, he has eight projects for the call for chapters from reputed publishing houses.

Reepu is an accomplished Associate Professor at Chandigarh University, India, with a PhD in Finance and a decade of academic expertise. Her extensive research contributions are showcased through numerous international and national conference presentations. Driven by innovation, she holds patents reflecting her commitment to advancing knowledge. Additionally, her publications in reputable journals indexed by Scopus, ABDC, and UGC CARE underscore her scholarly impact. With a rich blend of academic and research accomplishments, Dr Reepu is a dedicated professional who contributes significantly to the academic community and the field of finance.

Mohit Kukreti holds a PhD in Human Resource Development (HRD), with over 25 years of international expertise in roles such as higher education administration, academic quality assurance, and strategic planning for higher education institutions (HEIs). With a rich career, he has held academic leadership positions in Nepal, Ethiopia, and Sultanate of Oman. He had served as the Head of Departments, Program Director for the IBA Program at the Directorate General of six CAS Colleges in the Ministry of Higher Education in the Sultanate of Oman. He is presently associated with the recently established government's University of Technology and Applied Sciences (College of Economics and Business Administration-Ibri). Dr Kukreti's academic contributions extend to numerous articles and chapters published in peer-reviewed, ABDC and Scopus-indexed international Q1 journals and international books. His has participated and presented at conferences in the various countries. He has conducted various workshops, served as a session chair in conferences, undertaken editorial roles, and presently working as a reviewer for esteemed journals publishers such as Emerald, Routledge, IGI, and Inderscience. He has delivered talks at various universities, colleges and to the Ministry of Tourism officials, Government of India. His expertise extends to HEI quality assurance, HEI strategic Management, curriculum and courses designing at both undergraduate and postgraduate levels. He has lent his expertise as a PhD examiner at several universities in India. His research areas span HRD, Business Management, HEI's strategy development and quality assurance, entrepreneurship, and tourism.

Ercan Özen received his BSc in Public Finance (1994), MSc in Business-Accounting (1997), PhD in Business Finance (2008) from University of AfyonKocatepe. Now, he is a Professor of finance in department of Finance and Banking, Faculty of Applied Sciences, University of Uşak, Türkiye (Turkey). His current research interests include different aspects of finance. He served as the co-editor for books by eminent international publishing houses. And have publications more than 100, participated in many international conferences. He is a board member of five international conferences and workshops. Besides, chair of International Applied Social Sciences Congress. Co-editor of two international journals (Journal of Corporate Governance, Insurance, and Risk Management (JCGIRM) and Opportunities and Challenges in Sustainability (OCS)). The editor is also a certificated accountant, member of Agean Finance Association and member of TEMA (Turkey Combating Soil Erosion, for Reforestation and the Protection of Natural Resources Foundation).

About the Contributors

Anshul Agrawal is an Assistant Professor currently working at GNIOT Institute of Management Studies, India. She has a robust background encompassing eight in academia and corporate sectors, along with a dedicated tenure in research. Her specialization lies in finance, econometrics, time series analysis, security and derivative markets, and financial modeling. She has published her work in Scopus-indexed and ABDC category journals. She is proficient in various analytical tools such as SPSS, E-Views, Minitab, Microsoft Project Planner, and Advanced Excel.

Rachit Agarwal is working as an Assistant Professor at University School of Business, Chandigarh University, Mohali. He has more than 7 years of work experience in teaching and research. His areas of interest are financial analysis, investment behavior analysis, and behavioral study. He has published various papers in national and international journals including Scopus and ABDC listed journals. He has also organized many workshops and faculty development programs on Research Methodology and on different statistical tools.

Rakhi Arora is currently working as an Associate Professor of Finance at University School of Business, Chandigarh University, India. She has published research papers in ABDC category journals, Scopus-indexed journals, peer-reviewed journals, and chapters in Scopus-indexed edited books. She has a doctorate in Economics and Finance from University of Rajasthan, Jaipur. She has 15 years of experience in the Financial Services and Management Education Domain. Her area of specialization is finance and areas of interest in research are behavioral finance, financial services, and consumer behavior. She is a life member of Indian Commerce Association. She has presented papers in various national and international conferences and seminars. She has also attended national/international workshops and faculty development programs.

Mukul Bhatnagar is working as an Assistant Professor, University School of Business, Chandigarh University, Mohali, India. His areas of study are finance, banking, and insurance. He has more than 10 papers in Scopus and WOS database.

Vartika Bisht is a doctoral student at University School of Business, Chandigarh University, Mohali. She received her Master's of Commerce degree from Panjab University, Chandigarh. Her areas of interest are commerce and management, and she is engaged in research in the domain of marketing. She has participated in more than 70 workshops/FDPs and webinars. She has presented research papers at 12 national and international conferences till date and has 2 book chapters published with ISBNs.

Nasima Mohamed Hoosen Carrim is an Associate Professor at the University of Pretoria and the Chair for the Diversity and Inclusion Committee at the Economic and Management Sciences Faculty. She is also the President Elect (2023–2024) for the Society for Industrial and Organizational Psychology in South Africa (SIOPSA). Her research focuses on diversity and inclusion from an intersectionality and identity perspective. She has authored many articles in international journals such as in Gender, Work and Organization, The Journal of Men's studies among others. She has also published several book chapters in international publications such as in the Handbook on Diversity and Inclusion Indices: A Research Compendium, Research handbook on new frontiers of Equality and Diversity at work and others, including encyclopedia entries in The Wiley Blackwell Encyclopedia of Race, Ethnicity and Nationalism, and Oxford Research Encyclopedia of Business and Management. Prof Carrim sits on the Editorial Review Board for Equality, Diversity and Inclusion: An International Journal and is the Associate Editor for the Africa Journal of Management as well as the Section Editor for South African Journal of Industrial Psychology. She was a convenor for the Gender, Work and Organization conference that was held in Stellenbosch, South Africa, in 2023.

Bhupinder Pal Singh Chahal serves as an Adjunct Professor of Marketing at Yorkville University in Vancouver, BC, Canada, and concurrently holds roles as Faculty Administrator and Professor at Granville College, Vancouver. With a distinguished career spanning over 15 years in the realm of management education, he has established himself as a dedicated, accomplished, and respected academician and researcher. Dr Chahal's wealth of experience extends to conducting training and capacity-building programs at the national level. His innate expertise lies in team building, survey implementation, data analysis, competency enhancement, and strategic planning. With two international patents to his credit, Dr Chahal has demonstrated exceptional accomplishments in the realms of research and innovation.

Khem Chand is working as an Associate Professor in Mittal School of Business, Lovely Professional University, Phagwara, Jalandhar (Punjab). He has above 15 years' experience of academics and research. He holds an MCom, MBA (Marketing and HR), UGC-NET, JRF, and PhD in Management. He has completed PhD in regular mode from Guru Jambheshwar University of Science and Technology, Hisar (Haryana). He has worked as HOD in APIIT SD India, Panipat. He has published research papers in national and international journals.

Ajay Chandel is an Associate Professor at Mittal School of Business, Lovely Professional University, Punjab, who specializes in strategy and brand management. With 14 years of experience, he focuses on strategic management, business simulation, brand management, knowledge management, and social entrepreneurship.

He's contributed to Scopus and ABDC listed journals in topics like blockchain, branding, social media marketing, service quality, e-commerce, and consumer behavior. Additionally, he's published cases on SMEs and social entrepreneurship. He reviews for various journals including *The Case Journal*, *International Journal of Quality & Reliability Management*, and *Global Business Review*. He's developed E-content for MOOC on tourism marketing by EPG Pathshala and has undertaken consulting projects for companies like August Bioscience, Haveli Heritage Group, and VdoHire.

Abhishek Singh Chauhan is working as an Assistant Professor in Department of Management Studies, Graphic Era (Deemed to be University), Dehradun. He has extensive experience in teaching. He has published research papers in national and international journals.

Amit Gautam is an awardee of the Most Admiring Professor at the World Marketing Congress, Mumbai, 2021, and working as a Professor at Banaras Hindu University with a rich experience of more than 24 years in teaching, research, and consultancy. He has presented and contributed more than 60 research papers and articles in reputed national and international publications. He has completed various projects funded by UGC, Indian Oil, IOE BHU, and AICTE and has also published 10+ books from PHI, Himalaya Publishers, Excel Publishers, and ABC Publishing House. He is a reviewer of international publishers of repute, namely Sage, Emerald, Inderscience, and so forth.

Ashish Gupta is an Assistant Professor in the Department of Business Management, Maharishi University of Information Technology, Noida, UP. He has completed his PhD in Commerce, Department of Commerce, University of Lucknow, Lucknow, U.P (NAAC A++). He has qualified UGC-JRF in Commerce and UGCNET in Management. He has done MCom as well as MBA (Financial Management). He has published 18 research papers in different areas of commerce and management and has published in various national and international journals. He has been a resource person in many commerce- and management-related workshops. He is in the teaching profession for more than 6 years.

Munish Gupta is an Associate Professor at Chandigarh University's University School of Business. He focuses on behavioral studies, particularly in technology adoption. His research navigates people's and organizations' intricate decisions when encountering new technologies. He blends psychology, sociology, and economics to unravel these complex processes. Central to his studies is the cognitive aspect of adopting technology. He explores how people's thoughts, feelings, and beliefs shape their readiness to embrace new technological tools. His multidisciplinary approach combines information systems, psychology, and marketing knowledge to offer a well-rounded view of the factors influencing technology adoption. His work, documented in various studies, underscores the significance of usability, perceived benefits, and social influence in guiding decisions to adopt technology.

Swati Gupta is a dynamic individual with a doctoral degree and over 9 years of professional experience across various educational institutions and universities in diverse locations. She specializes in teaching subjects such as Consumer Behavior, Market Research, Marketing Management, Organizational Behavior, Sales and Distribution Management, Services Marketing, and Retail Management. Known for her energy and dedication, she possesses excellent analytical, problem-solving, and decision-making skills. Currently, she is working as an Assistant Professor at Chitkara Business School, Chitkara University, Punjab, India. Having served as the Editor for various books under renowned publishing houses including NOVA, Emerald, IGI Global, and AAP, she has contributed significantly to the academic field. Additionally, she has undertaken the role of a reviewer for IGI Global and has chapters indexed in Scopus covering topics in marketing, digital marketing, green business management, and consumer behavior, among others. Furthermore, she holds patent and copyrights under her name.

Amar Johri is an Assistant Professor in the College of Administrative and Financial Sciences at Saudi Electronic University, Dammam, Kingdom of Saudi Arabia since September 2019. He has more than 16 years of experience in academics. He obtained his doctorate (PhD) from Graphic Era University, Dehradun, Uttarakhand, India. His research interests include financial services, financial market, banking, investment, and accounting.

Dixit Kalra is an academician. He holds MBA and MCom degrees and is currently pursuing his PhD in Management from Punjabi University, Patiala, India. He has successfully cleared the UGC-National Eligibility Test for Lectureship (NET) twice. He has presented research papers at national and international conferences. In addition to it, he has written book chapters for international publishing houses and is also a reviewer with IGI Global. His research interests include AI in marketing, organic farming, sustainable marketing practices, and consumer behavior. He also contributed four book chapters on various topics.

Pawan Kumar has academic experience of 18 years and has done his PhD from Kurukshetra University, Kurukshetra. He has published more than 30 papers in national and international journals and has presented 35 papers in national and international seminars and conferences. He is also a Guest Editor in three journals (special issue of) indexed in Scopus. Furthermore, he has eight projects for the call for chapters from reputed publishing houses.

Sanjeet Kumar is an accomplished academician and researcher with a wealth of experience in the field of Business Administration. Dr Kumar currently serves as a Professor in the Department of Business Administration at Chaudhary Devi Lal University, Sirsa (India). In addition to his teaching responsibilities, he also holds significant administrative roles as the Director of the Incubation Center and the Director of Career Counseling and Industry Cell at the university. With over 16 years of experience in academia, Dr Kumar has made significant contributions to research and scholarship. He has successfully completed two research projects funded by the University Grants Commission, New Delhi. His dedication to research is evident through the publication of 46 research papers and the presentation of 33 papers at various national and international conferences and seminars. He has supervised nine PhD scholars to completion and is currently supervising three more. His commitment to academia, extensive research contributions, and dedication to student welfare makes Dr Sanjeet Kumar a respected figure in his field.

Tanya Kumar is working as an Assistant Professor at University School of Business, Chandigarh University, Mohali. She has work experience in teaching and research. She has completed her PhD in the area of Commerce from MAU, Baddi. Her areas of interest are financial analysis, investment behavior analysis, and behavioral study. She has published various papers in national and international journals including Scopus and ABDC listed journals.

Mehul Miglani is a dedicated Assistant Professor with a profound commitment to the higher education industry, demonstrated through continuous academic and professional achievements, currently serving at Chandigarh University. He has been significantly involved in research and teaching since December 2019. Mehul holds an M Com in Marketing and is pursuing a PhD in Commerce (HR) from the same university. He is a certified UGC NET JRF recipient, highlighting his expertise in commerce. Mehul's accolades include leading various academic workshops and seminars and contributing research papers focused on sustainable development and labor welfare. His strengths lie in communication, leadership, and maintaining high professional competence, which makes him an asset to his institution and his students.

Kaushal Kishore Mishra is working as a Professor of Marketing at the University School of Business, Chandigarh University, Mohali, Punjab. He has published 34 national and international research papers including five in Scopus-indexed journals, six book chapters Scopus indexed, and presented 29 papers at national and international conferences. He has four patent rights and three copyrights in his name. He has 24 years of teaching and research experience. He did his PhD in "Strategy formulation for marketing of services in rural Uttar Pradesh" from Uttar Pradesh Rajarshi Tandon University, Allahabad. He has guided two PhD scholars under his supervision.

Sunil Kant Mishra is working as a Professor in the Department of Commerce, CMP Degree College, University of Allahabad, Prayagraj, Uttar Pradesh, India. He specializes in HR and finance. He has more than 24 years of teaching experience.

Pawan Pant is working as an Associate Professor of Management at the University School of Business, Chandigarh University, Mohali, Punjab. He has published two research papers, one national and one international journal. He has 9 years of teaching experience and worked as an Assistant Manager (Purchase) at Pacific Industries Ltd., Udaipur (Rajasthan) for one year. His area of specialization is economics.

Priya is currently pursuing her PhD from Chandigarh University as a JRF research scholar. She has done her Bachelor degree as well as Master degree from Kurukshetra University Kurukshetra. She worked as an Assistant Professor for four years. She has attended and presented papers in more than 15 national and international conferences. She is an active researcher continuously contributing in the research field with her manuscripts.

Sonal Purohit, PhD, is an Associate Professor at Symbiosis Institute of Business Management in Marketing. She has served in several prestigious institutions in India over a period of 12 years. She has research publications in reputed journals such as the *Journal of Travel Research*, *Journal of Business Research*, *Technological Forecasting and Social Change*, *Journal of Retailing and Consumer Services*, and *Journal of Consumer Behavior*, among others. Her research interests include student engagement, technology adoption, services marketing, bottom of the pyramid marketing, teaching innovation, and social entrepreneurship.

Reepu is an accomplished Associate Professor at Chandigarh University, India, with a PhD in Finance and a decade of academic expertise. Her extensive research contributions are showcased through numerous presentations at both international and national conferences. Driven by innovation, she holds patents reflecting her commitment to advancing knowledge. Additionally, her publications in reputable journals indexed by Scopus, ABDC, and UGC CARE underscore her scholarly impact. With a rich blend of academic and research accomplishments, Dr Reepu stands as a dedicated professional contributing significantly to the academic community and the field of finance.

Kapil Sharma has more than 10 years of experience in teaching and administration and has completed the PhD in the year 2023 in Marketing. He has published more than five research papers in Scopus indexed journals.

Rajat Sharma is an Assistant Professor at Graphic Era Deemed to be University. He has achieved silver medal in Master's in Business Administration in the year 2021. He has several research papers and 7 patents published, and two are under the process of grant. His areas of interest include intellectual capital, mental wellbeing, psychology, etc.

Vikas Sharma is currently holding the position of Associate Professor at the University School of Business in Chandigarh University. His academic journey includes a specialized Master's in Business Administration (MBA) focusing on Finance, followed by a PhD in Management concentrated on Finance and Accounting, with a cumulative experience of 15 years in academia and professional spheres. His contributions encompass impactful research publications, showcasing his dedication to generating insightful content. In addition to his academic endeavors, he has cultivated competencies in administrative support and adeptly handles data analysis. He is actively pursuing an engaging opportunity within the finance sector to apply further and expand upon his expertise and capabilities.

Navpreet Kaur Sidhu is an Assistant Professor in Finance working at Chitkara Business School, Chitkara University, Punjab, India. A Former Banker who worked on the PAN India Project and represented it globally. Handled HNW1 clients and business houses and worked for business banking operations at Head Office in India. She is currently pursuing a Doctorate of Philosophy in Finance. She has presented research papers at national and international conferences and has written book chapters for international publishing houses and has also been a reviewer with IGI Global. She has also written and published an article for national newspapers and international journals. Her interest areas of research are climate finance, AI, machine learning, blockchain, and the like. Her dual experience in academia and industry puts her in a unique position to examine the integration of technology, particularly robo-advisors, into modern management approaches.

Animesh Singh is an Assistant Professor at the University School of Business, MBA department, Chandigarh University, Gharuan, Punjab. He has completed his MCom (Pure) and PhD from Lucknow University. He has also qualified for UGC NET (Commerce). He has more than eight years of work experience in finance. He has delivered lectures in more than 10 different institutions. He has also contributed to various research journals and books and has participated in multiple national and international seminars.

Divya Singh is currently working as a research scholar at Institute of Management Studies, Banaras Hindu University. She has authored a book entitled "Export Management". She has done MBA in International Business from Devi Ahilya University, Indore, Madhya Pradesh. She has qualified UGC NET and is also an ICSSR fellow. She has done research publications in journals of repute and presented research papers in various national and international conferences. She is dedicated towards conducting quality research and aspires to pursue her academic career in the field of international business.

Harvinder Singh is working as an Assistant Professor of Finance at the University School of Business, Chandigarh University, Mohali, Punjab. He has published eight national and international research papers including one in web of science indexed journals and one in an indexed book chapter and presented five papers at national and international conferences. He has 12 years of teaching and research experience. He did his PhD in Financial Inclusion from CT University, Ludhiana, Punjab. He has qualified for UGC–NET in Management as well as in Commerce.

Mandeep Singh is working as an Associate Professor, CSE, AIT APEX Chandigarh University, Mohali, India. His areas of research are computer sciences, management, and technology. Dr Mandeep Singh is an accomplished academician and technologist with a rich blend of academic and industry experience. With 14 years of dedicated service in academia, he has contributed significantly to the field of computer science education. Prior to his academic career, Dr Singh honed his skills in software development during his three-year stint in the industry. His expertise extends to system administration, where he spent another three years ensuring smooth operations in IT environments. Dr Singh's academic journey is distinguished by his prolific research output, with over 10 publications in Scopus-indexed journals. His academic qualifications include a Master's in Computer Applications (MCA), a Master's in Technology (MTech), and a Doctorate (PhD), reflecting his commitment to advancing knowledge in his field. Currently serving as an Associate Professor at Chandigarh University, Dr Singh continues to inspire and mentor the next generation of computer scientists while actively contributing to research and academic discourse.

Muskan Singh is a dedicated PhD scholar at Graphic Era University, specializing in a field yet to be explored. With a passion for research and a thirst for knowledge, she delves deep into her chosen subject, aiming to make significant contributions to academia. Her journey is marked by relentless curiosity, meticulous attention to detail, and an unwavering commitment to excellence. Outside academia, she is known for her creativity, resilience, and compassionate nature. Through her work, she aspires to inspire others and leave a lasting impact on her field. Muskan embodies the spirit of innovation and academic pursuit, shaping the future through her intellect and determination.

Rajesh Tiwari is working as a Professor, Academic Coordinator, and Chair Head-Finance in Graphic Era (Deemed to be University), Dehradun. He has over 20 years of rich experience in academics and industry. He holds an MBA (Finance), is a Chartered Financial Analyst (CFA), UGC-NET, and holds a PhD in Management. He has previously worked as Director in Indus University, Ahmedabad, United Group-Greater Noida (Affiliated to Guru Gobind Singh Indraprastha University, New Delhi), Sai Balaji Group-Pune. He has been Academic Coordinator for Management Programs of Staffordshire University, UK, and other reputed B Schools. He has published research papers in national and international journals.

Luan Vardari is an Assistant Professor of Finance in the Faculty of Economics at University "UKSHIN HOTI" Prizren. He received his Master's degree (MA) in Finance (Balkan Countries Stock Markets) in 2012 from Trakya University and finished his PhD in Business Administration at Trakya University in 2019. He teaches finance courses at graduate and undergraduate levels. His research interests include financial markets and institutions, portfolio optimizations, and international finance. Vardari is the Founder and the Editor-In-Chief of Prizren Social Science Journal and the Editor of book chapters and articles in national and international journals.

Azmee Zaheer is an Assistant Professor at the University School of Business, MBA department, Chandigarh University, Gharuan, Punjab. She has completed her PhD and MPhil in Management from Babasaheb Bhimrao Ambedkar University (A Central University) Lucknow, Uttar Pradesh. She received a Gold Medalist for MPhil's exemplary work. She has four years of research experience, 3.5 years of corporate experience in marketing, and 1.5 years of academic experience in marketing. She has also contributed to various research journals like Scopus, Web of Sciences, UGC Care, and Edited Book and has participated in multiple national and international seminars.

Foreword

I am excited and delighted to present "Data Alchemy in the Insurance Industry: The Transformative Power of Big Data Analytics." The insurance sector is poised for a significant upheaval in a time of unparalleled data proliferation and quickening advancements in technology. The capacity to leverage extensive data analyses' revolutionary potential has become an essential objective for insurers as they contend with changing client needs, competitive challenges, and regulatory demands.

A broad group of professionals and thought leaders wrote this groundbreaking book, which provides a thorough road map for negotiating the tricky nexus between data science and insurance. Each chapter offers priceless insights and doable techniques for realizing the complete potential of data analytics within the insurance ecosystem, from analyzing cutting-edge applications and developing patterns to comprehending the fundamentals of data alchemy.

Using cases, efficient methods, and valuable examples from the real world, "Data Alchemy in the Insurance Industry" gives readers the skills and information they require to thrive in a world that is becoming more and more data-driven. Whether the reader is a veteran looking to keep on top of things or a novice keen to learn how things work, this book provides a plethora of information and motivation for fostering creativity, improving judgment, and providing customers with real value.

I congratulate the writers for their commitment, knowledge, and enthusiasm in expanding the subject of data analytics in insurance as we start this amazing adventure together. This book will be a source of wisdom and motivation for policymakers, practitioners, researchers, and insurers as we use data alchemy's revolutionary potential to create a more robust, customer-focused, and profitable future for the insurance sector.

Dr Sanjeet Kumar
Professor
Chaudhary Devi Lal University, India

Preface

Welcome to "Data Alchemy in the Insurance Industry: The transformative power of Big Data Analytics." The insurance sector continues to evolve, and big data analytics has the potential to be highly revolutionary in this dynamic field where risk assessment, client interaction, and operation effectiveness are crucial. This book "Data Alchemy in the Insurance Industry: The transformative power of Big Data Analytics" explores the complex relationship between insurance and data science, revealing the alchemist techniques that transform unstructured data into valuable information and competitive advantages.

The insurance industry is facing never-before-seen data volumes, making utilizing this capability imperative rather than just advantageous. This book provides direction for industry experts, researchers, and others by using data analytics to shed light on how data may transform all aspects of insurance processes.

Each chapter examines the alchemy dynamics in action, including real-life instances, standards of excellence, and novel developments. Whether you're a seasoned finance professional, a data scientist, or an executive seeking to unlock new avenues for business optimization, this book provides an extensive outline for utilizing big data analytics to spur innovation, improve decision-making, and mold insurance prospects.

Moreover, by utilizing the knowledge of leading professionals, scholars, and scientists at the pinnacle of innovation based on data in insurance, this book builds a bridge between theorizing and doing. Readers obtain useful advice and state-of-the-art research synthesized into tactics for implementing data analytics solutions in their enterprises.

Eventually, "Data Alchemy in the Insurance Industry" is far greater than simply a book; it's a platform for creativity, an appeal to embrace statistics, and a guide for realizing the power of data analyses' fullest potential. Let's use the revolutionary potential of data alchemy to reimagine what is feasible in the insurance sector as we collectively set out on this adventure.

Introduction of the Book

Sanjay Taneja, Department of Management Studies, Graphic Era Deemed to be University, Dehradun, India
Reepu, Department of Management, Chandigarh University, Punjab, India

In an unprecedented digital revolution, the insurance industry has become a hub for innovative projects and prospects. Deriving relevant conclusions from the profusion of data – which is increasing in volume, pace, and diversity at an unfathomable rate – has become a critical strategic requirement for insurers worldwide. The blend of big data and analytics has surfaced as a transformative force in an ever-evolving terrain, enabling insurers to rethink conventional methods, streamline operations, and provide unmatched consumer value.

This book provides an extensive handbook for negotiating the complexities of innovation powered by data in the insurance industry against this background. This book reveals the alchemical methods that transform unprocessed data into tactical gold, empowering insurers to discover novel sources of worth, reduce risk, and promote economically viable expansion. It does this by synthesizing theoretical frameworks, case studies from the real world, and practical discernment.

This introduction lays the groundwork by examining the underlying theories of data alchemy and how it has revolutionized the insurance sector. We analyze the primary forces and patterns influencing the use of data analytics in various fields, including underwriting and more, drawing on the knowledge of notable experts and business pioneers.

In addition, this introduction presents readers with an overview of the book's organization and highlights the significant chapters and learning goals they might anticipate. Each chapter provides information and practical solutions for maximizing the transformative potential of big data analytics in the insurance industry, from comprehending the fundamental ideas of data science to navigating real-world obstacles and ethical dilemmas.

We warmly encourage readers to accompany us on this voyage of inquiry and revelation as we unravel the mysteries of data alchemy. We welcome a future in which data-driven innovation catapults the insurance sector to unprecedented resilience and success. By working together, being curious, and having an unwavering dedication to quality, we can fully utilize big data analytics to create a more promising future for insurers and insureds.

Chapter 1

Data Alchemy in Insurance: A Catalyst for Improving Financial Inclusion Levels and Insurance Penetration

Muskan Singh[a], *Rajat Sharma*[a] *and Mukul Bhatnagar*[b]

[a]Graphic Era Deemed to be University, India
[b]Chandigarh University, India

Abstract

Introduction: Data play a very significant role in solving the problem faced at micro and macro levels. Financial inclusion and insurance penetration have been a major problem of developing economies. These two economic indicators can be strengthened with the emergence of data alchemy.
Purpose: The present research study is conducted with the objective of measuring the impact of technological infrastructure, data alchemist techniques, and regulatory environment on insurance penetration and financial inclusion.
Methodology: To meet the research objectives, data were collected through a random sampling technique from the insurance agents in Mumbai, which can be considered the heart of insurance in India. On the data collected, the partial least squares (PLS) algorithm was applied using smart PLS software. PLS is a statistical method used for predictive modeling and analysis of complex data with multiple variables.
Findings: The final results revealed a significant relationship between data alchemy techniques and financial inclusion. Also, a significant impact on the financial inclusion level of the regulatory environment is also recorded. However, in a developing country like India, currently data alchemy techniques are not significantly impacting insurance penetration.

Keywords: Insurance; digitalisation; economic indicators; financial inclusion; tech infrastructure

Data Alchemy in the Insurance Industry, 1–12

doi:10.1108/978-1-83608-582-920241001

1. Introduction

By giving people and companies financial risk and safety reduction tools, the insurance sector significantly contributes to improving financial inclusion (Rafiuddin et al., 2023). Significant levels of insurance penetration and financial inclusion are still difficult to attain, particularly in emerging nations. Data alchemy in the insurance industry is the area where the future lies, thus bringing about some good in matters related to risk coverage (Kukreja, 2020). Data alchemy can be viewed as the creative synthesis of artificial intelligence (AI), machine learning, and big data analytics to the insurance industry to seek the pearls of insight in the sea of disparity data. Insurers may better know customers' flavor, tailor itineraries to different risk levels or population groups, and make it possible and reasonable to buy their services through data alchemy models (Patwardhan, 2018).

Knowledge alchemy in insurance represents a new generation of insurance in which insurers have shifted their data usage focus from apart to justifying their performance. In the past, insurance firms have always priced the policies and calculated risks with the help of actuarial formulas and statistics based on historical information. However, insurers operate now in an environment full of unstructured and structured data received from different data sources like social media, wearables, etc. as a result of the growth big data and training in advanced data analysis techniques as well(Sun, 2018). This kind of processing of the data with complex algorithms and models is called "data alchemy" and aims at uncovering hidden information in the patterns, trends, and insights that could be useful for decision-making. The insurance companies may exceed customer expectations, observe claims processing promptly, detect fraud more collectively, and design tailored products through data alchemy (Rawat et al., 2023).

The focus of this research study will be on the impact of data on insurance penetration and financial inclusion rates, with the industry under the insurance heading notably highlighted. The research study will address how insurers are adopting data alchemy techniques, the legal framework that governs the utilization of data in the insurance industry, and the technological systems which are needed to support insurance practices based on data mining (Sapovadia, 2018). Furthermore, in terms of the data alchemy technique, it will show how the quality of insurance products will perhaps be enhanced by way of reduced cost and better usability for broader users. This analysis is critical in that it could probably uncover ways through which information technology is efficient in promoting results that are advantageous for clients and businesses by enhancing access to financial services and insurance policies.

2. Literature Review

Local insurance firm, an insurance provider ensconced in the countryside of small hamlet sandwiched between undulating hills, is facing the following problem. Many people appeared to be uninsured even with the help of diverse insurance options and a poor knowledge about insurance being the prime cause for this entity (Rafiuddin et al., 2023). Insurance companies have indeed been determined to find a remedy, and historical data alchemy is the innovative strategy that it has come up with to stabilize the insurance sector using big data analytics as its backbone (Saygili & Ercan, 2020).

There has always been what is known as data magic, but it has not been in a brand-new form. However, Kukreja who is a scholar in this field have been, even before data analytics, discussing the pervasive power it has to completely redefine the industry of insurance (Kukreja, 2020). Insurers may provide specialized insurance products, given that they can develop them to match particular needs and make these products more affordable and relevant for the customers by utilizing large data volumes. The aforesaid data alchemy is beyond technology. Furthermore, it includes the purchase of suitable tech infrastructure as well as crossing through a myriad of enacted regulatory regimes because there are a myriad of enacted regulations (Tokutsu, 2020).

They even go through difficulties while the process of data transmutation has started. Security of the data and of the privacy also were blurred, besides authorities' doubts about the right regulation. In fact, insurance companies confer to legal advisors to determine what guidelines should be followed by the organization as well as they hire experienced information security experts to ensure that a modern data protection policy is implemented throughout the company (Dosso & Aysan, 2022).

As the results transformed the society, so did the head of the family, and every other member of the family in a revolutionary way. By means of the data alchemy, insurance companies were able to deliver targeted insurance covers that met the specific anticipation of their clients. One of the most important metrics, both in terms of cost and resolving claims, dropped mostly. In effect, a bigger number of people in the town join health insurance schemes, which raises the area's financial and insurance coverage as well as insurance prevalence (Alam et al., 2019).

To sum up, insurance companies' narrative management attention centers on the fact how data alchemy helps reach for enhanced financial inclusion and insurance coverage. Insurers may get advantage and better environment for their clients to work in this area by adopting data analytics and overcoming regulatory barriers; in the end, the industry will be more stable and also guarantee a safe future for everyone.

3. Research Methodology

For meeting the research objectives, conceptual model was framed based on the available review of literature. On identifying the significant variables, a questionnaire was framed on Likert scale and was made filled out by experts of 50 people. Once the questionnaire was validated by the experts, it was circulated to a larger sample set of 1,000 respondents containing insurance agents of Mumbai city. The reason behind choosing the city of Mumbai is because of its financial importance in the developing country like India. The head office that regulates all the insurance companies, i.e. IRDAI is located in Mumbai, and most of all head offices of insurance companies are located in this city. Out of 1,000 respondents, 190 people filled the questionnaire from which 29 were rejected because of incomplete information and seven were rejected because of repetition. The final sample size consisted of 154 respondents which can be considered appropriate as per the results of G*power software.

4. Data Analysis

The present section contains the results of the application of smart PLS software on the responses collected from the insurance agents.

5. Results

Fig. 1.1 contains the results of running the PLS algorithm on the frame conceptual model. In circles, there are variables, and in rectangles, there are items. Fig. 1.2 contains the results of bootstrapping the conceptual model.

Table 1.1 contains the results of measuring construct reliability and validity of the variables used in research is the first initiation toward drawing a conclusion through data analysis. The first indicator in the table is Cronbach alpha which have the cut-off rate of 0.75. Since all values of the given variables are greater than 0.75, the results can be considered reliable. Also, the last column contains average variance extracted, which has the cut-off rate of 0.5. Since all the values of the average variance extracted is greater than 0.5, data can be considered valid.

Table 1.2 contains the results of the heterotrait–monotrait (HTMT) ratio, which measures the discriminant validity between the constructs. Discriminant validity states that all constructs used in the research are different from each other. The cut-off rate for the same is 0.85, and since all values are less than 0.85, discriminant validity can be confirmed. Similarly, discriminant validity can be confirmed through the Fornell and Larcker criterion given in Table 1.3. However, the existence of discriminant validity is necessary between the items as well. The existence of discriminant validity in items of different variables is measured in Table 1.4 of cross-loadings. The results validate the difference among items.

Finally, Table 1.5 contains the results of hypothesis testing which contains the results regarding the significance of the relationship between the variables. Considering the first relationship which is measuring the impact of data alchemy techniques on financial inclusion levels, it can be observed that there is a statistically significant relationship between them as the *p*-value is 0.014. Also, there is a statistically significant influence of the regulatory environment on financial inclusion levels as their *p*-value is 0. All other relationships shown in the are found to be statistically insignificant as the p-value >0.05.

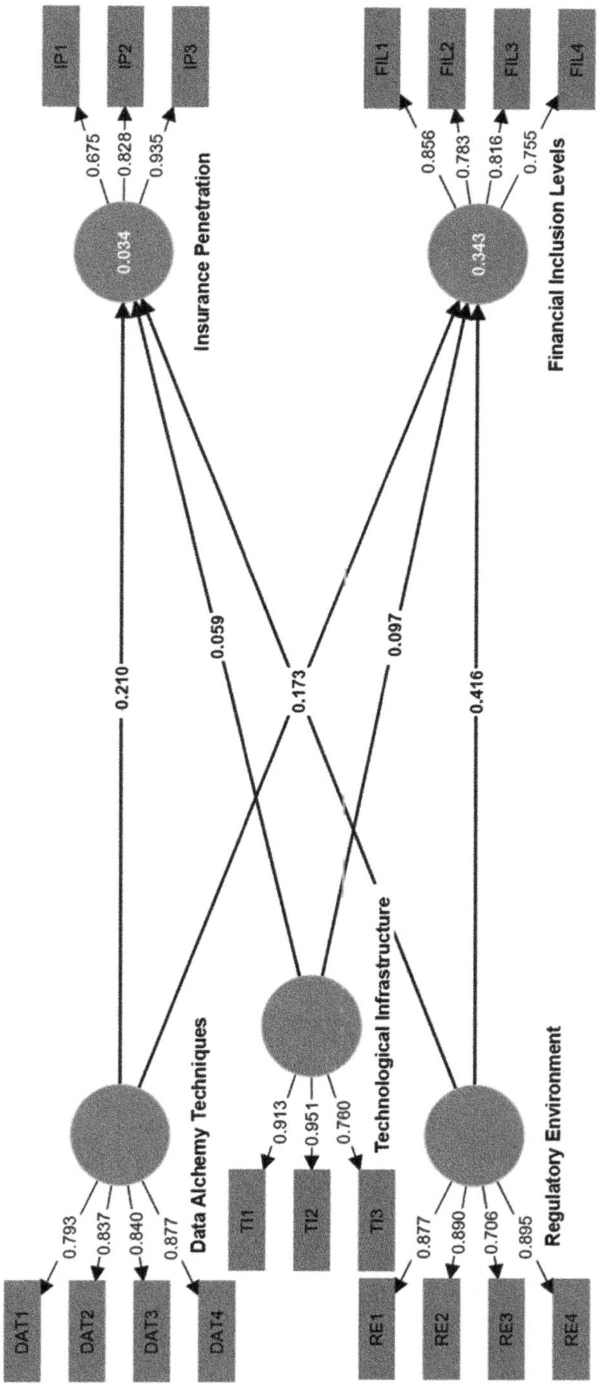

Fig. 1.1. PLS-Algorithm. *Source:* Author Compilations.

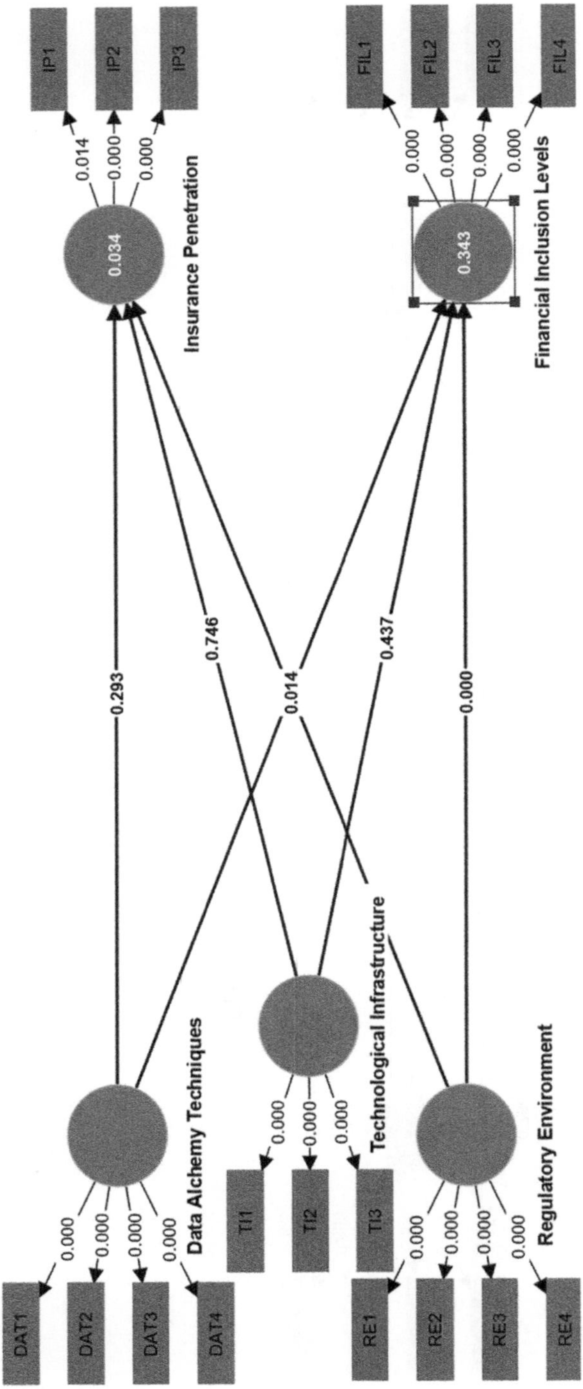

Fig. 1.2. Boot Strapping of Conceptual Model. *Source:* Author Compilations.

Table 1.1. Construct Reliability and Validity.

	Cronbach's Alpha	Composite Reliability (rho_a)	Composite Reliability (rho_c)	Average Variance Extracted (AVE)
Data alchemy techniques	0.859	0.888	0.904	0.701
Financial inclusion levels	0.825	0.87	0.879	0.646
Insurance penetration	0.834	0.641	0.858	0.671
Regulatory environment	0.868	0.914	0.909	0.715
Technological infrastructure	0.866	0.989	0.91	0.772

Source: Author Calculations.

Table 1.2. HTMT Inference.

	Data Alchemy Techniques	Financial Inclusion Levels	Insurance Penetration	Regulatory Environment	Technological Infrastructure
Data alchemy techniques					
Financial inclusion levels	0.513				
Insurance penetration	0.122	0.403			
Regulatory environment	0.68	0.577	0.096		
Technological infrastructure	0.666	0.332	0.105	0.765	

Source: Author Calculations.

6. Implications

Data alchemy in insurance is a real managerial challenge because it gives chances for the betterment of financial inclusion levels and insurance penetration that

Table 1.3. Fornell and Larcker Criterion.

	Data Alchemy Techniques	Financial Inclusion Levels	Insurance Penetration	Regulatory Environment	Technological Infrastructure
Data alchemy techniques	0.837				
Financial inclusion levels	0.499	0.804			
Insurance penetration	−0.075	0.294	0.819		
Regulatory environment	0.586	0.534	0.088	0.846	
Technological infrastructure	0.566	0.35	0.053	0.654	0.879

Source: Author Calculations.

Table 1.4. Cross Loadings.

	Data Alchemy Techniques	Financial Inclusion Levels	Insurance Penetration	Regulatory Environment	Technological Infrastructure
DAT1	0.793	0.302	−0.125	0.54	0.68
DAT2	0.837	0.359	−0.18	0.392	0.373
DAT3	0.84	0.421	−0.009	0.449	0.457
DAT4	0.877	0.535	0.015	0.574	0.445
FIL1	0.577	0.856	0.203	0.503	0.334
FIL2	0.213	0.783	0.316	0.342	0.16
FIL3	0.436	0.816	0.178	0.478	0.377
FIL4	0.233	0.755	0.325	0.332	0.177
IP1	0.106	0.275	0.675	0.065	0.129
IP2	−0.025	0.296	0.828	0.091	0.026
IP3	−0.08	0.247	0.935	0.071	0.071
RE1	0.604	0.509	0.064	0.877	0.624
RE2	0.407	0.411	0.035	0.89	0.538
RE3	0.489	0.272	0.003	0.706	0.633

Table 1.4. *(Continued)*

	Data Alchemy Techniques	Financial Inclusion Levels	Insurance Penetration	Regulatory Environment	Technological Infrastructure
RE4	0.49	0.54	0.152	0.895	0.487
TI1	0.545	0.324	0.015	0.581	0.913
TI2	0.518	0.372	0.093	0.637	0.951
TI3	0.417	0.103	−0.013	0.492	0.76

Source: Author Calculations.

together come as a synthesis with the potential to increase penetration levels in the insurance sector. Through use of big data and AI, insurers could obtain a larger amount of information on customers' interests and preferences helping them

Table 1.5. Hypothesis Testing.

	Original Sample (O)	Sample Mean (M)	Standard Deviation (STDEV)	T Statistics (|O/ STDEV|)	*P* Values
Data alchemy techniques → Financial inclusion levels	0.31	0.314	0.126	2.458	0.014
Data alchemy techniques → Insurance penetration	−0.21	−0.146	0.2	1.053	0.293
Regulatory environment → Financial inclusion levels	0.416	0.428	0.116	3.594	0
Regulatory environment → Insurance penetration	0.173	0.129	0.204	0.849	0.396
Technological infrastructure → Financial inclusion levels	−0.097	−0.102	0.125	0.777	0.437
Technological infrastructure → Insurance penetration	0.059	0.075	0.183	0.324	0.746

Source: Author Calculations.

understand and estimate their risks and come up with tailored products for those target groups which they did not serve before. This strategy is not only creating a larger customer pool for the company but also gives the administration a better rate of retaining its current clients by offering them a personalized experience. Furthermore, the insurers will be able to bring down their costs via data alchemy methods, which will also improve their risk estimating processes and detect frauds there by resulting in better profitability. Therefore, this method will help to create valuable partnerships with other areas such as the fin tech and telecom, so as to get to the bigger market and deliver original insurance products. Briefly, data alchemy is what has empowered the insurance sector with tools that make it easier to access, affordable and relevant to more people in the society. Moreover, it enables other stakeholders in the insurance sector to play their roles effectively in carving a niche toward the goal of insurance penetration. Ultimately, data alchemy is a critical component in realizing the wider harnessing of the insurance sector such that more members.

Social implications of the implementation of data alchemy in insurance are significant as it can lead to the increase of access and affordability to the insurance and thus the chances of financial exclusion get minimized. Through utilizing big data analytics and AI, insurance providers have a great opportunity to better understand the niche needs and the existing risks within the segment of the underserved population which comprises the low-income individuals and rural areas and then they can develop tailor-made insurance products that are customized to the specific requirements of the group. Besides this shields them of financial uncertainty creation, it also governs mental strength and independence among vulnerable communities. Also, data alchemy to some degree can make the economy get better not only by expanding insurance coverage but also by increasing financial inclusion. By doing this, data alchemy gives a safety net that clears the way for investment and business. Moreover, data alchemy implies in the process increased transparency and trust into the insurance sector because it helps getting more precise risk evaluation and price calculation which results in the exclusion of discrimination and consumer confidence growth. However, the societal pace of customer data use in insurance is remarkable, as it helps to take insurance to millions of people through the improvement of inclusion and fairness.

Data alchemy in insurance as a political implication has multiple attributes that may raise a flag to the attention of policymakers or regulators. The employment of sophisticated data analysis technologies and AI in insurance may result in improved regulation of the insurance industry, which is important for the job of the oversight bodies because precise checks of insurer statuses and identification of any risks are now possible. This, in turn, may create a strong and resilient insurance market, which is essential for safeguarding the soundness of the financial condition of a country. Furthermore, data alchemy implementation also encourages innovation in the insurance industry and consequently, the design of new products and services to meet the risks that do not exist today and also the social needs. Yet among the main issues concerns the issue of data privacy, security and ethics as personal data use in insurance raises questions related a to person's rights. Hence, political leaders must trade off the urge to harness innovation with protecting consumers, enabling the positive benefits of data alchemy in insurance to be utilized while any risks will be held in check through perfect regulations and oversight.

7. Conclusion

The results indicate that there are several key learnings regarding the relationship between data alchemy techniques, the regulatory environment, and financial inclusion levels. First, the use of data alchemy techniques has a statistically significant impact on financial inclusion, suggesting that advanced data analytics and AI can play a crucial role in improving access to financial services. Second, the regulatory environment also plays a significant role in shaping financial inclusion levels, highlighting the importance of regulatory frameworks in ensuring the accessibility and affordability of financial services. However, the study did not find any statistically significant relationships between financial inclusion levels and other variables, indicating that additional factors may need to be considered in understanding and promoting financial inclusion.

References

Alam, N., Gupta, L., & Zameni, A. (2019). Fintech and Islamic finance: Digitalization, development and disruption. In *Fintech and Islamic Finance: Digitalization, Development and Disruption*. Springer International Publishing. https://doi.org/10.1007/978-3-030-24666-2

Dosso, M., & Aysan, A. F. (2022). The technological impact in finance: A bibliometric study of fintech research. *Eurasian Studies in Business and Economics*, *22*, 193–209. https://doi.org/10.1007/978-3-030-94672-2_12

Kukreja, G. (2020). FinTech adoption in China: Challenges, regulations, and opportunities. In *Innovative Strategies for Implementing FinTech in Banking*. IGI Global. https://doi.org/10.4018/978-1-7998-3257-7.ch010

Patwardhan, A. (2018). Financial inclusion in the digital age. In *Handbook of Blockchain, Digital Finance, and Inclusion, Volume 1: Cryptocurrency, FinTech, InsurTech, and Regulation*. Elsevier Inc. https://doi.org/10.1016/B978-0-12-810441-5.00004-X

Rafiuddin, A., Gaytan, J. C. T., Mohnot, R., Sisodia, G. S., & Ahmed, G. (2023). Growth evaluation of fintech connectedness with innovative thematic indices – an evidence through wavelet analysis. *Journal of Open Innovation: Technology, Market, and Complexity*, *9*(2), 100023. https://doi.org/10.1016/j.joitmc.2023.100023

Rawat, R., Sharma, S., & Goyal, H. R. (2023). Intelligent digital financial inclusion system architectures for industry 5.0 enabled digital society. In *Winter Summit on Smart Computing and Networks. WiSSCoN 2023*. https://doi.org/10.1109/WiSSCoN56857.2023.10133858

Sapovadia, V. (2018). Financial inclusion, digital currency, and mobile technology. In *Handbook of Blockchain, Digital finance, and inclusion* (Vol. 2). Elsevier Inc. https://doi.org/10.1016/B978-0-12-812282-2.00014-0

Saygili, E., & Ercan, T. (2020). An overview of international fintech instruments using innovation diffusion theory adoption strategies. In *Innovative Strategies for implementing FinTech in Banking*. IGI Global. https://doi.org/10.4018/978-1-7998-3257-7.ch003

Sun, T. (2018). Balancing innovation and risks in digital financial inclusion-experiences of ant financial services group. *Handbook of Blockchain, Digital Finance, and Inclusion, 2*, 37–43. https://doi.org/10.1016/B978-0-12-812282-2.00002-4

Tokutsu, A. (2020). The 'independence day' of payments law? Fintech's impact on financial regulation in Japan. *Perspectives in Law, Business and Innovation*, 139–162. https://doi.org/10.1007/978-981-15-5819-1_8

Chapter 2

Unlocking the Power of Big Data in Insurance: The Role of Data Analytics

Divya Singh and Amit Gautam

Banaras Hindu University, India

Abstract

Introduction: The current study provides a conceptual base for big data analytics in the insurance industry that might be useful for academics, researchers, and practitioners conducting future studies in the respective field.
Purpose: This study intends to investigate the transformative impact of big data analytics in the insurance industry. It elaborates on how advanced data analytics techniques are reshaping the insurance landscape, from customer acquisition and retention to risk modeling, pricing, and claims management.
Methodology: The current study incorporates a thorough review of existing literature, industry reports and academic articles related to big data analytics in the insurance sector. The aim is to develop an in-depth comprehension of the subject by synthesizing key insights and trends.
Findings: The findings underscore the evolutionary potential of the insurance sector through big data analytics, emphasizing its role as a catalyst for innovation, efficiency, and growth. Embracing data-driven strategies is essential for insurers to adapt to evolving market dynamics, meet customer expectations, and maintain a competitive edge in the digital age.

Keywords: Insurance industry; big data; big data analytics; predictive analytics; insurance transformation

1. Introduction

The insurance industry contributes to economic expansion in three ways: enabling protection, capital formation, and increased trade (Saeed & Arshed, 2023). More than USD 6 trillion was brought in by the insurance industry globally in 2022

Data Alchemy in the Insurance Industry, 13–26

Published under exclusive licence by Emerald Publishing Limited
doi:10.1108/978-1-83608-582-920241003

which is an increment of about 10% from 2021, a sum that doubles the oil industry's intake and surpasses the gross domestic product (GDP) of some of the largest economies in the world which includes the United Kingdom (UK), India, Japan, Germany, Italy, Canada, and France (Hassani, Beneki, et al., 2020). By 2026, it is expected that the market will grow to nearly 8.4 trillion USD, with a compound annual growth rate of about 9% per year (Statista, 2024).The insurance industry is subjected to dynamism, and in today's rapidly evolving landscape, big data analytics, with its revolutionary potential for innovation and efficiency, has become an essential component of the industry. Due to the extensive growth of data and the widespread use of digital technologies, insurers are using advanced analytics techniques to extract useful information from large and complicated datasets (Ellili et al., 2023). Also, the insurance industry is growing its reliance on advanced technologies like big data, machine learning, and AI as the sector is dependent upon statistical methods of risk analysis (Frees & Huang, 2023).The insurance industry is transformed by big data analytics from the base, impacting every step of the value chain, from risk assessment and underwriting to claims management and customer engagement. To improve risk pricing and customize policies for individual customers, insurance organizations are utilizing analytics based on big data to compile and analyze data from a variety of sources, both structured and unstructured (Banu, 2022). Insurers can retain more customers and improve relationships with existing ones by analyzing consumer behavior patterns and using that information to create personalized policies and marketing campaigns (Rana et al., 2022). By harnessing the power of data alchemy, insurers can improve their ability to detect fraud and streamline these operations, leading to lower costs and improved customer satisfaction (Hassani, Beneki, et al., 2020). Embracing big data analytics is essential for insurers aiming to maintain a competitive edge in this ever-evolving market. As we delve deeper into the transformative potential of data alchemy, the advent of big data represents more than just a revolution; it signifies a paradigm shift that will alter the course of the insurance industry's future.

2. Global Insurance Industry

The insurance industry plays an important social and economic role by providing financial protection for individuals and businesses in the event of unforeseen events. Also, it is an important part of the economy due to the size of premiums collected and investments made. The insurance industry endures the effects of growing global risks, both in terms of number and cost, caused by factors like cybercrime and climate change. In 2023, the global insurance market has been valued at more than six billion USD, and it is expected to grow significantly in the coming years (Statista, 2024) (Fig. 2.1). In the view of risk management professionals around the world, cybercrime poses the greatest threat to the businesses. Losses due to natural disasters have also increased in cost over the last 20 years. The sustainability of the insurance industry will be supported by the likelihood that these risks will increase in the years to come (Rudden, 2023b). In terms of

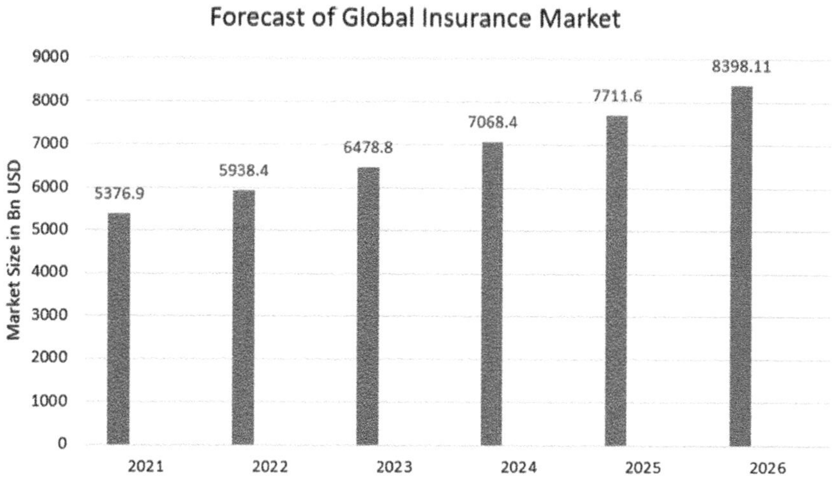

Fig. 2.1. Size of Global Insurance Market. *Source:* http://www.statista.com

market size, the USA is the largest insurance market in the world. The United States' (US) insurance market saw the highest value of life and non-life direct premiums in 2022. In terms of market size, China was the second biggest, although the US market was over four times larger than China's. After the US, the insurance markets of the UK, Germany, Japan, and France ranked highest among the Organization for Economic Co-operation and Development (OECD) countries. In terms of market capitalization, insurance companies from these nations were among the biggest globally (Rudden, 2023c).

US-based insurers dominated the global insurance market by market capitalization. With revenues of more than 458 billion USD in 2023, American insurer United Health is the largest insurer in the world. The remaining two insurance giants were Chinese firms, China Life Insurance and Ping An Insurance (Rudden, 2023a).

3. Big Data

In today's time, it becomes nearly impossible to design, monitor, and evaluate effective policies without reliable and high-quality data that address the appropriate issues at the right time. Therefore, data is regarded as a crucial element for decision-making and serves as the foundation for accountability. In the 21st century, data has taken center stage due to the massive amount of data being generated. These data are playing a pivotal role in the transformation of markets and industries by creating a new "digital universe." There was a record-breaking influx of new and duplicated data in the year 2020, where the amount of data generated, stored, transferred, and used on a global scale went from 41 zettabytes to 64.2. zettabyte, and by 2025, the same will rise upto 180 zettabyte (Taylor, 2023b) (Fig. 2.2). The advent of a new age, "Big data," is defined by this digital information generated from intricate and diverse data that can originate from any point and at any moment (Vassakis et al., 2018).

"Big data" can be used as a hypernym which covers different range of data, technologies and applications. Big data has been a challenging concept to define, both formal and informal definitions of big data exist, sharing their set of similarities and differences (Bedi et al., 2014; Demchenko et al., 2013), but in general, it is used to describe the gathering, transforming, analyzing, and illustrating extremely large datasets. It can also be defined as datasets that are so large that they cannot be adequately processed, stored, or analyzed using conventional software. Big data refers to structured and unstructured datasets that are both extremely large and dynamic, indicating their expansion both in terms of size and pace (Balne, 2020).

Organizations that want to be data-driven rely on big data as a foundation because it allows them to make informed choices that improve operational efficiency and strategic foresight. Businesses can enhance their decision-making processes by discovering hidden patterns and insights in vast datasets through effective management and analysis (Shrestha et al., 2021).The flexibility that comes with processing data in real-time, also allows for innovation and adaptation, which accelerates the development and deployment of new features and products (Zicari, 2014).The continuous intelligence process ensures constant discovery of growth opportunities through the seamless integration of automated data streams and advanced analytics.

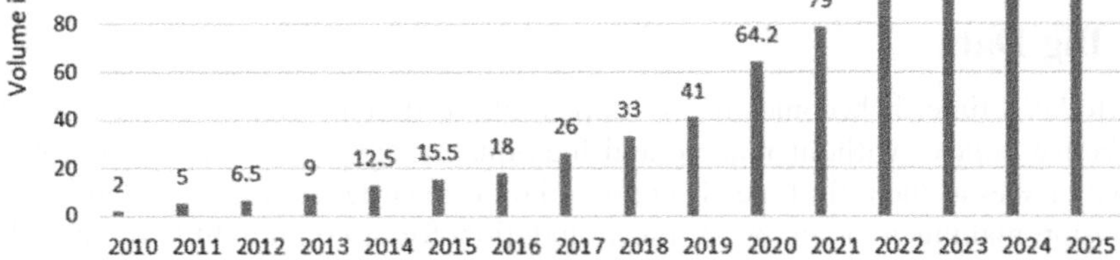

Fig. 2.2. Volume of Data Created, Captured, Copied, and Consumed Worldwide. *Source:* http://www.statista.com

4. Big Data Challenges

To fully realize the potential of big data, despite the fact that the benefits are factual and significant, there are a multitude of difficulties that need to be addressed as it is hard to understand what exactly constitutes a big dataset because what seems enormous now will certainly seem smaller in the future (Ekbia et al., 2015). There are several challenges regarding big data which are subject to its own characteristics, models and methods of analysis and present a data analytics system (Jin et al., 2015; Vassakis et al., 2018). The existing literature on challenges related to big data has focused on problems with defining dig data, deciding what data to generate, and collect, and privacy and ethical concerns related to data mining. Companies are constantly improving their approaches in order to tackle the challenge of creating a viable solution for complex and massive amounts of data. A human analyst is often needed to sort through data in order to build useful information. Another significant challenge is that, although the computing capabilities needed to process these data are rapidly improving, the human skills and knowledge that are required to fully utilize big data are falling behind (Crawford, 2013; Hargittai, 2015; Lazer et al., 2009; Tole, 2013; Zicari, 2014). Data, processes, and management challenges have been put together according to the data life cycle which comprises the three main groups into which the overall challenges of big data fall (Fig. 2.3). Data challenges are related to the features of the data (data volume, velocity, quality, veracity, volatility, variety, discovery, and dogmatism); process-related challenges are the relevant techniques for capturing, integrating, transforming, and selecting the optimal model for analysis and providing the results of the data. Management challenges cover the aspects of security, privacy, ethics, and governance (Akerkar, 2014; Zicari, 2014).

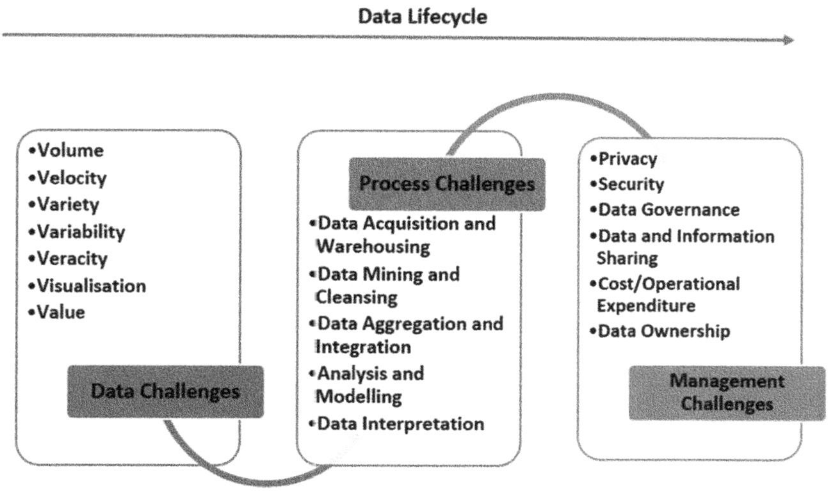

Fig. 2.3. Big Data Challenges. *Source:* Adapted from Akerkar (2014); Zicari (2014).

5. Big Data Analytics

The term "big data analytics" pertains to the intricate mining process of massive datasets for useful information that can guide strategic decision-making. These data may contain previously unseen correlations, patterns, market trends, or consumer preferences. Big data analytics includes applying advanced analytic methods for diverse and big datasets ranging in size from terabytes to zettabytes. These sets may contain structured, semi-structured, and unstructured data as well as information gathered from a variety of sources (Himeur et al., 2023).

The application of analytics to the decision-making process is nothing new; in fact, business analytics first emerged in the mid-1950s, Analytics 1.0, alongside the tools as a result of which business intelligence tools could generate and store more data in enterprise data warehouses and identify patterns at a rate that exceeded that of human brains (Vassakis et al., 2018). When it came to making decisions, managers in that first era reached a level of data-based comprehension that went beyond intuition. Up until the middle of the 2000s, businesses had to wait for a new phase, Analytics 2.0, to arrive before they could take advantage of the opportunities presented by the exponential proliferation of datasets and the rise of big data. The big difference between eras is the expertise needed for data analysis, which is why businesses acted swiftly to acquire the skills and knowledge needed to glean insights from big data as soon as the need for new, innovative technologies arose (Davenport, 2013). The succussing era known as Analytics 3.0 or the "data economy" is defined by a massive increase in the generation of data caused by the expansion of the Internet of Things (IoT) with about 8.4 billion connected devices in the year 2017 characterized by developing goods and services that are based on analytics (Vailshery, 2023) (Fig. 2.4). Machine learning and other

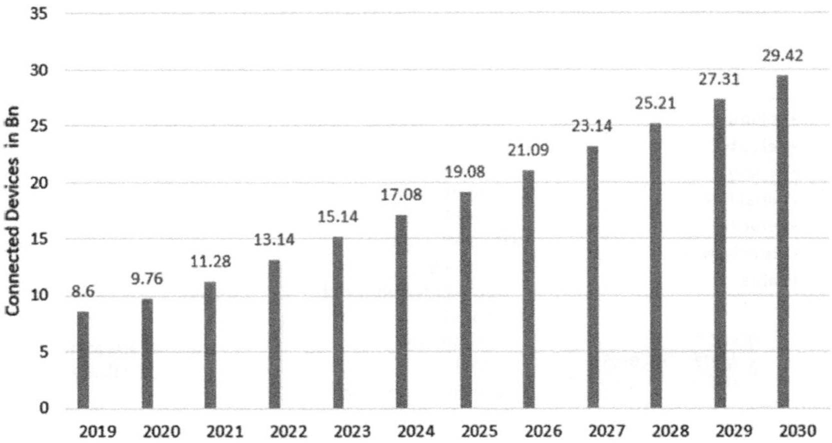

Fig. 2.4. Number of IoT Connected Devices Worldwide. *Source:* http://www.statista.com

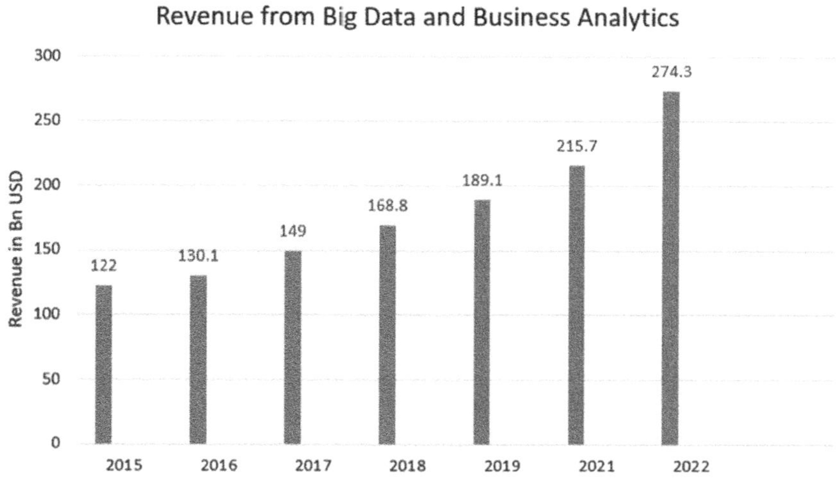

Fig. 2.5. Revenue From Big Data and Business Analytics Globally. *Source:* http://www.statista.com

cognitive technologies are part of the newest analytics era, Analytics 4.0, which is all about augmenting human decision-making and action with dynamic machine automation (Soori et al., 2023). Enterprises and organizations in the modern analytics era must overcome technological challenges to gain greater access to quality data, as new technologies are constantly increasing data generation. In the year 2022, the worldwide market for big data and business analytics had been estimated for more than 270 billion USD, with the leading sectors investing in this space, being manufacturing, government, banking, and professional services (Taylor, 2023a) (Fig. 2.5).

Hence, businesses must focus their efforts on extracting value from data by means of analytical methods and techniques (Gavin, 2019). In order to gain a competitive edge through the introduction of new and improved products, businesses can use big data analytics to analyze trends and find new ones. Decision-making that is derived from data makes a significant and positive impact on the productivity and profitability of a business (Niu et al., 2021). Advances in performance can be achieved through the use of big data analytics for making predictions, greater ROI, reduced risk, and more transparency because big data provides in-depth knowledge about an organization's various departments.

6. The Role of Big Data Analytics in Insurance Transformation

As the insurance industry continues to become more digitized, a significant increase in the amount of data that is being generated as a result of customers conducting product research, reviews, and comparisons online is observed (Brown

& Goolsbee, 2002).The insurance value chain has undergone a paradigm shift as a result of the exponential growth in data volume. Insurers are now utilizing advanced analytical tools to derive meaningful insights and make informed decisions. To improve operational efficiency and effectiveness, insurers can optimize resource allocation and budgeting by scientifically deconstructing the results of various activities and campaigns (Bose, 2009). Insurance companies' data repositories have been even more enriched by the proliferation of end-to-end servicing and sales channels in general, health, and life insurance, which has given analytics-driven strategies a valuable feed. Claims modeling, catastrophe modeling, rating algorithms, and fraud detection are just a few areas where data analytics is making impacts in the insurance industry (Mckinsey Analytics, 2016).The rate of adoption is different across industries, though, and some are moving more slowly than others. Insurers are enhancing their analytical capacities by utilizing open data sources offered by government agencies. These sources include massive datasets on energy, worker safety, education, and health (Eckert & Osterrieder, 2020). Insurers are also encouraged to take a strategic approach by data analytics, which leads them to reevaluate their distribution channels, business models, and product offerings along with risk assessment, product development, and customer service strategies (Rana et al., 2022). Furthermore, it stresses the significance of data protection policies and strong data governance frameworks for protecting sensitive customer information and maintaining trust in data handling procedures. By embracing analytics, insurers can better navigate this data-rich landscape, discover new growth opportunities, and fulfill the changing needs of their stakeholders and customers with value-driven solutions (Banu, 2022).

7. The Types of Data in Insurance Industry

Tools for predictive analytics, pattern recognition, and machine learning have recently arisen as potent resources that, when strategically used, can generate substantial business impact. But moving from just being aware of these capabilities to actually do something useful with them calls for a methodical and well-informed strategy, which calls for early engagement and dedication (Jin et al., 2015). The four main categories of big data analytics – prescriptive, predictive, diagnostic, and descriptive – produce useful insights that may influence organizational performance and strategic decision-making.

7.1 Prescriptive Data Analysis

This type of analysis delves into determining optimal actions and recommendations for future strategies. In order to improve their strategic decision-making processes, organizations can use prescriptive analytics to build calculated plans and perform scenario-based "what-if" analyses (Lepenioti et al., 2020). By revealing the best actions to take in different scenarios, these insights not only help with product design and strategy development, but they also optimize operations for the insurers.

7.2 Predictive Analytics

Predictive analytics focuses on forecasting likely future scenarios based on historical data patterns (Seyedan & Mafakheri, 2020). It is revolutionizing the insurance industry, especially in the underwriting and risk assessment processes. Insurers can optimize profitability and reduce losses by predicting risks and recognizing emerging trends to make well-informed decisions. Predictive analytics in health insurance can help identify and treat health conditions early, leading to cost savings and better outcomes for patients.

7.3 Diagnostic Data Analysis

Diagnostic analysis involves examining past performance to identify underlying reasons and factors contributing to outcomes. In order to assess performance, spot trends, and comprehend the reasons behind achievements or setbacks, this sort of analysis is valuable (Ridzuan & Wan Zainon, 2021). A number of areas of the insurance industry operations can be aided by diagnostic analysis. These include staff performance reviews, claims data trend analysis, and the discovery of measures to enhance customer service.

7.4 Descriptive Data Analysis

Descriptive analysis, on the basis of past performance, summarizes the historical data for formulating future strategies. Organizations can optimize their business processes and make better decisions by analyzing large datasets to learn more about past trends, successes, and problems (Hussain & Lee, 2016). Marketing, sales, operations, and finance are just a few of the insurance industry's functional areas that can benefit from descriptive analysis when it comes to optimizing premiums, planning contracts, and making strategic decisions.

8. Data Analytics in Insurance

Data are vital to the insurance industry because key decisions are based on the insights gained from comprehensive analyses. In order to find useful information to back up strategic initiatives, big data analysis – a systematic process of organizing and evaluating raw and big data – is crucial (Saeed & Arshed, 2023). Insurers in the modern digital era are banking on data analytics to revolutionize their industry and overcome persistent issues. A new era of possibilities is dawning for insurers as big data projects, driven by innovations in sensor networks and natural language processing, are revolutionizing the way data is collected and transformed (Thayyib et al., 2023). Key focus areas across all lines of insurance include customer acquisition and retention, risk modeling and pricing, and claims management.

8.1 Customer Acquisition and Retention

It is critical for insurers to acquire and keep customers in order to maintain growth and profitability. Insurers can benefit from more targeted and personalized marketing strategies by gaining deeper insights into customer behavior, preferences, and needs through data analytics. Insurers can find highly engaged market segments by analyzing demographic data, buying habits, and communication preferences and then craft messages that are specific to those segments (Campbell et al., 2020).

The insurers can optimize their customer acquisition channels through data analytics. This includes both digital and traditional channels, including websites, social media, and mobile apps, in addition to more traditional ones like agents and brokers. Insurance companies can narrow their marketing efforts to reach the most receptive customers by using predictive analytics to determine which demographics are most likely to buy (Bose, 2009).

Insurers can enhance customer satisfaction and loyalty by proactively addressing the issues identified through the analysis of customer feedback, service interactions, and claims history (Rane, 2023). The personalized communication and offerings with data-driven insights can strengthen customer relationships and increases long-term retention rates.

8.2 Risk Modeling and Pricing

The insurance industry relies on risk modeling and pricing in order to accurately evaluate risks and price them in a way that ensures profitability. Insurers can improve their risk modeling skills with the help of data analytics by utilizing advanced statistical methods and machine learning algorithms (Hassani, Unger, & Beneki, 2020).

The risk prediction and quantification models can be improved by studying past data, including claims data, demographic information, and external variables like economic trends and natural disasters (Wagenaar et al., 2020).With the help of these models, insurers can set more reasonable rates for their policies, reflecting the actual risk that each policyholder faces.

In addition, insurers are able to modify their risk models in response to new trends and shifting market conditions with the help of data analytics. Insurers can stay competitive and profitable by adopting dynamic pricing strategies that reflect changing risk profiles and market dynamics (Mills, 2009). This is made possible by leveraging real-time data streams and predictive analytics.

8.3 Claims Management

Processing, evaluating, and settling insurance claims are all parts of claims management, which is an essential part of the insurance industry. Claims management processes can be made more efficient and accurate with the help of data analytics. Insurance companies can mitigate fraudulent activities and financial losses by analyzing claim data and patterns to find possible fraud indicators and detect anomalous claim behavior (Wang et al., 2018).

In addition, insurers can better allocate resources and guarantee adequate reserves to fulfill future claim obligations with the help of data analytics, which enables more accurate loss reserving and claim forecasting (Fang et al., 2016).

Data analytics can be used to improve customers' claims experiences by making the claims process more efficient, cutting down on processing times, and increasing communication and transparency.

9. Conclusion

The incorporation of big data analytics into the insurance sector represents a significant transformation in the manner in which insurers conduct their business and provide service to their clients. Insurers are utilizing data analytics to improve various aspects of their business, including customer acquisition and retention, risk modeling and pricing, and claims management. This is made possible by the exponential growth of data as well as advancements in technology. Insurers can better cater their products and services to each customer's unique needs by gaining valuable insights into customer behavior, preferences, and needs through data analysis. In addition, insurers can boost operational efficiency and profitability with data analytics by improving the accuracy of risk assessments, optimizing pricing strategies, and detecting fraudulent activities. Embracing big data analytics is crucial for insurers to stay competitive and address the evolving needs of stakeholders and customers in the changing insurance industry. The shift towards data-driven decision-making in the insurance industry promises a future where innovation, efficiency, customer-centricity, and risk management are interconnected.

References

Akerkar, R. (2014). *Big data computing*. CRC Press, Taylor and Francis Group.

Balne, S. (2020). Analysis on research methods in bigdata applications. *Nternational Journal of Innovative Research in Computer and Communication Engineering*, *8*(10), 4059–4063. https://doi.org/10.2139/ssrn.3734043

Banu, A. (2022). Big data analytics – tools and techniques – application in the insurance sector. In K. Sood, R. K. Dhanaraj, B. Balusamy, S. Grima, & M. Uma (Eds.), *Big data: A game changer for insurance industry (Emerald Studies in Finance, Insurance, and Risk Management)* (pp. 191–212). Emerald Publishing Limited. https://doi.org/10.1108/978-1-80262-605-620221013

Bedi, P., Jindal, V., & Gautam, A. (2014). Beginning with big data simplified. In *2014. International Conference on Data Mining and Intelligence Computing (ICDMIC)* (pp. 1–7). http://doi.org/10.1109/ICDMIC.2014.6954229

Bose, R. (2009). Advanced analytics: Opportunities and challenges. *Industrial Management & Data Systems*, *109*(2), 155–172. https://doi.org/10.1108/02635570910930073

Brown, J. R., & Goolsbee, A. (2002). Does the Internet make markets more competitive? Evidence from the life insurance industry. *Journal of Political Economy, 110*(3), 481–507. https://doi.org/10.1086/339714

Campbell, C., Sands, S., Ferraro, C., Tsao, H. Y. (Jody), & Mavrommatis, A. (2020). From data to action: How marketers can leverage AI. *Business Horizons, 63*(2), 227–243. https://doi.org/10.1016/j.bushor.2019.12.002

Crawford, K. (2013). The hidden biases of big data. *Harvard Business Review Blog*. http://blogs.hbr.org/2013/04/the-hidden-biases-in-big-data/

Davenport, T. H. (2013). Analytics 3.0. *Harvard Business Review*. https://hbr.org/2013/12/analytics-30

Demchenko, Y., Grosso, P., De Laat, C., & Membrey, P. (2013). Addressing big data issues in scientific data infrastructure. In *International Conference on Collaboration Technologies and Systems (CTS)* (pp. 48–55). 40–55. http://doi.org/10.1109/CTS.2013.6567203

Eckert, C., & Osterrieder, K. (2020). How digitalization affects insurance companies: Overview and use cases of digital technologies. *Zeitschrift Fur Die Gesamte Versicherungswissenschaft, 109*(5), 333–360. https://doi.org/10.1007/s12297-020-00475-9

Ekbia, H., Mattioli, M., Kouper, I., Arave, G., Ghazinejad, A., Bowman, T., Suri, V. R., Tsou, A., Weingart, S., & Sugimoto, C. R. (2015). Big data, bigger dilemmas: A critical review. *Journal of the Association for Information Science and Technology, 68*(8), 1523–1545. https://doi.org/10.1002/asi.23294

Ellili, N., Nobanee, H., Alsaiari, L., Shanti, H., Hillebrand, B., Hassanain, N., & Elfout, L. (2023). The applications of big data in the insurance industry: A bibliometric and systematic review of relevant literature. *The Journal of Finance and Data Science, 9*, 100102. https://doi.org/10.1016/j.jfds.2023.100102

Fang, K., Jiang, Y., & Song, M. (2016). Customer profitability forecasting using big data analytics: A case study of the insurance industry. *Computers & Industrial Engineering, 101*, 554–564. https://doi.org/10.1016/j.cie.2016.09.011

Frees, E. W., & Huang, F. (2023). The discriminating (pricing) actuary. *North American Actuarial Journal, 27*(1), 2–24. https://doi.org/10.1080/10920277.2021.1951296

Gavin, M. (2019). *Business analytics: What it is & why it's important*. Harvard Business School, Business Insights. https://online.hbs.edu/blog/post/importance-of-business-analytics

Hargittai, E. (2015). Is bigger always better? Potential biases of big data derived from social network sites. *The Annals of the American Academy of Political and Social Science, 659*(1), 63–76. https://doi.org/10.1177/0002716215570866

Hassani, H., Beneki, C., Unger, S., Mazinani, M. T., & Yeganegi, M. R. (2020). Text mining in big data analytics. *Big Data and Cognitive Computing, 4*(1), 1–34. https://doi.org/10.3390/bdcc4010001

Hassani, H., Unger, S., & Beneki, C. (2020). Big data and actuarial science. *Big Data and Cognitive Computing, 4*(4), 1–29. https://doi.org/10.3390/bdcc4040040

Himeur, Y., Elnour, M., Fadli, F., Meskin, N., Petri, I., Rezgui, Y., Bensaali, F., & Amira, A. (2023). AI-big data analytics for building automation and management systems: A survey, actual challenges and future perspectives. In *Artificial intelligence review* (Vol. 56, Issue 6). Springer. https://doi.org/10.1007/s10462-022-10286-2

Hussain, S., & Lee, S. (2016). Visualization and descriptive analytics of wellness data through big data. In *The 10th International Conference on Digital Information Management, ICDIM 2015* (pp. 69–71). Icdim. https://doi.org/10.1109/ICDIM.2015.7381878

Jin, X., Wah, B. W., Cheng, X., & Wang, Y. (2015). Significance and challenges of big data research. *Big Data Research*, *2*(2), 59–64. https://doi.org/10.1016/j.bdr.2015.01.006

Lazer, D., Pentland, A., Adamic, L., Aral, S., Barabási, A., Brewer, D., Christakis, N., Contractor, N., Fowler, J., Gutmann, M., Jebara, T., King, G., Macy, M., Roy, D., & Alstyne, M. Van (2009). Computational social science. *Science*, *323*(February), 721–723.

Lepenioti, K., Bousdekis, A., Apostolou, D., & Mentzas, G. (2020). Prescriptive analytics: Literature review and research challenges. *International Journal of Information Management*, *50*(May 2019), 57–70. https://doi.org/10.1016/j.ijinfomgt.2019.04.003

Mckinsey Analytics. (2016). *The age of analytics: Competing in a data-driven world.* McKinsey & Company. (Issue December). http://www.mckinsey.com/business-functions/mckinsey-analytics/our-insights/the-age-of-analytics-competing-in-a-data-driven-world

Mills, E. (2009). A global review of insurance industry responses to climate change. *The Geneva Papers on Risk and Insurance - Issues and Practice*, *23*, 323–359. https://doi.org/10.1057/gpp.2009.14

Niu, Y., Ying, L., Yang, J., Bao, M., & Sivaparthipan, C. B. (2021). Organizational business intelligence and decision making using big data analytics. *Information Processing & Management*, *58*(6), 102725. https://doi.org/10.1016/j.ipm.2021.102725

Rana, A., Bansal, R., & Gupta, M. (2022). Big data: A disruptive innovation in the insurance sector. In P. Marano, K. Sood, B. Balusamy, & S. Grima (Eds.), *Big Data Analytics in the Insurance Market (Emerald Studies in Finance, Insurance, and Risk Management)* (pp. 165–183). Emerald Publishing Limited. https://doi.org/10.1108/978-1-80262-637-720221009

Rane, N. (2023). *Enhancing customer loyalty through Artificial Intelligence (AI), Internet of Things (IoT), and Big Data Technologies: Improving Customer Satisfaction, Engagement, Relationship, and Experience.* Available at SSRN: https://ssrn.com/abstract=4616051 or http://dx.doi.org/10.2139/ssrn.4616051

Ridzuan, F., & Wan Zainon, W. M. N. (2021). Diagnostic analysis for outlier detection in big data analytics. *Procedia Computer Science*, *197*, 685–692. https://doi.org/10.1016/j.procs.2021.12.189

Rudden, J. (2023a). *Biggest 50 insurance companies worldwide May 2023, by market cap.* Statista.Com. https://www.statista.com/statistics/431547/leading-insurance-companies-worldwide-by-market-cap/

Rudden, J. (2023b). *Global insurance industry - statistics & facts.* Statista.Com. https://www.statista.com/topics/6529/global-insurance-industry/#topicOverview

Rudden, J. (2023c). *Market share of the total insurance market worldwide.* Statista.Com. https://www.statista.com/statistics/1045207/market-share-of-insurance-worldwide-by-country/

Saeed, M., & Arshed, N. (2023). Big data analytics technology adoption in Kenya insurance industry: A systematic literature review chronicle abstract. *Asian Bulletin of Big Data Managment*, *3*(1), 1–17.

Seyedan, M., & Mafakheri, F. (2020). Predictive big data analytics for supply chain demand forecasting: Methods, applications, and research opportunities. *Journal of Big Data*, *7*(1). https://doi.org/10.1186/s40537-020-00329-2

Shrestha, Y. R., Krishna, V., & Krogh, G. von (2021). Augmenting organizational decision-making with deep learning algorithms: Principles, promises, and challenges. *Journal of Business Research*, *123*(February), 588–603. https://doi.org/10.1016/j.jbusres.2020.09.068

Soori, M., Arezoo, B., & Dastres, R. (2023). Artificial intelligence, machine learning and deep learning in advanced robotics, a review. *Cognitive Robotics*, *3*(March), 54–70. https://doi.org/10.1016/j.cogr.2023.04.001

Statista. (2024). *Forecast of the global insurance market in 2021 and 2022, with forecasts from 2023 to 2026*. https://www.statista.com/statistics/1192960/forecast-global-insurance-market/

Taylor, P. (2023a). *Revenue from big data and business analytics worldwide from 2015 to 2022*. Statista.Com. https://www.statista.com/statistics/551501/worldwide-big-data-business-analytics-revenue/

Taylor, P. (2023b). *Volume of data/information created, captured, copied, and consumed worldwide from 2010 to 2020, with forecasts from 2021 to 2025*. Statista.Com. https://www.statista.com/statistics/871513/worldwide-data-created/

Thayyib, P. V., Mamilla, R., Khan, M., Fatima, H., Asim, M., Anwar, I., Shamsudheen, M. K., & Khan, M. A. (2023). State-of-the-Art of artificial intelligence and big data analytics reviews in five different domains: A bibliometric summary. *Sustainability*, *15*(5), 4026. https://doi.org/10.3390/su15054026

Tole, A. A. (2013). Big data challenges. *Database Systems Journal*, *4*(3), 31–40. https://doi.org/10.4172/2324-9307.1000133

Vailshery, L. S. (2023). *Number of IoT connected devices worldwide 2019-2023, with forecasts to 2030*. Statista.Com. https://www.statista.com/statistics/1183457/iot-connected-devices-worldwide/

Vassakis, K., Petrakis, E., & Kopanakis, I. (2018). Big data analytics: Applications, prospects and challenges. In G. Skourletopoulos, G. Mastorakis, C. Mavromoustakis, C. Dobre, & E. Pallis (Eds.), *Big mobile data. Lecture notes on data engineering and communications technologies* (Vol. 10, pp. 3–20). https://doi.org/10.1007/978-3-319-67925-9_1

Wagenaar, D., Curran, A., Balbi, M., Bhardwaj, A., Soden, R., Hartato, E., Mestav Sarica, G., Ruangpan, L., Molinario, G., & Lallemant, D. (2020). Invited perspectives: How machine learning will change flood risk and impact assessment. *Natural Hazards and Earth System Sciences*, *20*(4), 1149–1161. https://doi.org/10.5194/nhess-20-1149-2020

Wang, Y., Kung, L. A., & Byrd, T. A. (2018). Big data analytics: Understanding its capabilities and potential benefits for healthcare organizations. *Technological Forecasting and Social Change*, *126*, 3–13. https://doi.org/10.1016/j.techfore.2015.12.019

Zicari, R. V. (2014). *Big data: Challenges and opportunities. Big data computing*. CRC Press, Taylor and Francis Group.

Chapter 3

AI-Driven Personalized Risk Management in the Insurance Sector

Anshul Agrawal[a], *Tanya Kumar*[b], *Rachit Agarwal*[b] *and Ashish Gupta*[c]

[a]GNIOT Institute of Management Studies, India
[b]Chandigarh University, India
[c]Maharishi University of Information Technology, India

Abstract

Introduction: In the fiercely competitive insurance landscape, embracing personalized risk management offers insurers a strategic advantage, enabling the provision of innovative, customer-centric solutions tailored to individual policyholders.

Purpose: The purpose of the study was to identify AI factors that supports risk management in the insurance sector to assist investors and users to manage their risk using different AI tools.

Methodology: In the current study, primary data are collected by using simple random sampling from 372 respondents. A questionnaire was sent to more than 500 respondents, but the final sample size was 372 based on their complete responses and data provided in the questionnaire. Target audience was insurance services/policy users. The study is empirical in nature, and data analysis was done using factor analysis.

Findings: It was found that there are three major factors which can affect risk management in insurance such as better risk management, acceptance as well as anticipation, and better customization can be possible for the customers by utilizing AI-driven technology in insurance. The early identification of fraudulent behavior can enable the insurers in loss reduction as well as promoting competitive price policy for honest customers. An automative mechanism can be helpful in adjusting premiums on the basis of real-time assessment of risk factors.

Keywords: Artificial intelligence; insurance; risk management; chatbots; competitive policy

Data Alchemy in the Insurance Industry, 27–39

doi:10.1108/978-1-83608-582-920241006

1. Introduction

In today's dynamic insurance landscape, the integration of AI has sparked a revolution in risk management practices. This transformation, known as personalized risk management, has become indispensable for insurance firms seeking to not only boost customer satisfaction but also optimize underwriting processes and mitigate risks effectively (Mall et al., 2023). The rapid advancement of AI technologies, including machine learning algorithms, natural language processing (NLP), and predictive analytics, has empowered insurers to explore vast datasets, extracting actionable insights for personalized risk assessment and management. Departing from the traditional one-size-fits-all approach, insurers are now embracing a more tailored paradigm, crafting insurance offerings that resonate deeply with individual characteristics, behaviors, and preferences (Dhieb et al., 2020). This transition has been fueled by AI-driven solutions that exhibit remarkable capabilities in enhancing underwriting accuracy through sophisticated data analytics techniques.

Furthermore, personalized risk management embodies a customer-centric ethos, as insurers strive to comprehend and address the unique needs and concerns of each policyholder, thus fostering deeper engagement and loyalty. However, the widespread adoption of AI in insurance has brought forth ethical considerations surrounding data privacy, algorithmic biases, and transparency in decision-making processes (Edgington & Kasztelnik, 2024). Intensified regulatory scrutiny underscores the necessity for compliance with data protection regulations, as well as ensuring fairness and accountability in AI-driven decision-making (Thiruma Valavan, 2023). Understanding consumer perceptions and attitudes toward AI-driven personalized insurance solutions is pivotal for their acceptance and adoption (de Andrés-Sánchez & Gené-Albesa, 2023). Moreover, AI-powered risk management systems not only enhance risk assessment accuracy but also streamline operational processes, such as claims processing, leading to improved efficiency and cost effectiveness (Zarifis & Cheng, 2022). In the fiercely competitive insurance landscape, embracing personalized risk management offers insurers a strategic advantage, enabling the provision of innovative, customer-centric solutions tailored to individual policyholders (Tereszkiewicz & Południak-Gierz, 2021).

The seamless integration of AI technologies into insurance services holds the potential to enrich the overall customer experience by furnishing real-time insights, personalized recommendations, and responsive support (Skandali et al., 2023). As consumer expectations evolve and technology progresses, the insurance market undergoes significant transformations, with personalized risk management emerging as a pivotal differentiator for industry players (Zarifis & Cheng, 2021). Nonetheless, while AI-driven personalized risk management presents numerous opportunities for innovation and growth, it also poses challenges related to data security, regulatory compliance, and the imperative for ongoing investment in technology and talent (El Hajj & Hammoud, 2023). Overall, the transformative impact of AI integration in reshaping the insurance landscape enables insurers to offer customized solutions, fostering meaningful customer relationships and driving competitiveness (Ahmadi, 2024; Dhieb et al., 2020; Mall et al., 2023; Adeoye et al., 2024; Singh, 2017; Tereszkiewicz & Południak-Gierz, 2021).

The research study aims to contribute significantly to both academia and industry in the domain of AI-driven personalized insurance solutions. By investigating consumer perceptions, preferences, and experiences, the study intends to offer actionable insights into insurance companies, facilitating the development of more effective personalized risk management strategies that can enhance customer satisfaction, loyalty, and profitability (Méndez-Aparicio et al., 2017). Furthermore, the study aims to identify and address ethical and regulatory challenges associated with AI-driven personalized insurance, thereby aiding in the alignment of policies and practices with regulatory requirements and ethical standards (Edgington & Kasztelnik, 2024). Policymakers and regulatory bodies stand to benefit from the study's insights, which could inform the development of regulations aimed at promoting fairness, accountability, and consumer protection within the insurance industry. Additionally, the research endeavors to advance academic knowledge by expanding the understanding of the intersection between AI technologies and personalized risk management in the insurance sector, generating novel insights and theories that enrich the field of insurance studies and related disciplines (Thiruma Valavan, 2023).

The novelty of this study is employing the structural equation modeling (SEM) using SMART PLS approach (Pandey & Rai, 2023). This study can assess structural relationships between constructs, identifying key drivers of consumer behavior toward AI-driven personalized insurance and predicting outcomes such as purchase intentions and satisfaction (Zarifis & Cheng, 2021). This structured approach not only enhances the robustness of the research findings but also provides valuable insights for strategic decision-making among insurance companies seeking to refine their personalized risk management strategies (Pandey & Rai, 2023).

2. Literature Review

The insurance industry is evolving through AI adoption, notably in personalized products tailored to individual needs (Tereszkiewicz & Południak Gierz, 2021). Machine learning enables data analysis for accurate predictions (Grize et al., 2020), while predictive analytics forecasts events for personalized interventions (Adeoye et al., 2024). NLP extracts insights from text data for effective communication (Zia & Kalia, 2022), and AI-powered chatbots enhance customer support (Bala et al., 2024). These efforts boost customer satisfaction and risk assessment accuracy, driving business growth (Ahmadi, 2024; Adeoye et al., 2024). Overall, AI-driven personalization is reshaping the insurance landscape to better meet individual customer needs. The detailed description of previous studies is mentioned in Table 3.1.

Table 3.1. The Description of Exiting Studies.

Author	Methodology	Findings
Tereszkiewicz and Południak Gierz (2021)	A qualitative analysis of AI's role in personalized insurance through case studies and expert interviews.	AI enables tailoring of insurance products and services to meet individual customer needs, preferences, and risk profiles, enhancing relevance and value proposition.
Grize et al. (2020)	A quantitative study analyzing the effectiveness of machine learning algorithms in personalizing insurance offerings based on historical data and customer profiles.	Machine learning algorithms facilitate accurate predictions and recommendations, allowing insurers to personalize offerings and improve customer satisfaction.
Adeoye et al. (2024)	A mixed-methods approach incorporating both quantitative analysis of predictive analytics outcomes and qualitative interviews with insurance professionals to understand its impact on personalized interventions.	Predictive analytics aids in anticipating customer behavior, assessing risks, and enabling personalized interventions, leading to proactive risk management and improved customer experiences.
Zia and Kalia (2022)	A qualitative content analysis of NLP applications in the insurance sector, examining its effectiveness in understanding customer sentiment and preferences from textual data.	NLP enables the analysis of text-based data to understand customer sentiment, preferences, and trends, facilitating personalized communication and offerings.
Bala et al. (2024)	A case study approach evaluating the implementation of chatbots and virtual assistants in insurance companies, assessing their impact on	Chatbots and virtual assistants provide real-time customer support and personalized recommendations, enhancing customer

Table 3.1. *(Continued)*

Author	Methodology	Findings
	customer satisfaction and interaction efficiency.	satisfaction and interaction efficiency.
Adeoye et al. (2024)	Mixed-methods research combining quantitative analysis of AI-driven personalized insurance outcomes and qualitative interviews with industry experts and customers to explore its effectiveness and challenges.	AI technologies such as machine learning, predictive analytics, NLP, and chatbots enhance risk assessment accuracy and customer experience, driving personalization in insurance.
Ahmadi (2024)	A comprehensive review synthesizing qualitative and quantitative findings from existing literature on the transformative impact of AI integration in the insurance industry, with a focus on personalized solutions.	AI integration in insurance offers customized solutions, fosters customer relationships, and enhances competitiveness through personalization.
Sosa and Montes (2022)	Qualitative research involving interviews and surveys with insurance professionals and customers to understand the implementation and impact of AI in personalized risk management.	AI integration in insurance optimizes underwriting processes, boosts customer satisfaction, and fosters engagement through personalized risk management.
Yang et al. (2024)	A quantitative analysis of AI technologies' penetration and adoption rates in the insurance sector, supplemented by qualitative interviews with industry stakeholders to explore challenges and opportunities.	AI technologies rapidly advance personalized risk assessment and management in the insurance sector, presenting opportunities for improved efficiency and customer satisfaction.
de Andrés-Sánchez and	A mixed-methods study combining the quantitative	Transition to tailored insurance solutions driven

(Continued)

Table 3.1. *(Continued)*

Author	Methodology	Findings
Gené-Albesa (2023b)	analysis of market trends and qualitative interviews with insurance executives to investigate the transition to tailored insurance solutions driven by AI.	by AI emphasizes customer engagement and loyalty, shaping the insurance industry landscape.
Huang et al. (2011)	A qualitative analysis of insurers' strategies and approaches to address customer needs through personalized risk management, incorporating interviews and case studies.	Insurers' efforts to address unique customer needs through personalized risk management foster engagement and loyalty, driving customer-centricity in the insurance sector.
Arthur and Owen (2022)	An ethnographic study exploring ethical considerations in AI adoption in insurance, involving interviews, observations, and document analysis to understand stakeholders' perspectives and concerns.	Ethical considerations in AI adoption in insurance emphasize the importance of compliance with regulations, transparency, and fairness in decision-making processes.
de Andrés-Sánchez and Gené-Albesa (2023)	A survey-based research study assessing consumer perceptions and attitudes toward AI-driven personalized insurance, capturing quantitative data on acceptance and qualitative insights into factors influencing adoption.	Consumer perceptions and attitudes toward AI-driven personalized insurance influence market acceptance and adoption, highlighting the importance of addressing concerns and building trust.
Addy et al. (2024)	A case study analysis of insurance companies implementing AI-powered risk management systems, examining quantitative outcomes such as efficiency	AI-powered risk management systems offer operational benefits such as improved efficiency and cost-effectiveness for

Table 3.1. *(Continued)*

Author	Methodology	Findings
	gains and qualitative feedback from stakeholders.	insurers, enhancing overall performance.
Liu et al. (2007)	A comparative analysis of insurers' strategies for personalized risk management through case studies and interviews with industry leaders, identifying key success factors and challenges.	Embracing personalized risk management provides insurers with a strategic advantage in a competitive landscape, driving differentiation and market positioning.
Mall et al. (2023)	The meta-analysis of existing literature on AI's impact on the insurance landscape, synthesizing qualitative and quantitative findings to provide insights into broader trends and implications.	AI's broader impact reshapes the insurance landscape, empowering insurers to offer customized solutions and enhancing competitiveness.
Dhieb et al. (2020)	An action research approach collaborating with insurance companies to implement AI-driven technologies and evaluating their impact on operational efficiency and customer experiences through qualitative feedback and performance metrics.	AI streamlines insurance operations and enhances customer experiences, improving efficiency for insurers and driving customer satisfaction.
Singh (2017)	A longitudinal study examining the relationship between customer engagement strategies and business outcomes in the insurance sector, combining quantitative analysis of engagement metrics and qualitative interviews with industry professionals.	Customer engagement drives loyalty and business growth for insurers, emphasizing the importance of effective engagement strategies in the insurance industry.

Source: Authors' Compilation.

3. Methodology

In the current study, primary data are collected by using simple random sampling from 372 respondents. A questionnaire was sent to more than 500 respondents, but the final sample size was 372 based on their complete responses and data provided in questionnaire. Target audience was insurance services/policy users. The study is empirical in nature, and data analysis was done using factor analysis.

3.1 Data Analysis

The data analysis is conducted using factor analysis. As shown in Table 3.2, the value of Kaiser–Meyer–Olkin (KMO) was 0.873, which is above 0.6 and is found to be satisfactory for the study. The chi-square value was 3409.04, which was found to be significant.

Table 3.2. KMO and Barlett's Test.

Kaiser–Meyer–Olkin Measure of Sampling Adequacy.		**0.873**
Bartlett's test of sphericity	Approx. Chi-square	3409.043
	Df	66
	Sig.	0.000

Source: Factor Analysis, Primary Data.

As highlighted in Table 3.3, the eigen values of 12 statements are used in analysis for making the factors. The average percentage of variance are 27.35 approximately. The cumulative percentage of variance is 27.793, 55.142 and 77.540, respectively.

Table 3.4 provides the information regarding rotated component matrix, and three factors were determined on the analysis namely, better risk management, adoption and anticipation, and better customization.

4. Factor 1: Better Risk Management

AI-driven chatbots are to be utilized toward personalized risk management for improving insurance outcomes as well as enhancement of customer satisfaction. This risk management process can improve the overall profitability level of insurance companies. Respondents also believe that the adoption of AI in the insurance sector can help to reduce fraudulent claims in insurance industry by developing fair price strategies as per individuals' risk profile.

Table 3.3. Total Variance Explained.

	Initial Eigenvalues			Extraction Sums of Squared Loadings			Rotation Sums of Squared Loadings		
Component	**Total**	**% of Variance**	**Cumulative %**	**Total**	**% of Variance**	**Cumulative %**	**Total**	**% of Variance**	**Cumulative %**
1	5.968	49.731	49.731	5.968	49.731	49.731	3.335	27.793	27.793
2	2.113	17.612	67.343	2.113	17.612	67.343	3.282	27.349	55.142
3	1.224	10.196	77.540	1.224	10.196	77.540	2.688	22.398	77.540
4	0.614	5.117	82.657						
5	0.441	3.673	86.330						
6	0.413	3.441	89.770						
7	0.314	2.613	92.383						
8	0.256	2.137	94.520						
9	0.206	1.714	96.234						
10	0.189	1.573	97.807						
11	0.154	1.283	99.090						
12	0.109	0.910	100.000						

Extraction method: Principal component analysis.

Source: Factor Analysis, Primary Data.

Table 3.4. Rotated Component Matrix.

S. No.	Statements	Component 1	Component 2	Component 3
1	I believe that utilizing AI-driven personalized risk management can significantly improve insurance outcomes.	0.912		
2	I trust that AI-driven personalized risk management can enhance customer satisfaction in the insurance industry.	0.815		
3	I trust that AI-driven risk management can improve the overall profitability of insurance companies.	−0.802		
4	I believe that AI-driven risk management can contribute to reducing fraudulent claims in the insurance industry.	0.702		
5	I feel that AI-driven risk management can lead to fairer pricing strategies based on individual risk profiles.	0.666		
6	I believe that AI can help insurance companies better anticipate and mitigate potential risks for their customers.		0.867	
7	I am optimistic about the potential of AI to streamline insurance processes and reduce operational costs.		0.826	
8	I am confident that AI algorithms can adapt to changing risk factors and provide real-time insights.		0.811	
9	I am open to adopting AI-driven personalized risk management solutions in my insurance practices, whether as a consumer or a provider.		0.797	
10	I am comfortable with the idea of sharing personal data if it leads to more accurate risk assessments and tailored insurance products.			0.933
11	I perceive AI-driven risk management as a valuable tool for promoting proactive risk prevention and mitigation measures.			0.923
12	I perceive AI technologies as effective tools for accurately assessing individual risks in insurance.			0.820

Source: Factor Analysis, Primary Data.

5. Factor 2: Adoption and Anticipation

The adoption of AI can be helpful for insurance companies in better anticipation as well as the mitigation of potential risks of customers. The level of optimism can be improved through potential AI in streamlining the insurance process by reducing operational costs. Moreover, AI algorithms can easily adapt the changing risk factors by providing real-time insights toward it as they provide efficient solutions toward risk management in insurance practices.

6. Factor 3: Better Customization

The other derived factor is that AI-driven chatbots lead to better customization as it provides accurate risk assessment to the customers who share their personal data as by tailoring insurance products as per their requirement. Furthermore, it is one of the valuable tools that can promote proactive risk prevention as well as risk mitigation measures. People also believe that AI technology can be one of the effective tools which assess the risk of individuals accurately in the insurance sector.

7. Conclusion

In conclusion, it can be stated that AI-driven personalized risk management resulted in transformative shift toward insurance industry which provides the ability to individuals in risk assessment and mitigation. AI fulfills specific needs as well as risk profiles of customers through dynamic underwriting, personalized pricing, proactive intervention and fraud detection by offering them with better customer experience. AI introduces a great level of sophistication through leveraging machine learning algorithms in analyzing data related to individual behavior patterns, lifestyle choices, tailoring insurance offerings, real-time data streaming and so on. Moreover, the implementation of AI-driven risk management represents privacy and ethical challenges that need to be addressed. Policy holders need to prioritize their accountability, transparency as well as regulatory compliance in order to ensure risk mitigation. Furthermore, regular monitoring and evaluation of AI systems is necessary to identify as well as address the issues. With the advancement in technology, the available options need to be availed using AI-driven solutions.AI-driven technology provide assistance to insurers by fulfilling their regulatory requirements by the adoption of automated mechanism through check upon antimoney laundering and maintaining data privacy as per industry standards. These algorithms can help to detect anomalous patterns in case of any inconsistency of provided information. The early identification of fraudulent behavior can enable the insurers in loss reduction as well as promoting competitive price policy for honest customers. An automative mechanism can be helpful in adjusting premiums on the basis of real-time assessment of risk factors.

References

Ahmadi, S. (2024). A comprehensive study on integration of big data and AI in financial industry and its effect on present and future opportunities. *International Journal of Current Science Research and Review*, *07*(01). https://doi.org/10.47191/ijcsrr/V7-i1-07

Arthur, K. N. A., & Owen, R. (2022). A micro-ethnographic study of big data-based innovation in the financial services sector: Governance, ethics and organisational practices. In *Business and the ethical implications of technology* (pp. 57–69). Springer Nature. https://doi.org/10.1007/978-3-031-18794-0_4

Adeoye, O. B., Okoye, C. C., Ofodile, O. C., Odeyemi, O., Addy, W. A., & Ajayi-Nifise, A. O. (2024). Integrating artificial intelligence in personalized insurance products: A pathway to enhanced customer engagement. *International Journal of Management & Entrepreneurship Research*, *6*(3), 502–511. https://doi.org/10.51594/ijmer.v6i3.840

Addy, W. A., Ajayi-Nifise, A. O., Bello, B. G., Tula, S. T., Odeyemi, O., & Falaiye, T. (2024). Transforming financial planning with AI-driven analysis: A review and application insights. *World Journal of Advanced Engineering Technology and Sciences*, *11*(1), 240–257. https://doi.org/10.30574/wjaets.2024.11.1.0053

Bala, D. E., Stancu, S., Pernici, A., & Vulpe, M. I. (2024). *Impact of personalization on improving a chatbot's performance. Case study for a banking virtual assistant* (pp. 259–270). https://doi.org/10.1007/978-981-99-6529-8_22

de Andrés-Sánchez, J., & Gené-Albesa, J. (2023). Assessing attitude and behavioral intention toward chatbots in an insurance setting: A mixed method approach. *International Journal of Human–Computer Interaction*, 1–16. https://doi.org/10.1080/10447318.2023.2227833

Dhieb, N., Ghazzai, H., Besbes, H., & Massoud, Y. (2020). A secure AI-driven architecture for automated insurance systems: Fraud detection and risk measurement. *IEEE Access*, *8*, 58546–58558. https://doi.org/10.1109/ACCESS.2020.2983300

Edgington, S., & Kasztelnik, K. (2024). The ethical considerations of business artificial intelligence exploration through the lenses of the global AI technology acceptance model. *Journal of Strategic Innovation and Sustainability*, *19*(1). https://doi.org/10.33423/jsis.v19i1.6749

El Hajj, M., & Hammoud, J. (2023). Unveiling the influence of artificial intelligence and machine learning on financial markets: A comprehensive analysis of ai applications in trading, risk management, and financial operations. *Journal of Risk and Financial Management*, *16*(10), 434. https://doi.org/10.3390/jrfm16100434

Grize, Y., Fischer, W., & Lützelschwab, C. (2020). Machine learning applications in nonlife insurance. *Applied Stochastic Models in Business and Industry*, *36*(4), 523–537. https://doi.org/10.1002/asmb.2543

Huang, L.-S., Quaddus, M., Rowe, A. L., & Lai, C.-P. (2011). An investigation into the factors affecting knowledge management adoption and practice in the life insurance business. *Knowledge Management Research & Practice*, *9*(1), 58–72. https://doi.org/10.1057/kmrp.2011.2

Liu, J., Li, B., Lin, B., & Nguyen, V. (2007). Key issues and challenges of risk management and insurance in China's construction industry. *Industrial Management & Data Systems*, *107*(3), 382–396. https://doi.org/10.1108/02635570710734280

Mall, S., Panigrahi, T. R., & Verma, S. (2023). Bibliometric analysis on big data applications in insurance sector: Past, present, and future research directions. *Journal of Financial Management, Markets and Institutions*, *11*(01). https://doi.org/10.1142/S2282717X23300015

Méndez-Aparicio, M. D., Izquierdo-Yusta, A., & Jiménez-Zarco, A. I. (2017). Consumer expectations of online services in the insurance industry: An exploratory study of drivers and outcomes. *Frontiers in Psychology*, *8*. https://doi.org/10.3389/fpsyg.2017.01254

Pandey, P., & Rai, A. K. (2023). Consumer adoption of AI-powered virtual assistants (AIVA): An integrated model based on the SEM–ANN approach. *FIIB Business Review*. https://doi.org/10.1177/23197145231196066

Singh, I. (2017). *The interrelationships between selected relationship marketing constructs, customer engagement and behavioural intentions in the life insurance industry*. Master's thesis. University of Pretoria.

Skandali, D., Magoutas, A., & Tsourvakas, G. (2023). Artificial intelligent applications in enabled banking services: The next frontier of customer engagement in the era of chatGPT. *Theoretical Economics Letters*, *13*(05), 1203–1223. https://doi.org/10.4236/tel.2023.135066

Sosa, I., & Montes, Ó. (2022). Understanding the InsurTech dynamics in the transformation of the insurance sector. *Risk Management and Insurance Review*, *25*(1), 35–68. https://doi.org/10.1111/rmir.12203

Tereszkiewicz, P., & Południak-Gierz, K. (2021). Liability for incorrect client personalization in the distribution of consumer insurance. *Risks*, *9*(5), 83. https://doi.org/10.3390/risks9050083

Thiruma Valavan A. (2023). AI ethics and bias: Exploratory study on the ethical considerations and potential biases in AI and data-driven decision-making in banking, with a focus on fairness, transparency, and accountability. *World Journal of Advanced Research and Reviews*, *20*(2), 197–206. https://doi.org/10.30574/wjarr.2023.20.2.2245

Yang, J., Blount, Y., & Amrollahi, A. (2024). Artificial intelligence adoption in a professional service industry: A multiple case study. *Technological Forecasting and Social Change*, *201*, 123251. https://doi.org/10.1016/j.techfore.2024.123251

Zarifis, A., & Cheng, X. (2021). Evaluating the New AI and Data Driven Insurance Business Models for Incumbents and Disruptors: Is there Convergence? *Business Information Systems*, 199–208. https://doi.org/10.52825/bis.v1i.58

Zarifis, A., & Cheng, X. (2022). AI Is Transforming Insurance With Five Emerging Business Models. In *Encyclopedia of Data Science and Machine Learning* (pp. 2086–2100). IGI Global. https://doi.org/10.4018/978-1-7998-9220-5.ch124

Zia, A., & Kalia, P. (2022). Emerging Technologies in Insurance Sector: Evidence from Scientific Literature. In *Big Data: A Game Changer for Insurance Industry* (pp. 43–63). Emerald Publishing Limited. https://doi.org/10.1108/978-1-80262-605-620221004

Chapter 4

Ethical Considerations in Data Analytics: Challenges, Principles, and Best Practices

Kapil Sharma[a], *Pawan Kumar*[a] *and Ercan Özen*[b]

[a]Chandigarh University, India
[b]University of Uşak, Turkey

Abstract

Introduction: In the era of data-driven decision-making, ethical considerations are central. This chapter examines the complex ethical landscape of data analytics, addressing challenges such as privacy and bias. It outlines guiding principles and best practices, aiming to foster responsible data stewardship and uphold integrity in an increasingly interconnected world.
Purpose: The main aim of this study is to explore the ethical dimensions of data analytics, addressing key challenges, principles, and best practices in various sectors of society.
Methodology: The study explores the ethical dimensions of data analytics using multi-faceted approaches. Since, new dimensions have to be explored, the study chosen is exploratory.
Findings: This study explores the ethical dimensions of data analytics. Addressing these ethical dimensions requires a multi-faceted approach involving technical, organizational, and regulatory measures. By proactively identifying and addressing ethical challenges, organizations can foster trust, accountability, and responsible innovation in data analytics. Additionally, ongoing dialog and collaboration among stakeholders are essential to navigating the complex ethical landscape of data analytics effectively.
Implications: This study on ethical considerations in data analytics serves as a valuable resource for organizations, policymakers, educators, and society at large. By integrating ethical principles into data analytics practices, stakeholders can harness the transformative potential of data while upholding ethical standards and safeguarding individual rights and societal well-being.

Data Alchemy in the Insurance Industry, 41–48

doi:10.1108/978-1-83608-582-920241008

Keywords: Data analytics; integral; exploratory; ethical dimension; framework; guidelines; complexities; digital landscape

1. Introduction

In today's data-driven world, organizations harness the power of data analytics to gain insights, drive innovation, and enhance decision-making. However, the ethical implications of data analytics are profound, spanning privacy, transparency, fairness, and accountability (Barocas & Selbst. 2016). This chapter delves into the ethical considerations inherent in data analytics, offering guidance on ethical decision-making and responsible data governance (Gao, Barbier, & Goolsby, 2011).

2. Key Ethical Challenges

2.1 Privacy and Data Protection

- The collection, storage, and analysis of personal data raise concerns about privacy infringement and data misuse.
- Ensure ethical data analytics by implementing robust privacy safeguards, informed consent mechanisms, and adhering to data protection regulations like General Data Protection Regulation (GDPR) and California Consumer Privacy Act (CCPA) (Kitchin, 2014).

2.2 Transparency and Accountability

- **Transparency in data analytics** involves disclosing the purposes, methodologies, and potential implications of data analysis to stakeholders (Narayanan & Shmatikov, 2008).
- **Organizations must be accountable** for their data practices, ensuring transparency, fairness, and integrity throughout the data **lifecycle.**

2.3 Bias and Fairness

- Algorithmic biases and discriminatory outcomes pose ethical challenges in data analytics, perpetuating social inequalities and systemic injustices.
- Ethical data analytics requires mitigating biases, ensuring fairness, and promoting diversity and inclusion in data collection, analysis, and decision-making (Barocas & Selbst, 2016).

3. Ethical Principles in Data Analytics

3.1 Respect for Individuals

Data analytics should respect individuals' autonomy, privacy, and dignity, upholding their rights to informed consent and data privacy. Organizations should prioritize data minimization, anonymization, and pseudonymization to protect individuals' privacy and confidentiality (Hagendorff & McCusker, 2020).

3.2 Transparency and Accountability

Transparency entails openness, honesty, and clarity in data analytics processes, ensuring stakeholders understand the purposes, methods, and implications of data analysis (Kitchin, 2014). Accountability involves taking responsibility for data practices, addressing concerns, and remedying harms caused by unethical data use (Barocas & Selbst, 2016).

3.3 Fairness and Equity

Data analytics should strive for fairness, equity, and impartiality in decision-making, avoiding biases and discrimination based on protected attributes such as race, gender, or socioeconomic status. Organizations should implement fairness-aware algorithms, conduct bias assessments, and promote diversity and inclusivity in data analytics teams (O'Neil, 2016).

4. Best Practices for Ethical Data Analytics

4.1 Ethical Governance and Oversight

Organizations should establish ethical governance structures, policies, and procedures to guide responsible data use. Ethical review boards, data ethics committees, and privacy impact assessments can help ensure ethical compliance and accountability (Zliobaite, 2015).

4.2 Data Transparency and Consent

Organizations should provide clear and accessible information about data collection, processing, and sharing practices to users. Obtaining informed consent from individuals for data collection and analysis is essential for respecting their autonomy and privacy rights (Solove, 2006).

4.3 Bias Detection and Mitigation

Organizations should implement bias detection techniques, fairness metrics, and algorithmic audits to identify and mitigate biases in data analytics. Regular monitoring, evaluation, and adjustment of algorithms can help minimize discriminatory outcomes and promote equitable decision-making (Pedreschi et al., 2009).

5. Methodology

This research study is exploratory The nature, and data for this research were collected by a survey of four northwestern Indian states namely, Punjab, Himachal, Delhi and Haryana (as shown in Table 4.1) for ethical concerns of data in four different sectors of economy by taking a sample size of 100 respondents spread out in the regions in these sectors.

Table 4.1 shows respondents'profile in data use. Maximum respondents were males. Most of the respondents' were from 39 to 48 year old age group. Most of the respondents hailed from Punjab, and lastly, majority of the respondents belonged to the financial service sector.

Table 4.1. Respondents' Profile.

Respondents	Sample Size = 100
a. Gender	
Male	63
Female	37
b. Age (Years)	
<28	10
29–38	27
39–48	33
49–58	23
59–68	7
c. State	
Punjab	32
Haryana	21
Himachal Pradesh	5
Delhi	42
d. Employment Sector	
Financial sector	32
Health services	16
Information Technology	26
Higher Education sector	26

Source: Primary Data, 2024.

Next, Table 4.2 explains ethical concern factors and their solutions as envisaged by the respondents belonging to different sectors in which they are employed.

- *Privacy Concerns: Unauthorized access to personal data, lack of transparency in data collection practices*

To address privacy concerns, organizations should implement robust privacy policies, which outline clear guidelines for data collection, storage, and usage. Encryption and anonymization techniques can be employed to protect sensitive information from unauthorized access. Furthermore, it is imperative for organizations to establish transparent consent mechanisms, ensuring individuals comprehend how their data will be utilized and have the option to opt-out if they choose. Adhering to pertinent data protection regulations like GDPR or CCPA is vital to maintain compliance and uphold individuals' privacy rights.

- *Bias and Fairness: Biased algorithms leading to discriminatory outcomes, perpetuation of societal biases*

Organizations should prioritize fairness in their data analytics processes by regularly auditing algorithms for bias. Diversifying datasets can help mitigate

Table 4.2. Ethical Concerns Raised by the Respondents and Solutions as Advised.

Ethical Concern Factor	Employment Sector	Ethical Concerns Raised by Total Number of Respondents
Privacy concerns	Financial sector	29
Bias and fairness	Health services	13
Transparency	Health services	12
Accountability	Information technology	23
Consent and data ownership	Higher education	22
Security and cyber security risks	Financial sector	29
Potential harm and unintended consequences	Information technology	21

Source: Primary data, 2024.

biases by ensuring representation from diverse demographic groups. Fairness metrics should be incorporated into model evaluation to assess and address potential discriminatory outcomes. Moreover, involving diverse stakeholders in the development process can help identify and mitigate biases from the outset, promoting fairness and equity in data analytics.

- *Transparency and Explainability: The Lack of transparency in algorithmic decision-making processes, black-box models*

Transparency and explainability are essential for building trust and accountability in data analytics. Organizations should use interpretable machine learning models that provide insights into how decisions are made. Providing explanations for algorithmic decisions helps individuals understand the reasoning behind outcomes and promotes trust in the system. Documenting data sources and model assumptions is crucial for transparency, enabling stakeholders to assess the reliability and validity of results. Promoting transparency in data processing practices fosters accountability and ethical decision-making.

- *Accountability: The Lack of accountability for the consequences of data analytics decisions, unclear roles and responsibilities*

Establishing clear accountability frameworks is essential for ensuring responsible data analytics practices. Organizations should designate responsible parties for data governance, defining roles and responsibilities for data stewardship and oversight. Implementing oversight mechanisms, such as regular audits and reviews, helps hold individuals and organizations accountable for ethical breaches. By establishing accountability structures, organizations can promote ethical decision-making and mitigate the risks associated with data analytics.

- *Consent and Data Ownership: Inadequate consent mechanisms, ambiguity regarding data ownership and usage rights.*

Securing explicit consent for data collection and processing is crucial for honoring individuals' privacy rights. Organizations must offer clear details regarding data usage and solicit consent from individuals before proceeding with data collection or processing. Providing options for data sharing preferences empowers individuals to control how their data is shared and used. Respecting data ownership rights involves acknowledging individuals' rights to their data and ensuring that data are used in accordance with their preferences and consent.

- *Security and Cybersecurity Risks: Vulnerabilities in data storage, unauthorized access, and data breaches*

Implementing strong cybersecurity measures is crucial for safeguarding data from security threats. Organizations need to employ encryption and access controls to secure both data storage and transmission channels. Conducting routine security audits aids in pinpointing vulnerabilities and upholding compliance with industry standards for data protection. Adhering to cybersecurity protocols and regulations assists in mitigating the risks associated with unauthorized access and data breaches, thereby protecting sensitive information from potential security breaches.

- *Potential Harm and Unintended Consequences: The misuse of data leading to societal harm, unintended consequences of algorithmic decisions*

Conducting ethical impact assessments is essential for evaluating the potential risks and benefits of data analytics projects. Organizations should assess the potential societal impacts of their actions and prioritize ethical considerations in decision-making processes. Evaluating the potential harms and unintended consequences of algorithmic decisions helps organizations identify and mitigate risks before they occur. Establishing mechanisms for addressing and mitigating harms ensures that data analytics projects contribute positively to society while minimizing negative impacts.

6. Conclusion

In summary, ethical considerations play a crucial role in data analytics, influencing responsible decision-making and fostering trust and integrity in data-driven processes. By prioritizing ethical principles, promoting transparency, and embracing accountability, organizations can effectively utilize the transformative potential of data analytics while respecting individual rights and societal values. Ethical data analytics is not just a legal or regulatory obligation but a moral obligation to advocate for fairness, equity, and social welfare in the digital era.

References

Barocas, S., & Selbst, A. D. (2016). Big data's disparate impact. *California Law Review*, *104*(3), 671–732.

Gao, H., Barbier, G., & Goolsby, R. (2011). Harnessing the crowdsourcing power of social media for disaster relief. *IEEE Intelligent Systems*, *26*(3), 10–14.

Hagendorff, T., & McCusker, R. (2020). Ethical considerations of COVID-19 apps. *Nature*, *582*(7810), 29.

Kitchin, R. (2014). *The data revolution: Big data, open data, data infrastructures and their consequences*. Sage.

Narayanan, A., & Shmatikov, V. (2008). Robust de-anonymization of large sparse datasets. In *Proceedings of the 2008 IEEE Symposium on Security and Privacy* (pp. 111–125).

O'Neil, C. (2016). *Weapons of math destruction: How big data increases inequality and threatens democracy*. Crown.

Pedreschi, D., Ruggieri, S., & Turini, F. (2009). Discrimination-aware data mining. In *Proceedings of the 15th ACM SIGKDD International Conference on Knowledge Discovery and Data Mining* (pp. 560–568).

Solove, D. J. (2006). A taxonomy of privacy. *University of Pennsylvania Law Review*, *154*(3), 477–564.

Zliobaite, I. (2015). *A survey on measuring indirect discrimination in machine learning*. arXiv preprint arXiv:1511.00148.

Chapter 5

Analyzing Two and a Half Decades of Health Insurance and Big Data Analytics Research: A Bibliometric Study

Vartika Bisht[a], *Priya*[a], *Sanjay Taneja*[b] *and Amar Johri*[c]

[a]Chandigarh University, India
[b]Graphic Era Deemed to Be University, India
[c]Saudi Electronic University, Saudi Arabia

Abstract

Purpose: Health insurance and big data analytics have become increasingly intertwined in recent years, offering both opportunities and challenges for the industry. Thus, the primary aim is to utilize bibliometric analysis for comprehensive literature reviews in health insurance and big data analytics.
Design/methodology/approach: Scopus, chosen for its broad coverage, is utilized to extract 493 manuscripts meeting the inclusion criteria set (year and language) for a 25-year period. The tools employed in the study include VOSViewer and Biblioshiny package (R-programming).
Findings: An emerging trend has been observed in the field of health insurance and big data analytics for 25 years. The US has been observed as the topmost leading country to contribute to the subject under study. The Ministry of Science and Technology of Taiwan is at the top first rank of top leading institutions contributing 20 documents to the field of health insurance and big data analytics. Moreover, thematic mapping and word cloud is done to find the most relevant keywords in the study. Furthermore, co-occurrence analysis revealed the relationship of keywords for health insurance and big data mining.
Implications: The implications of the research extend beyond academic insights and have practical implications for stakeholders involved in healthcare policy, practice, and research.
Originality/Value/Implications: The novelty in the manuscript has been brought in by focusing on one of the many types of insurance, i.e., health.

Data Alchemy in the Insurance Industry, 49–64

doi:10.1108/978-1-83608-582-920241010

Moreover, big data analytics in relation to health insurance for such a range of time period serves as the original presentation of the work with regards to the matter under study.

Keywords: Big data; bibliometric; Biblioshiny; health insurance; VOSViewer

1. Introduction

The insurance industry holds a significant position in the world economy due to its role in risk management (Kiptoo et al., 2021) and financial protection (Amponsah et al., 2022). It is a multitrillion-dollar industry (Ortikov & Uktamova, 2022) that provides essential services to individuals, businesses, and governments globally. As healthcare systems worldwide continue to grapple with issues such as rising costs, aging populations, and the need for more personalized medicine (Shukla et al., 2023), the use of big data analytics in healthcare, including health insurance, has become increasingly important. Health insurance industry covers medical expenses incurred by the insured individual, providing access to healthcare services (Lieberthal, 2016) and helping to mitigate the financial burden of illness or injury. Furthermore, big data analytics refers to the "process of examining large and complex data sets to uncover hidden" patterns, correlations, trends, and other valuable insights that can inform decision-making, strategic planning and problem-solving (Ikegwu et al., 2024). The integration of big data analytics within the health insurance industry (Rehman et al., 2022) has become increasingly prevalent, revolutionizing various aspects of healthcare management and delivery. By leveraging large volumes of structured and unstructured data, including patient records, claims data, demographic information, and even real-time health monitoring data from wearable devices(Nayak et al., 2019), health insurance companies can gain valuable insights into patient behavior and health outcomes. Eckert and Osterrieder (2020) underscore the significance of pivotal technologies such as the "Internet of Things (IoT), artificial intelligence, blockchain, machine learning, big data analytics, and insurance management platform" in the realm of data analytics in insurance industry.

Judijanto et al. (2024) assessed the influence of digital revolution transformations on health research, particularly through the lens of bibliometric analysis. It has been previously mentioned in the study of Mall et al. (2023) about the bibliometric image of insurance sector. Therefore, conducting a bibliometric analysis specifically focused on the overlap between health insurance and big data analytics becomes the need of the hour. Ziwei et al. (2024) in his five-year bibliometric analysis revealed recent advancements in the IoT have within the realm of intelligent healthcare. Moreover, Litvinova et al., 2024 conducted a bibliometric examination of employing digital technologies to mitigate adverse drug reactions. Emerging technologies' bibliometrics in this sector has been observed by Akhil (2022) and customer loyalty by Singla & Sawhney (2023). Additionally, bibliometric insights have been observed in the work on health insurance (Mureşan, 2023), while the use of big data analytics in this field has been neglected.

A systematic literature review was done by Inamdar et al. (2021) in the area of big data analytics. It has been covered in relation to the banking sector (Nobanee et al., 2021) and the education sector (Baig et al., 2020). The healthcare big data has been emphasized in the work of insurance sector (Lv & Qiao, 2020) and its use by Batko & Ślęzak (2022). Khang et al. (2024) have talked about the usage of big data for providing solutions in the subject area of medicine. It has also been highlighted by Sarker (2024) about the revolutionary role of healthcare sector due to machine learning. Thus, the research gap found is that the previous studies have conducted bibliometric analysis in insurance as a whole; however, the "health insurance in relation to big data" still remains an unexplored area. Thus, the present research aims to plan a comprehensive understanding of the big data analytics in health insurance industry by providing a 25-year bibliometric work on the manuscripts extracted. Thus, the study queries the research questions in relation to the bibliometric framework of health insurance and big data analytics, specifically emphasizing on the yearly publication trend, co-occurrence analysis of keywords, sponsoring institutions and thematic mapping.

2. Research Methodology

The author's main goal is to use bibliometric analysis to enhance how well literature reviews are conducted in the field of health insurance and big data analytics. It is a useful method for offering analysis regarding the most recent developments in qualitative research (Chawla & Goyal, 2022). The extraction model for the 493 manuscripts that were sorted using the Scopus database is shown in Fig. 5.1. Because Scopus is an extensive database that includes a broad range of scientific publications, this study has chosen to use it as its major source for retrieving publication records (Pranckutė, 2021). The inclusion and exclusion criterion shows that the time period covered in the study is of 25 years (2000-2024), giving 506 documents. Additionally, the filtration criterion when put for the "Language" sets to 493 overall manuscripts being counted in relation to health insurance and big data analytics.

VOS Viewer software was used in conjunction with the biblioshiny R package to examine the extracted manuscript results. The most effective tool for evaluating bibliographic data is VOS Viewer (Van Eck & Waltman, 2010), especially when it comes to visualizing networks. Additionally, the Biblioshiny R package provides a full toolkit for performing bibliometric analysis (Chambers, 2008).

3. Data Analysis and Interpretation

The portion of the study relates to the analytical description by the use of VOS Viewer and Biblioshiny package of R-programming of the 493 manuscripts for health insurance and big data analytics.

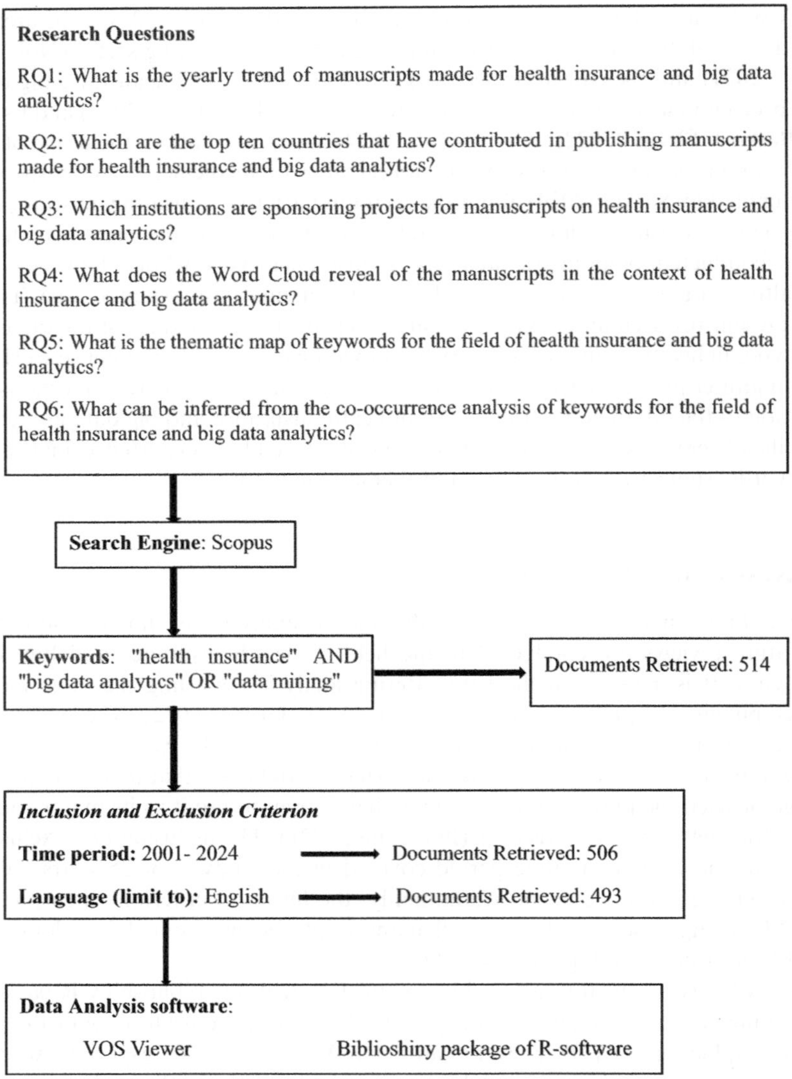

Fig. 5.1. Data Extraction Model. *Source:* Authors.

3.1 The Yearly Trend of Manuscripts Made for Health Insurance and Big Data Analytics

Over the past 25 years, there has been a notable increase in the annual trend of manuscript publications in the fields of big data analytics and health insurance. A single manuscript in 2001 has been observed, followed by three publications in 2002. But since 2008, there has been a steady rising trend, suggesting that interest in the topic with regards to health insurance industry is increasing. There has been a consistent rise in the number of manuscripts, with 17 in 2011, 28 in 2013, 34 in 2016, and 44 in 2018. The number of publications in 2021 is down significantly, at only 29. Following that, a noteworthy point is of the 35 manuscripts that are published in 2023 and 18 in 2024, even when it is just the first three months of the year 2024 that have been considered in the study.

The interpretation from the yearly publication trend is that over the past two decades, there has been a rapid advancement in technology, particularly in the field of data analytics. This has made it easier and more feasible for researchers to collect, analyze, and interpret large datasets related to health insurance, leading to an increased interest in publishing manuscripts in this area. Changes in healthcare policies and regulations, particularly those related to data privacy and security, may have also serve a probable reason that influenced the publication trends displayed below in Fig. 5.2.

3.2 Top 10 Countries That Have Contributed in Publishing Manuscripts Made for Health Insurance and Big Data Analytics

Table 5.1 and Fig. 5.3 illustrates the top 10 leading countries with the highest number of publications being contributed in the field of health insurance and big data analytics. It is observed that the US stands at the top giving a total count of

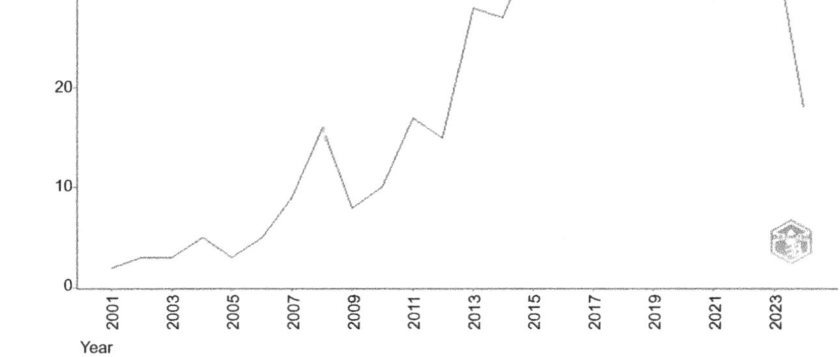

Fig. 5.2. Yearly Publication Trend Measured by Annual Scientific Production. *Source:* Authors.

Table 5.1. Top 10 Leading Countries.

S.No.	Country	Documents
1	United States	159
2	Taiwan	88
3	India	45
4	South Korea	35
5	China	27
6	Australia	24
7	Canada	16
8	United Kingdom	14
9	Indonesia	13
10	Iran	12

Source: Authors.

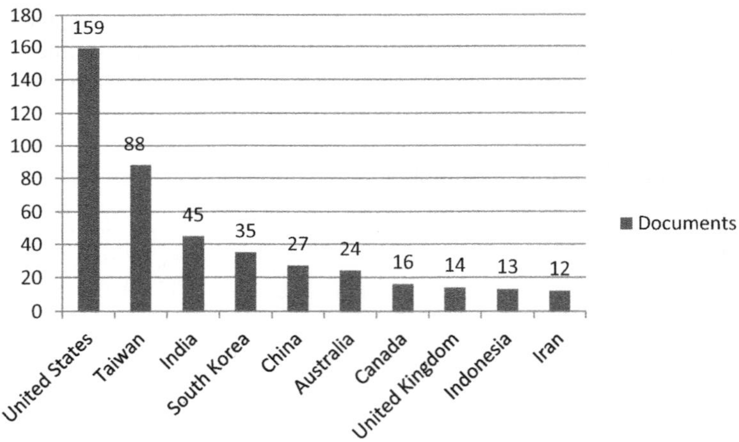

Fig. 5.3. Graphical Representation of Top 10 Leading Countries.
Source: Authors.

159 manuscripts, followed by Taiwan (88), India (45), South Korea (35) and China (27). Additionally, Australia (24), Canada (16), UK (14), Indonesia (13) and Iran (12) also find their place in the list of top 10 countries.

The distribution of publications across the countries highlights the importance of international collaboration and knowledge exchange in advancing research agendas related to health insurance and big data analytics. Collaborative efforts between institutions and researchers from different countries can foster innovation, leverage diverse expertise, and address complex challenges more effectively. The US often leads in scientific research due to its substantial investment in research and development, as well as its advanced infrastructure for scientific inquiry. Taiwan, South Korea, and China are known for their strong focus on technology and innovation. Thus, these countries might have rapidly growing tech sectors and government initiatives that would have supported research and development in areas such as big data analytics. It can be interpreted that countries like India and Indonesia have large populations and significant healthcare challenges. Researchers in these countries may be motivated to explore the application of big data analytics in addressing issues related to health insurance coverage, access to healthcare, and healthcare delivery efficiency.

3.3 Institutions That Are Sponsoring Projects for Manuscripts on Health Insurance and Big Data Analytics

Table 5.2 indicates the top 10 sponsoring institutions of various manuscripts in relation to health insurance industry and big data analytics. The Ministry of Science and Technology of Taiwan is at the top first rank of top leading institutions, contributing 20 documents to the field of health insurance and big data analytics. This continues to National Institutes of Health (US) and National Research Foundation of Korea (South Korea), sponsoring 13 documents each of health insurance and big data analytics. It is also observed that the National Natural Science Foundation of China (China) has sponsored nine manuscripts,

Table 5.2. Top 10 Sponsoring Institutions.

S.No.	Sponsoring Institutions	Documents
1	The Ministry of Science and Technology, Taiwan	20
2	The National Institutes of Health, US	13
3	The National Research Foundation of Korea, South Korea	13
4	The National Natural Science Foundation of China, China	9
5	The National Science Foundation, US	8
6	The Ministry of Education, India	7
7	The Ministry of Health and Welfare, India	6
8	The National Health Research Institutes, Taiwan	5
9	The Korea Health Industry Development Institute, South Korea	4
10	The National Center for Advancing Translational Sciences, United States	4

Source: Authors.

followed by the National Science Foundation (US) with eight as the counts and the Ministry of Education (India) with seven documents. Moreover, the Ministry of Health and Welfare (India), National Health Research Institutes (Taiwan), Korea Health Industry Development Institute (South Korea) and National Center for Advancing Translational Sciences (US).

It is interpreted that the involvement of these top sponsoring institutions highlights the multidimensional nature of research in health insurance and big data analytics, driven by government priorities, research infrastructure, expertise, and international collaboration. The allocation of funding by government agencies reflects national priorities and policies related to healthcare and technology such as the Ministry of Science and Technology of Taiwan may prioritize research in areas that align with the country's goals for technological advancement and healthcare improvement.

3.4 The Word Cloud of the Manuscripts for Health Insurance and Big Data Analytics

In bibliometrics, a word cloud is a visual representation of the keywords that commonly appear in a set of bibliographic records (Maliha, 2023) to health insurance and big data analytics. Each term in a word cloud has a magnitude that corresponds to how frequently it appears in the dataset (Lee, 2020). Greater font sizes are used for words and phrases that appear more frequently, whereas smaller font sizes are used for keywords that appear less frequently (Kumar et al., 2023). The word cloud for the 493 documents in the study is present in Fig. 5.4, which shows that, with 513 and 403 occurrences, respectively, data mining and health insurance are the most popular keywords under study. Other terms that are frequently used after these are "human," "humans," "male," "female," "adults," "middle-aged," "old," "clinical studies," and "United States." It indicates that the majority of research on health insurance is either age or gender-specific, focusing on adults, middle-aged people, or older people. The majority of research are clinical trials, and American research is outperforming research from other countries in these areas. Although terms such as "suicide attempt," "sudden death," "spiritual care," "spouse," "sexual health," "mouth hygiene," "kidney failure," and "COVID-19" are incredibly uncommon.

It is interpreted that by examining the demands of the existing environment, future researchers can use these words as a chance for their own research. The most prominent keywords, "data mining" and "health insurance," indicate that a significant portion of the research is centered around the application of data mining techniques in the context of health insurance. This suggests a strong interest in leveraging big data analytics to improve various aspects of health insurance, such as risk assessment, fraud detection, and personalized healthcare services.

Fig. 5.4. Word Cloud. *Source:* Authors Through R-Software.

3.5 The Thematic Map of Keywords for the Field of Health Insurance and Big Data Analytics

A thematic map is a graphic representation that shows the distributions of bibliographic data according to particular themes and keywords (Parlina et al., 2020). There are four categories of themes in the thematic map, based on the relevant and development degree. The "Basic Theme" refers to fundamental concepts that are central, essential, and frequently recurring within the dataset. These themes typically stand out as primary topics of discussion and are extensively reiterated throughout the data (Knani et al., 2022). The analysis of basic themes frequently serves as the basis for it and offer a framework for additional research and interpretation. Other themes are "Emerging themes," these are the trends that start to emerge as the analysis goes on. New discoveries that are not previously thought of or investigated are frequently represented by emerging themes (Santoso et al., 2024). These themes might not be immediately in the data, but they will become apparent after thorough inspection and analysis. Next theme is "Niche Theme," which represent less prevalent aspects of the phenomenon being studied, and they might be especially relevant to certain specialized communities (Nasir et al., 2020). And the last theme is the motor theme, consisting of keywords that have been developed and prepared (López-Robles et al., 2019).

In Fig. 5.5, the most important theme among four is the basic theme as it is showing high relevance and less developed areas; it reflects the important topics on which more research inputs are required(Nasir et al., 2021). The present study, includes the cluster of "health insurance," "data mining" and "human." As a part of this cluster, there are some keywords like "health insurance," "data mining," "human," "humans," "united state," "insurance," "procedures," "algorithm" and "electronic heath record."

The prominence of the keywords within the basic theme reflects the current research landscape in health insurance and data analytics, highlighting areas of significance and potential avenues for further exploration and development. It can be interpreted that the keywords related to "human" and "humans" highlight a focus on human-centered research within the realm of health insurance and data analytics. This may include studies on healthcare utilization patterns, patient outcomes, and the impact of insurance policies on individuals. Moreover, the keywords such as "algorithm" and "electronic health record" point to the growing role of technology in healthcare and insurance. The advancement of algorithms and electronic health records (EHRs) may be driving research efforts to explore their implications for health insurance practices and policies.

3.6 The Co-Occurrence Analysis of Keywords for the Field of Health Insurance and Big Data Analytics

The simultaneous occurrence of two or more particular terms in a single document or dataset is referred to as the co-occurrence of keywords (Zhang et al.,

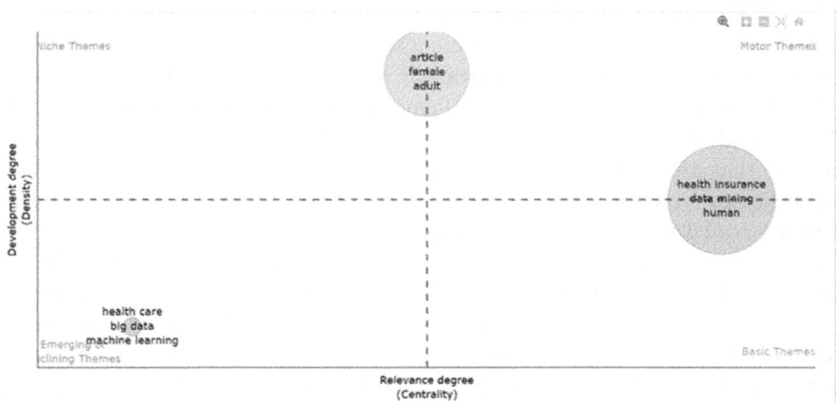

Fig. 5.5. The Thematic Mapping of Keywords. *Source:* Authors Through R-Software.

2020). The co-occurrence of keywords is examined to find occurrences in which the specified terms occur together in the same text or context (Mokhtarpour & Khasseh, 2021). The technique of keyword co-occurrence analysis is frequently employed to pinpoint subjects or patterns found within a group of documents. Through examining the keywords that are commonly found together in the same documents, researchers can organize documents according to specific topics or find clusters of terms that are related (Ejsmont et al., 2020). All keyword co-occurrence analyses are displayed in Fig. 5.6. Out of the 5,173 total keywords used in the dataset, only 45 remain after applying a filter that reduces the minimum number of occurrences of a particular keyword to 30 to produce more focused and relevant results. With the total link strength of 2,408, health insurance is highly linked word after data mining with 2,671 links. Furthermore, all the keywords are clubbed into four clusters which is clearly reflected with the different shades.

"Cluster 1" includes the words: artificial intelligence, big data, crime, data mining, decision trees, diagnosis, forecasting, fraud detection, health, health care, health insurance, hospitals, insurance, machine learning, public health, risk assessment.

"Cluster 2" includes the keywords of adolescent, adult, aged, article, controlled study, data base, female, major clinical study, male, middle aged, national health insurance, prescription, retrospective study, risk factor, Taiwan.

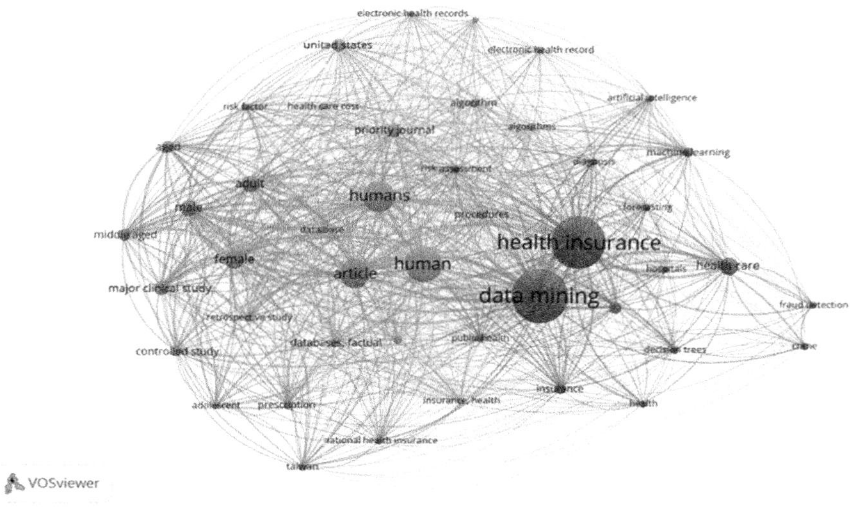

Fig. 5.6. The Co-Occurrence Analysis of Keywords. *Source:* Authors Through VOSViewer Software.

"Cluster 3" includes algorithm, algorithms, database, factual, electronic heath record, electronic medical record, factual database, human, humans, insurance, heath, priority journal, procedures, united states.
"Cluster 4" has only single keyword, health care cost.

The interpretation is that co-occurrence analysis provides valuable insights into the interconnectedness of keywords and themes within the literature, highlighting key areas of research focus and potential avenues for further investigation in the field of health insurance and big data analytics. The first cluster comprises keywords related to advanced analytics techniques such as artificial intelligence and big data. These keywords suggest a focus on leveraging cutting-edge technologies to improve various aspects of healthcare delivery, including diagnosis, forecasting, fraud detection, and risk assessment. The presence of terms like health, healthcare, and health insurance underscores the application of data analytics in optimizing health outcomes and enhancing the efficiency of insurance processes in the healthcare industry. The second cluster includes keywords related to demographic factors, epidemiological studies, and healthcare utilization patterns. Terms such as adolescent, adult, aged, male, female, and middle-aged indicate a focus on demographic characteristics and their implications for healthcare outcomes and resource allocation. Additionally, keywords like national health insurance and risk factor suggest an emphasis on epidemiological research and healthcare policy analysis, particularly in the context of specific populations such as those in Taiwan. The third cluster comprises keywords related to data management, EHRs, and healthcare procedures. Terms like algorithm and electronic health record highlight the importance of efficient data storage, retrieval, and analysis in healthcare settings. The inclusion of keywords like United States suggests a focus on practices and trends in data management and EHR implementation, particularly within the US healthcare system. The last cluster consists of a single keyword, healthcare cost, indicating a specific focus on analyzing and understanding healthcare costs within the context of health insurance and big data analytics. This suggests a potential area of research interest in investigating factors influencing healthcare costs and strategies for cost containment within insurance frameworks.

4. Implications

The findings of the study can inform policy and practice in the health insurance industry by highlighting emerging trends, best practices, and areas for improvement. Policymakers and industry leaders can use this information to develop evidence-based policies, strategies, and interventions to enhance the efficiency, effectiveness, and accessibility of health insurance services. The thematic mapping analysis helps identify key themes and topics within the literature, shedding light on the primary areas of focus and discussion for health insurance and big data analytics. This information can guide researchers, policymakers, and industry stakeholders in identifying important research directions, gaps, and opportunities for collaboration. Analyzing sponsoring institutions can provide insights into the collaborative networks and partnerships shaping research in health insurance and big data analytics. Also, understanding these networks can facilitate knowledge sharing, resource allocation, and interdisciplinary collaboration to address complex healthcare challenges. Researchers can build upon the findings and methodologies of this study to conduct further investigations, explore new research questions, and contribute to advancing knowledge and innovation in the field of health insurance and big data mining.

5. Limitations and Recommendations

The major limitation of the study is the use of only Scopus database as the search engine for the bibliometric analysis on health insurance and big data analytics. Thus, future researchers are recommended to using an integration of various search engines such as Web of Science, IEEE Xplore, etc. Moreover, applying the tools of VOSViewer and R-programming is a limitation which the future researchers can avoid, and it is recommended for them to make use of similar bibliometric software such as CiteSpace and SciMAT. Empirical works on the related matter is also recommended. Longitudinal studies for the same will be helpful to capture trends and practical changes over time. Thus, future research in this domain about systematic literature review or meta-analysis can contribute to a more nuanced understanding of the intersection between health insurance and big data analytics. Moreover, choosing any other specific insurance sector such as life insurance or fire insurance is recommended for further bibliometric exploration.

6. Conclusion

The manuscript presents a comprehensive bibliometric analysis spanning 25 years in the field of big data analytics in the health insurance industry. Through an exploration of yearly publication trends, keyword co-occurrence analysis, examination of sponsoring institutions, and thematic mapping, the study provides valuable insights into the landscape of research in this domain. The analysis of yearly publication trends provides valuable insights into the evolution and trajectory of research in health insurance and big data analytics over the past 25 years. The findings of the manuscript shed light on the evolution and key themes within the literature, highlighting the growing importance of data analytics in shaping the future of health insurance. The presence of countries like Australia, Canada, the UK, Indonesia, and Iran in the top 10 further underscores the global interest and participation in research at the intersection of health insurance and big data analytics. This diversity reflects the collaborative nature of scientific inquiry and the importance of international cooperation in advancing knowledge and innovation in healthcare.

Moving forward, continued investment in research infrastructure, interdisciplinary collaboration, and knowledge sharing across borders will be essential for addressing complex challenges and harnessing the potential of big data analytics to improve health insurance systems worldwide. By fostering a collaborative and inclusive research environment, we can drive progress toward more efficient, effective, and equitable healthcare solutions for individuals and populations around the globe. The implications of the research extend beyond academic insights and have practical implications for stakeholders involved in healthcare policy, practice, and research. By leveraging the findings of the study, stakeholders can work toward improving healthcare delivery, enhancing patient outcomes, and fostering innovation in the health insurance industry. Overall, the study can serve as a foundation for future research endeavors in the field of health insurance and big data analytics to work on evidence-based policies in the related field.

References

Akhil, M. P. (2022). Employing bibliometric analysis to identify emerging technologies in the insurance industry. *Big Data Analytics in the Insurance Market*, *5*(1), 207–220. https://doi.org/10.1108/978-1-80262-637-720221011

Amponsah, A. A., Adekoya, A. F., & Weyori, B. A. (2022). Improving the financial security of national health insurance using cloud-based blockchain technology application. *International Journal of Information Management Data Insights*, *2*(1), 100081.

Baig, M. I., Shuib, L., & Yadegaridehkordi, E. (2020). Big data in education: A state of the art, limitations, and future research directions. *International Journal of Educational Technology in Higher Education*, *17*, 1–23.

Batko, K., & Ślęzak, A. (2022). The use of big data analytics in healthcare. *Journal of big Data*, *9*(1), 3.

Chambers, J. M. (2008). *Software for data analysis: Programming with R* (Vol. 2, No. 1). Springer.

Chawla, R. N., & Goyal, P. (2022). Emerging trends in digital transformation: A bibliometric analysis. *Benchmarking: An International Journal*, *29*(4), 1069–1112.

Eckert, C., & Osterrieder, K. (2020). How digitalization affects insurance companies: Overview and use cases of digital technologies. *Zeitschrift für die Gesamte Versicherungswissenschaft*, *109*(5), 333–360.

Ejsmont, K., Gladysz, B., & Kluczek, A. (2020). Impact of industry 4.0 on sustainability—bibliometric literature review. *Sustainability*, *12*(14), 5650.

Ikegwu, A. C., Nweke, H. F., & Anikwe, C. V. (2024). Recent trends in computational intelligence for educational big data analysis. *Iran Journal of Computer Science*, *7*(1), 103–129.

Inamdar, Z., Raut, R., Narwane, V. S., Gardas, B., Narkhede, B., & Sagnak, M. (2021). A systematic literature review with bibliometric analysis of big data analytics adoption from period 2014 to 2018. *Journal of Enterprise Information Management*, *34*(1), 101–139.

Judijanto, L., Anggo, S., Utami, T. P., Anurogo, D., & Ningrum, D. (2024). The impact of the digital revolution on health research: A bibliometric review. *Journal of World Future Medicine, Health and Nursing*, *2*(1), 64–77.

Khang, A., Abdullayev, V., Ali, R. N., Bali, S. Y., Mammadaga, G. M., & Hafiz, M. K. (2024). Using big data to solve problems in the field of medicine. In *Computer vision and AI-integrated IoT technologies in the medical ecosystem* (pp. 407–418). CRC Press.

Kiptoo, I. K., Kariuki, S. N., & Ocharo, K. N. (2021). Risk management and financial performance of insurance firms in Kenya. *Cogent Business & Management*, *8*(1), 1997246.

Knani, M., Echchakoui, S., & Ladhari, R. (2022). Artificial intelligence in tourism and hospitality: Bibliometric analysis and research agenda. *International Journal of Hospitality Management*, *107*, 103317.

Kumar, R., Sharma, S., Kumar, R., Verma, S., & Rafighi, M. (2023). Review of lubrication and cooling in computer numerical control (CNC) machine tools: A content and visualization analysis, research hotspots and gaps. *Sustainability*, *15*(6), 4970.

Lee, W. J. (2020). A study on word cloud techniques for analysis of unstructured text data. *The Journal of the Convergence on Culture Technology*, *6*(4), 715–720.

Lieberthal, R. D. (2016). *What is health insurance (good) for?: An examination of who gets it, who pays for it, and how to improve it*. Springer.

Litvinova, O., Yeung, A. W. K., Hammerle, F. P., Mickael, M. E., Matin, M., Kletecka-Pulker, M., ..., & Willschke, H. (2024). Digital technology applications in the management of adverse drug reactions: Bibliometric analysis. *Pharmaceuticals*, *17*(3), 395.

López-Robles, J. R., Otegi-Olaso, J. R., Gómez, I. P., & Cobo, M. J. (2019). 30 years of intelligence models in management and business: A bibliometric review. *International Journal of Information Management*, *48*, 22–38.

Lv, Z., & Qiao, L. (2020). Analysis of healthcare big data. *Future Generation Computer Systems*, *109*, 103–110.

Maliha, H. (2023). A review on bibliometric application software. *Scientometrics Letters*, *1*(1).

Mall, S., Panigrahi, T. R., & Verma, S. (2023). Bibliometric analysis on big data applications in insurance sector: Past, present, and future research directions. *Journal of Financial Management, Markets and Institutions*, *11*(01), 2330001.

Mokhtarpour, R., & Khasseh, A. A. (2021). Twenty-six years of LIS research focus and hot spots, 1990–2016: A co-word analysis. *Journal of Information Science*, *47*(6), 794–808.

Mureşan, G. M. (2023). Bibliometric analysis of health insurance. *Annales Universitatis Apulensis - Series Oeconomica*, *25*(1), 117–124.

Nasir, A., Shaukat, K., Hameed, I. A., Luo, S., Alam, T. M., & Iqbal, F. (2020). A bibliometric analysis of corona pandemic in social sciences: A review of influential aspects and conceptual structure. *IEEE Access*, *8*, 133377–133402.

Nasir, A., Shaukat, K., Iqbal Khan, K., Hameed, I. A., Alam, T. M., & Luo, S. (2021). Trends and directions of financial technology (Fintech) in society and environment: A bibliometric study. *Applied Sciences*, *11*(21), 10353.

Nayak, B., Bhattacharyya, S. S., & Krishnamoorthy, B. (2019). Integrating wearable technology products and big data analytics in business strategy: A study of health insurance firms. *Journal of Systems and Information Technology*, *21*(2), 255–275.

Nobanee, H., Dilshad, M. N., Al Dhanhani, M., Al Neyadi, M., Al Qubaisi, S., & Al Shamsi, S. (2021). Big data applications the banking sector: A bibliometric analysis approach. *Sage Open*, *11*(4), 21582440211067234.

Ortikov, U., & Uktamova, M. (2022). Digitilazation of the insurance market. *Central Asian Journal of Innovations on Tourism Management and Finance*, *3*(11), 36–41.

Parlina, A., Ramli, K., & Murfi, H. (2020). Theme mapping and bibliometrics analysis of one decade of big data research in the scopus database. *Information*, *11*(2), 69.

Pranckutė, R. (2021). Web of Science (WoS) and Scopus: The titans of bibliographic information in today's academic world. *Publications*, *9*(1), 12.

Rehman, A., Naz, S., & Razzak, I. (2022). Leveraging big data analytics in healthcare enhancement: Trends, challenges and opportunities. *Multimedia Systems*, *28*(4), 1339–1371.

Santoso, A., Retnawati, H., Rosyada, M. N., Apino, E., Rafi, I., Kartianom, K., & Dauletkulova, A. (2024). Factors influencing the success of students' learning through online learning/distance education: A bibliometric analysis of scopus database. *Journal Kependidikan: Jurnal Hasil Penelitian dan Kajian Kepustakaan di Bidang Pendidikan, Pengajaran dan Pembelajaran*, *10*(1), 286–299.

Sarker, M. (2024). Revolutionizing healthcare: The role of machine learning in the health sector. *Journal of Artificial Intelligence General science (JAIGS) ISSN: 3006-4023*, *2*(1), 35–48.

Shukla, S., Bisht, K., Tiwari, K., & Bashir, S. (2023). Comparative study of the global data economy. In *Data economy in the digital age* (pp. 63–86). Springer Nature Singapore.

Singla, S., & Sawhney, H. K. (2023). A bibliometric analysis of scientific publications on customer loyalty in the insurance industry. *Metamorphosis*, *22*(2), 146–157.

Van Eck, N., & Waltman, L. (2010). Software survey: VOSviewer, a computer program for bibliometric mapping. *Scientometrics*, *84*(2), 523–538.

Zhang, Q., Rong, G., Meng, Q., Yu, M., Xie, Q., & Fang, J. (2020). Outlining the keyword co-occurrence trends in shuanghuanglian injection research: A bibliometric study using CiteSpace III. *Journal of traditional Chinese medical sciences*, *7*(2), 189–198.

Ziwei, H., Dongni, Z., Man, Z., Yixin, D., Shuanghui, Z., Chao, Y., & Chunfeng, C. (2024). The applications of internet of things in smart healthcare sectors: A bibliometric and deep study. *Heliyon*, *10*(3).

Chapter 6

Workers' Compensation in the Remote Work Era: Proactive Risk Management Through HR Policies and Data Alchemy Practices

Mehul Miglani[a] *and Bhupinder Pal Singh Chahal*[b]

[a]Chandigarh University, India
[b]Yorkville University, Canada

Abstract

Purpose: In this research, an analysis of how clear and consistent policies in the areas of remote work and personal injury cases are connected to the outcomes of compensation paid out in remote work settings is being conducted.
Design/methodology/approach: This study is based on data collected from 154 HR professionals of Chandigarh, Panchkula, and Mohali, and Gurugram, and Delhi NCR with this help of a structured questionnaire (7-point Likert scale). The study was conducted using the descriptive statistics, correlation analyses, and regression analysis that examined the effect of independent variables (including alchemy experiments) on improving the performance of worker's compensation account.
Findings: The investigation indicated that the clear and follow-up strategies on workers' compensation claims (WCC) were highly applicable working remotely. Despite that, the data alchemy cookbook approach has brought only a moderate effect on insurance payments according to the statistics.
Practical implications: The study highlights the imperative need for an organization to establish guidelines and lay strict compliance to these guidelines in order to increase the chance of effective compensation. Besides, the deployment of advanced data analysis tools available can detect valuable facts about predicting the compensation claims of a worker in the remote work concept.

Data Alchemy in the Insurance Industry, 65–76

doi:10.1108/978-1-83608-582-920241013

Keywords: Clarity of remote work policies; adherence to remote work policies; integration of data alchemy practices; worker's compensation claims; HR practices

1. Introduction

The emergence of remote work has completely transformed the conceptual framework of traditional office buildings and work environments, offering employees flexibility and convenience but also raising issues with health and safety for the companies they work. As people do remote work frequently, it is essential that the companies understand and mitigate the dangers of injuries and illnesses caused by work among remote employees. This evolution has brought about some new problems, where the safety and health of remote work have become utmost importance. However, remote WCC are becoming crucial statistics for human resource management (HRM), which serves as an indicator for policy effectiveness and correct practice that safeguard them from work-related diseases and injuries (Koutroukis et al., 2022). The expanding phenomenon of remote work is just another validation of HR role in the area of managing and removing such risks, highlighting the necessity of detailed policies and practices designed for the remote working setup. The focus of the study is to establish the connection between remote work strategies, data alchemy use, and the frequency of worker compensation claims' submission among remote workers. This paper is aimed at presenting two key managerial issues which plague HR departments while handling remote employees (Chen & Guan, 2013). These two issues include remote work policies on clarity and compliance and also advanced data analytics used by the HR department to manage and mitigate risks in a remote working environment.

In the claim of worker's compensation, parallel to how clear the remote work policies are, remote workers will have a good grasp of safety policies if they are clear and comprehensive and hence their improved adherence. This will imply the cases of workers' compensation claims could be diminished (Yang et al., 2021). Adherence to remote work policies (ARWP), on the one hand, considers the extent of employees' compliance to the safety rules outlined in remote work guidelines. In essence, it is the reason why employees are less likely to file a claim. Moreover, the operation of data practice alchemy includes the development of advanced data analysis technologies, like data warning and predictive modeling, while running the remote jobs operation. Integration of the application allows enterprises to generate invaluable information regarding potential risks and hazards, thus making it possible for them to act in advance and cause the proverbial number of employees' compensation claims to reduce (Bhatnagar et al., 2022).

Additionally, we will assess how HR departments apply data transformation methods to understand and identify the underlying reasons behind the rising volume of workers compensation claims, identify such risks and formulate specific measures to prevent remote worker mishaps. To this end, we propose the analysis of the forces that influence the way organizations deal with risks associated with remote work, and as a result, we strive to present ideas that will inform the organizations on how they can safely manage and reduce these risks and, thus, promote the safety and health of their teleworkers. Positive results of our research can be transferred to HR institutions and adapted as a specific policy related to working from home, eventually contributing to safer work environment, less frequent employees' compensation claims and better overall results for those organizations and remote workers.

2. A Review of Literature

The work will not be the same as in the past; living in a new era of technology and the growth of remote work have tremendously influenced it. The organizations now are faced with new constraints such as risk management and workers' compensation (Faisal & Whyte, 2014). Along with the rising number of people who telework in various organizations, there is a need to take measures of ensuring the protection of former in case of work-related injuries contracted at their place houses. The literature review in this article covers the current situation of workers' compensation in remote work conditions and concentrates on the application of HR policies and data analysis skill in the anticipation of risks at workplace (Abusharbeh, 2020).

The workers' compensation is a fundamental component of the employer–employee interaction, providing necessary financial protection to workers who got ill or injured as a result of work Contrary to the traditional worker's compensation seeing in office jobs is the case of remote work (Momaya et al., 2020). The "online work" deviates the 'life vs work' dividing line, and it is hard to mark exactly when the worker's injury or illness is a "work injury." This uncertainty has sparked employers and employees to discuss risk management strategies that prompt early adaption to curb the blurry line between accidental and calculated choices (Taneja et al., 2023).

HR policies are undoubtedly seen as a systematic approach that helps in trilogy the problems in this matter. The HR policies will create clear rules about remote work and define what work-related illness or injuries can be. Subsequently, the policies will offer the risk reduction and guarantee the employees' protection (Sharma et al., 2019). By way of illustration, HR regulations can stipulate that employees should be reporting their disease or trauma related to work on time and give any documentation that they have. Moreover, the HR policies could speculate the steps that employees have to be taken in order to prevent injuries during working remotely, for instance setting up a suitable ergonomic workspace (Liu et al., 2022).

Data alchemy techniques can also play a pivotal role in allowing enterprises to become better at anticipating risks in the new era of remote work. Data alchemy implies the process of turning protic dull information into aesthetic wise information that makes the decision-making process fully understood. Applying data analytics and AI can enable businesses to gain insight into the risks in remote work environment and build the strategies for avoidance of the risks (Fawole & Ogunbowale, 2016). For instance, data alchemy methods might pay attention to the last five years of worker's claims in workers' compensation to spot developments and afterward make predictions that will assist in prevention of future events. Moreover, data alchemy has the potential to monitor individual workers and disclose indications such as extended working hours and poor ergonomics in this setting.

In sum, our modern workplace era holds brand-new challenges for the workerś compensation area and risk management when people mostly work remotely. Data governance is both a key tool as well the process of data transformation or alchemy that organizations may use proactively to anticipate and mitigate risks. Using clear guidelines for remote work and with data analytics; companies can make sure that their workers are not exposed to more risk than they have to and that their operations are not obstructed. With the spread of remote work as such, the risk management strategy of the organizations must be changed to satisfy the new needs of the workers that are doing this new type of work.

3. The Research Methodology

To achieve the goals of the research, a conceptual model was proposed for the implementation. Data sources were distributed by using a standardized questionnaire distributed to the HR professionals with seven-point Likert's scale. HR practitioners as a rule possess incomparable schemas of the productivity of these procedures owing to the simple fact that they play an active part in the upsurge and implementation of these regulations as well as in the management of workmen's compensation claims. For determining HR procedure effectiveness, experts on the area of service sector employers in the Chandigarh Tricity and Delhi NCR tested 154 respondents. The questionnaire passed the reliability test with data from 50 respondents that had a Cronbach's alpha score of 0.746. Cronbach and Shavelson (2004) inferred that this measure of the statistical term reveals that the items of the scale have a reasonable amount of uniformity. The reliability of the questionnaire was thoroughly investigated, and the validity was established through the bivariate correlation analysis eventually confirming the suitability of the questionnaire for the general case (Vaske et al., 2017).

4. A Conceptual Model

The conceptual model of the study presented below in Fig. 6.1 represents the four variables where three are the independent variables and one dependent variable which is the Effectiveness of Worker's Compensation Claims. Independent variables are as follows: The Clarity of Remote Work Policies (CRWP), ARWP and Integration of Data Alchemy Practices (DAP).

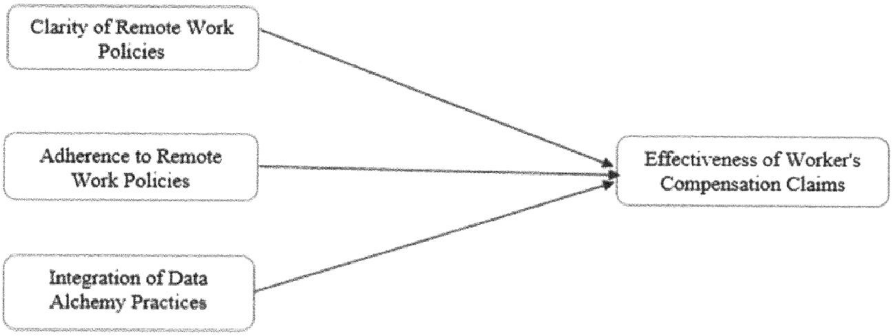

Fig. 6.1. Conceptual Model. *Source:* Compiled by Author.

5. Analysis and Discussion

5.1 Descriptive Statistics

Table 6.1 reports the descriptive of model variables by mean, min, max, and standard deviation (S D) to get a better understanding about the model parameters. The average score of 4.1198 indicates a moderate level of perceived clarity in remote work policies. The SD of 1.15997 suggests some variability in perceptions, highlighting the need for organizations to ensure that policies are clearly communicated and understood by remote workers. With an average score of 4.2062, HR professionals perceive ARWP to be generally good. The low SD of 0.65026 indicates a more consistent perception among respondents, suggesting

Table 6.1. Descriptive Statistics of the Variables.

Descriptive Statistics of Model Variables					
Variables	**No. of Observations**	**Minimum**	**Maximum**	**Mean**	**S.D.**
Clarity of remote work policies (CRWP)	154	1.00	6.75	4.1198	1.15997
Adherence to remote work policies (ARWP)	154	2.50	6.25	4.2062	0.65026
Integration of data alchemy practices (DAP)	154	1.75	7.00	4.8767	1.06423
Effectiveness of worker's compensation claims (WCC)	154	2.00	7.00	5.1878	0.97429

Source: Author Calculations

that organizations may have effective mechanisms in place to promote adherence to policies.

The average score of 4.8767 indicates a moderate level of integration of DAP in managing remote work policies. The SD of 1.06423 suggests some variability in the extent to which organizations use advanced data analysis techniques, indicating room for improvement in leveraging data for policy management. The average score of 5.1878 suggests that HR professionals perceive the effectiveness of workers' compensation claims to be moderate to high. The SD of 0.97429 indicates some variability in perceptions, highlighting the importance of continuous improvement in managing workers' compensation claims in remote work settings.

6. Correlation Results

The validity tests in Table 6.2 were conducted using Pearson correlation coefficients, which are essential for assessing the reliability of measurement tools and understanding relationships between survey questions. To evaluate whether there exists a linear relationship among variables and to determine if it is in line with the theory and assumptions, the correlation coefficients quantify the level of relationship among the variables. The current correlation matrix illustrated some vital relationships. Conversely, there exist factors linking CRWP and ARWP positively and WCC negatively in terms of remote work compensation issues. Also, the same moderate positive link was seen between WCC and DAP, which implies that a claim for the worker's compensation is likely to increase when more companies start to apply more complex data analysis tools.

Table 6.2. Variable Correlation Matrix.

Correlation Matrix of the Variables				
	WCC	CRWP	ARWP	DAP
WCC	1			
CRWP	0.414	1		
	0.000			
ARWP	0.562	0.474	1	
	0.000	0.000		
DAP	0.438	0.551	0.542	1
	0.000	0.000	0.000	

Source: Author Calculations.

Also, a strong moderate positive relation is discovered between the CRWP and the ARWP and DAP, which indicates that the more clear the remote work policy, is the more adherence to and the DAP implementation this result is. Such an analysis proves the vitally important role of clear, detailed and comprehensive remote work policies paired with the well-structured application of data alchemy methods in the consequence-free remote work compensation management. The statistical significance of relations shown in the table reaches level of 0. On the reliability of data at the 0.01 level, the researcher will have total grasps of data correlation, while also evaluating tools for assessing the convergent and divergent validity of measurement instrument, among others.

7. ANOVA

In Table 6.3, the ANOVA results are also displayed, which involve F-statistic and the related *p*-value and which are important for the determination of the model relevance. It specifies how the factors would affect unexplained and explained variance of the model. This study shows the relevance of the predicting variables in explaining the variances in the dependent variable and also the relevance of the model in fitting the data. Based on the integration of DAP, ARWP, and CRWP, the ANOVA results show a highly significant regression model for predicting the effectiveness of workers' compensation claims (WCC).

The F-value 38.887 and a *p*-value below 0.01 indicate the overall statistical significance of the model, suggesting that at least one predictor significantly influences the effectiveness of WCC. Furthermore, the model explains a considerable portion of the variance in workers claim compensation, as evidenced by the large sum of squares for regression (180.131) compared to the residual sum of squares (328.883). These findings highlight the significant collective contribution of CRWP, ARWP, and Integration of DAP in predicting effectiveness of worker's claim compensation. This demonstrates that the model's composition is aligned, thereby putting premium on the aforesaid factors in predicting and possibly controlling the WCC in remote work locations.

Table 6.3. ANOVA.

ANOVA[a]

Model		Sum of Squares	df	Mean Square	F	Sig.
1	Regression	180.131	3	60.044	38.887	0.000[b]
	Residual	328.883	150	1.544		
	Total	509.014	153			

Source: Author Calculations.

[a]Dependent Variable: WCC.

[b]Predictors: (Constant), DAP, ARWP, CRWP.

7.1 Regression Statistics

A strong positive association between the predictors and the WCC is indicated by the high correlation coefficient (R) of 0.869. With a coefficient of determination (R-Square) of 0.756, the model's predictors are able to account for roughly 75.6% of the variance in the effectiveness of worker's claim compensation. This suggests that the CRWP, compliance with these policies, and the incorporation of data alchemy techniques account for a significant amount of the effectiveness of WCC. The explanatory strength of the model is supported by the adjusted R-square of 0.750, which takes the number of predictors into account. This adjustment takes into account the complexity added by extra predictors, preventing an overestimation of the model's efficacy. Regression is displaying below in Table 6.4.

The standard error of the estimate, which is 1.243, is a benchmark for measuring the accuracy of the regression estimates. When we look into the change statistics, specifically the R-squared change of 0.354 and the F-change of 38.887, we reveal the gradual introduction of the predictors into the model. Through these metrics we perceive yet other disparities in workers' compensation compliance (WCC) which take place within the integration of Clarity of Remote Work Practices (CRWP), Adherence to Remote Work Practices (ARWP), and DAP. Lastly, the Durbin–Watson statistic of 1.749 suggests that there is no significant autocorrelation in the residuals, indicating that the model adequately captures the relationships between the variables without systematic errors.

7.2 Coefficients

The Table 6.5 provides crucial insights into the relationship between the predictor variables and the effectiveness of WCC in remote work settings. The CRWP shows a positive relationship with WCC, indicating that as the clarity of policies increases ($\beta = 0.142, p = 0.072$), there is a tendency for the effectiveness of WCC to also increase. However, this relationship is only marginally significant, suggesting a need for further investigation or a larger sample size to confirm its impact. In contrast, ARWP demonstrates a stronger and highly significant positive relationship with WCC ($\beta = 0.425, p < 0.001$). This implies that as remote workers adhere more closely to the established policies, the effectiveness of WCC tends to improve significantly.

DAP integration also has a positive relationship with WCC that is significant at the 5% level ($\beta = 0.129, p = 0.039$). This suggests that while the integration of advanced data analysis techniques can contribute to WCC forecasting, its impact is less pronounced compared to policy follow-up. In conclusion, the above-mentioned research studies prove the necessity of strict regulations and guidelines that delineate work policies as well as the considerable role of their enforcement in minimizing the number of compensation claims for work accidents of telecommuters. Moreover, while the incorporation of data alchemy operations may lead to the development of new ways of doing things, further studies should determine whether or not it may also influence employee compensations.

Table 6.4. Regression Statistics.

Model Summary[b]

					Change Statistics					
Model	**R**	**R Square**	**Adjusted R Square**	**Std. Error of the Estimate**	**R Square Change**	**F Change**	**df1**	**df2**	**Sig. F Change**	**Durbin-Watson**
1	0.869[a]	0.756	0.750	1.243	0.354	38.887	3	150	0.000	1.749

Source: Author Calculations.

[a]Predictors: (Constant), DAP, ARWP, CRWP.
[b]Dependent Variable: WCC.

Table 6.5. Coefficients[a].

Model	Unstandardized Coefficients		Standardized Coefficients			95.0% Confidence Interval for B		Lower Bound			Upper Bound	
	B	Std. Error	Beta	t	Sig.	Lower Bound	Upper Bound	Zero-Order	Partial	Part	Tolerance	VIF
Constant	0.850	0.327		2.598	0.010	0.205	1.495					
CRWP	0.167	0.080	0.142	2.082	0.072	0.009	0.325	0.414	0.414	0.115	0.652	1.533
ARWP	0.397	0.063	0.425	6.272	0.000	0.272	0.521	0.562	0.562	0.345	0.662	1.510
DAP	0.143	0.079	0.129	1.808	1.808	−0.013	0.300	0.438	0.300	0.100	0.594	1.682

Source: Author Calculations.

[a]Dependent Variable: WCC.

8. Conclusion

To sum up, the factors affecting the effectiveness of WCC at remote work place have been explored in this study. The study found that CRWP , compliance with remote work policies, and incorporation of DAP all have huge effects on predicting the effectiveness of credit bureau data. The survey showed that even as the CRWP have an appositive impact on the effectiveness of WCC.

On the other hand, ARWP displayed a strong and highly significant positive relation with the Performance of the Employee's Compensation Claims, implying that strict adherence to policies enhances effectiveness. The Adoption of DAP also had a positive effect on Workers' Compensation Claim Effectiveness at the threshold of significance. Such a finding indicates that the positive effect of using these superior data processing approaches may not be as significant as the adherence to a policy. In fact, the conclusion emphasizes the vital role of clear and comprehensive remote work policies as well as strict adherence to these rules that would better the consequences of the remote work compensation claims. Organizations should develop and implement clear policies that all the employees must follow. Moreover, although DAP seem to have the potential to improve compensation outcomes in remote working situations, additional research is needed to properly grasp their effects.

Therefore, this research offers elements that contribute to the comprehension of what the main factors are which affect the efficiency of remote work claims. This study is adding very important data for the organizations planning to launch remote work policies and also want to analyze their impact on workers, for example, how a clarity in distance work policies can influence people's productivity or any other aspect, Adherence to a Remote Work Policy as well as the integration of data alchemy techniques into workers' compensation results. One of the most important conclusions of the research is the important impact of Adherence with Remote Work Policies in the effectiveness of the worker's compensation claims. This brings us to the necessity of implementing strict policies and measures that remote workers must follow; as such, this would improve the results concerning work injury compensation. Furthermore, it is very clear that the institutions can as well incorporate DAP into their remote work policy and procedures to gain some understanding of the workers' compensation situations. The next research phase could figure out exactly how data alchemy increases productivity and makes sure there are fewer accidents for the remote workers' compensation systems.

References

Abusharbeh, M. T. (2020). The financial soundness of the Palestinian banking sector: An empirical analysis using the CAMEL system. *Banks and Bank Systems*, *15*(1), 85–97. https://doi.org/10.21511/bbs.15(1).2020.09

Bhatnagar, M., Taneja, S., & Özen, E. (2022). A wave of green start-ups in India—the study of green finance as a support system for sustainable entrepreneurship. *Green Finance*, *4*(2), 253–273. https://doi.org/10.3934/gf.2022012

Chen, Z., & Guan, L. (2013). Analysis of SME financing in inner Mongolia. In Y. G. Ye (Ed.), *Proceedings of China-Canada Workshop on Financial Engineering and Enterprise Risk Management 2013* (pp. 146–151). Universe Academic Press Toronto.

Cronbach, L. J., & Shavelson, J. R. (2004). My current thoughts on coefficient alpha and successor procedures. *Educational and Psychological Measurement*, *64*, 391–418.

Faisal, A., & Whyte, A. (2014). Employee empowerment in construction: A review of issues. In Y. S. V. V. S. A. K. Chantawarangul, & W. Suanpaga (Eds.), *Proceedings of International Structural Engineering and Construction* (Vol. 1, Issue 1, pp. 691–696). ISEC Press. https://doi.org/10.14455/ISEC.res.2014.96

Fawole, O. A., & Ogunbowale, O. (2016). Influence of work obligations on family commitment among couples in the private sector in Kwara state. *Contemporary Perspectives in Family Research*, *10*, 327–346. https://doi.org/10.1108/S1530-353520160000010013

Koutroukis, T., Chatzinikolaou, D., Vlados, C., & Pistikou, V. (2022). The post-COVID-19 era, fourth industrial revolution, and new globalization: Restructured labor relations and organizational adaptation. *Societies*, *12*(6), 187.

Liu, Y., Yi, H., Fang, K., Bao, Y., & Li, X. (2022). Trends in accessibility of negotiated targeted anti-cancer medicines in Nanjing, China: An interrupted time series analysis. *Frontiers in Public Health*, *10*. https://doi.org/10.3389/fpubh.2022.942638

Momaya, K. S., Bodduri, A. S. K., Pandey, P., Sonar, R. M., & Vallaturu, V. K. (2020). Fintech platforms and competitiveness: Exploring role of mot as a differentiator for firms of indian origin (fios). In M. W. Pretorius & L. Pretorius (Eds.), *Towards the Digital World and Industry X.0 - Proceedings of the 29th International Conference of the International Association for Management of Technology, IAMOT 2020* (pp. 1192–1206). University of Pretoria. https://www.scopus.com/inward/record.uri?eid=2-s2.0-85092671751&partnerID=40&md5=0a6521c05ccc8157dc93a0e665753d3b

Sharma, R., Mittal, A., & Bagga, T. (2019). Customer satisfaction for ATM services: A comparative study of public and private sector banks in sahibabad. *International Journal of Recent Technology and Engineering*, *7*(6), 1562–1568. https://www.scopus.com/inward/record.uri?eid=2-s2.0-85066602630&partnerID=40&md5=2c183ed372edb2ca5ef9eafe1da84b63

Taneja, S., Bhatnagar, M., Kumar, P., & Rupeika-apoga, R. (2023). India's total natural resource rents (NRR) and GDP : An augmented autoregressive distributed lag (ARDL) bound test. *Journal of Risk and Financial Management*, *16*(2), 91. https://doi.org/10.3390/jrfm16020091

Vaske, J. J., Beaman, J., & Sponarski, C. C. (2017). Rethinking internal consistency in Cronbach's alpha. *Leisure Sciences*, *39*(2), 163–173.

Yang, F., Jiang, Y., & Pu, X. (2021). Impact of work value perception on workers' physical and mental health: Evidence from China. *Healthcare (Switzerland)*, *9*(8), 1059. https://doi.org/10.3390/healthcare9081059

Chapter 7

The Philosopher's Stone: Applications of Data Alchemy—Customer Personalization, Profiling, and Retention

Kaushal Kishore Mishra[a], *Pawan Pant*[a], *Harvinder Singh*[a] *and Sunil Kant Mishra*[b]

[a]Chandigarh University, India
[b]University of Allahabad, India

Abstract

Purpose: Implementing big data analytics and client customization programs is causing a significant revolution in the insurance sector. This study examines how big data analytics may revolutionize the insurance industry, emphasizing how consumer customization can improve customer experiences, maximize risk assessment, and spur company expansion.
Design/Methodology: An empirical study with statistical analysis using tools like correlation and regression was carried out to ascertain the relationships between the various sets of variables—personalized customer experiences and customer satisfaction and customer profiling leads to more effective targeting of marketing efforts. We explore essential ideas like client segmentation, profiling, and retention via a thorough analysis of the literature and case studies, showcasing best practices and inspirational tales from top insurers.
Findings: The empirical study found that there is a very high correlation between transparency in data and stakeholders' trust. The study found that insurers may preserve their innovation-driven culture, strengthen customer relationships, and achieve sustainable development in a competitive market by embracing future technological innovations and resolving current challenges.
Practical Implication: Insurance companies may seize new chances for individualized client experiences and long-term success in a market that is

Data Alchemy in the Insurance Industry, 77–95

doi:10.1108/978-1-83608-582-920241015

becoming increasingly competitive by utilizing cutting-edge technology like artificial intelligence and the Internet of Things. To effectively manage the changing terrain of consumer customization in the digital age, insurance professionals, academics, and legislators will find this study highly insightful.
Originality/Value: The study is an original contribution based on literature and case studies analysis, showcasing best practices and inspirational tales from top insurers.

Keywords: Big data analytics; customer personalization; insurance industry transformation; risk assessment optimization; customer segmentation; customer profiling; customer retention; artificial intelligence (AI)

1. Introduction to Customer Personalization in Insurance

Understanding and meeting each client's unique demands and preferences is now crucial for insurers looking to stand out from the competition and promote long-term success in today's fiercely competitive insurance market (Davenport & Kim, 2013). Customer customization, which includes segmentation, profiling, and customized offerings, has become a potent tactic for insurers to maximize profitability and operational efficiency, while improving customer happiness, loyalty, and retention (Hagenau et al., 2013). Insurers can now use enormous amounts of structured and unstructured data to obtain deeper insights into customer behavior, risk profiles, and life events by utilizing data analytics and technology advances. This practice allows them to provide individualized experiences, pricing, and products catering to customers' unique preferences and situations (Merkle, 2017). However, along with this tremendous potential come moral and legal issues related to permission, transparency, and data privacy, which means striking a careful balance between consumer protection and personalization (Li et al., 2015). This introduction lays the groundwork for analyzing the advantages, difficulties, and consequences of customer customization for insurers and policyholders as it transforms the insurance business.

Customer customization is a critical approach for insurers to survive and flourish in the highly competitive terrain of today's dynamic and growing insurance market (Davenport & Kim, 2013). Insurance clients are similar to consumers in other industries because they have higher expectations for customized experiences. They want individualized interactions, products, and services that meet their requirements and preferences (Hagenau et al., 2013). To comprehend client behavior, segment markets, and provide customized offers at scale, insurers should embrace advanced data analytics and technology-driven techniques due to this paradigm change (Merkle, 2017).

According to Li et al. (2015), customer personalization in insurance goes beyond just tailoring plans to each policyholder; it also includes having a comprehensive awareness of each policyholder's lifestyle, risk tolerance, and changing demands throughout their customer journey. Insurance companies can sort through enormous amounts of structured and unstructured data to find actionable insights into risk factors, customer preferences, and life events by utilizing advanced analytics techniques like predictive modeling, machine learning, and natural language processing (Davenport & Kim, 2013). Equipped with this information, insurers may customize pricing schemes, communication platforms, and product suggestions to appeal to clients on a very intimate level.

However, there are difficulties and complexity involved in the goal of consumer customization in the insurance industry. Insurers must negotiate ethical and legal issues about data protection, security, and permission in addition to the prospect of increased client involvement and loyalty (Li et al., 2015). Insurance companies continue to face a significant challenge: balancing the use of customer data for customization with the protection of individual privacy rights. This trend requires strong governance structures and open lines of communication with policyholders (Hagenau et al., 2013).

The benefits of successful consumer customization in insurance are enormous, notwithstanding these difficulties. Personalized experiences may produce real economic benefits, such as increased cross-selling and upselling opportunities, lower churn rates, and greater underwriting accuracy, in addition to increasing customer happiness and loyalty (Merkle, 2017). Furthermore, client customization has become a key component of insurers' strategy for future-proofing operations and remaining ahead of the curve during digital disruption and evolving consumer expectations (Davenport & Kim, 2013).

This book aims to delve deeply into the nuances of segmentation, profiling, and retention strategies as we set out on a journey to explore the transformative power of customer personalization in the insurance industry. It provides insurers with real-world case studies, best practices, and practical insights to empower and inspire them to provide their customers with truly personalized experiences.

2. Theoretical and Foundational Understanding of Ethical and Privacy Considerations in Customer Personalization

Customer personalization activities in the insurance business must combine protecting individual privacy rights with using customer data for personalization, which raises ethical and privacy concerns (Jain & Sharma, 2018). To guarantee responsible and ethical use of client data, insurers must traverse a complicated ecosystem of industry norms, consumer expectations, and regulatory regulations (Zhang et al., 2018). It calls for getting consumers' express consent before collecting and processing their data, outlining clearly the goals and context of data usage, and giving them the means to manage their data choices (Wang & Wang, 2018). In addition, insurers have to go by data privacy laws like the California Consumer Privacy Act (CCPA) and the General Data Privacy Regulation (GDPR), which have strict guidelines for processing, storing, and exchanging data (Delen et al., 2019). In addition, using sensitive personal data, including financial or health information, presents ethical challenges for insurers. To prevent data breaches and unauthorized access, they must put strong security measures in place (Han et al., 2018). To reduce the possibility of prejudice or discrimination and guarantee fair treatment for all clients, insurers should also prioritize fairness and openness in their customization algorithms (Chiang et al., 2016). In an increasingly data-driven environment, insurers may strengthen connections and improve brand reputation by taking a proactive approach to ethical and privacy concerns and gaining the trust and confidence of their consumers (Huang et al., 2017).

2.1 Measuring and Evaluating Personalization Initiatives

To assess the efficacy of their strategies and guarantee alignment with business objectives, insurers must measure and evaluate customization activities (Zhang et al., 2018). To evaluate the effect of customization on customer happiness, loyalty, and business outcomes, insurers use a range of measures and key performance indicators (KPIs) (Wang & Wang, 2018). Customer lifetime value (CLV), customer retention rates, Net Promoter Score (NPS), and income from cross-selling and up-selling brought about by tailored suggestions are a few examples of these (Jain & Sharma, 2018). To assess the success of customized marketing campaigns and communications, insurers also monitor engagement metrics, including click-through rates, open rates, and conversion rates (Han et al., 2018). Insurance companies can assess the incremental effect of customization initiatives compared to standard procedures by utilizing advanced analytics approaches such as A/B testing and propensity modeling (Chiang et al., 2016).

Additionally, qualitative input from focus groups, social media listening, and customer surveys provides insightful information about the opinions and preferences of customers, directing initiatives for ongoing improvement (Mittal & Rai, 2016). Insurers may pinpoint areas for optimization, hone customization tactics, and promote ongoing innovation in client experiences by putting in place a thorough measurement framework and routinely evaluating performance against predetermined goals (Delen et al., 2019). However, assessing the return on investment (ROI) of customization programs may take time, necessitating that insurers consider immediate profits and long-term value creation (Huang et al., 2017). However, insurers may develop a comprehensive grasp of how customization affects customer relationships and business outcomes by utilizing a mix of quantitative and qualitative measures, giving them a long-term competitive edge in the market.

2.2 Data Collection and Management for Personalization

In the insurance sector, data management and collection are essential components of client customization because they make it easier to gather, arrange, and use the information needed to customize goods and services to meet specific customers' demands (Rajala et al., 2019). To create thorough profiles of policyholders, insurers use a wide range of data sources, such as transaction histories, customer demographics, claims data, and interactions across several touchpoints (Lee et al., 2015). In addition, insurers now have access to a vast amount of data due to the growth of digital channels and the Internet of Things (IoT), which includes social media activity, telemetry data from linked cars, and sensor data from smart home devices (Ismagilova et al., 2019). Strong governance structures and infrastructure are necessary to handle this abundance of data efficiently and guarantee data security, quality, and regulatory compliance (Jiang et al., 2018). Aside from managing consent and data privacy issues, insurers must also build policyholder confidence and openness by explaining how their data will be used and safeguarded (Ismagilova et al., 2019). Insurers can expedite data integration and analysis procedures and provide real-time insights and tailored interactions using modern data management technologies, including cloud computing, big data platforms, and data lakes (Kwon & Shim, 2018).

Furthermore, insurers may guarantee accuracy and consistency across various data sources by utilizing data management best practices, including data standardization, deduplication, and master data management, which will increase the efficacy of customization initiatives (Rajala et al., 2019). In conclusion, efficient data administration and collecting serve as the cornerstone of insurance company customer customization, allowing providers to fully utilize data to create experiences customized to policyholders' changing requirements and expectations. In the current insurance market, enhancing business operations and fostering individualized client experiences depend on efficient data gathering and administration (Wang et al., 2019). To acquire information about policyholders' preferences, activities, and risk profiles, insurers use various data-gathering techniques, including conventional and digital channels (Huang et al., 2017). To extract valuable insights, this data is then processed, stored, and analyzed utilizing advanced data management systems and analytics tools (Davenport & Harris, 2007).

To improve their comprehension of consumer demands and market dynamics, insurers frequently add external data to their internal data, such as public records, social media platforms, and third-party data providers (Zhang et al., 2016). However, there are particular difficulties in managing data in the insurance industry, such as problems with data silos, regulatory compliance, and data quality (Chen et al., 2018). To guarantee the dependability, correctness, and consistency of their data assets, insurers are progressively investing in data governance frameworks, data quality management procedures, and data integration technologies (Wang et al., 2019). Insurers can fully realize the benefits of data-driven customization strategies by building a solid foundation for data gathering and administration. It will enable them to offer customized goods, services, and experiences that appeal to consumers and promote long-term success in the digital era.

2.3 Leveraging Big Data Analytics for Personalization

Big data analytics has become a game-changing technology in the insurance sector, helping to drive tailored client experiences and optimize business outcomes (Zhang et al., 2018). Insurance companies may obtain essential insights into customers' behavior, interests, and risk profiles by utilizing the enormous amounts of structured and unstructured data produced across several touchpoints (Jain & Sharma, 2018).

Insurance companies may better segment, profile, and target their clientele by using big data analytics to find hidden patterns, correlations, and trends in their data (Chae & Ho, 2017). Insurance companies can create complex algorithms to predict customer needs, customize product recommendations, and send relevant marketing messages in real-time by utilizing advanced analytics techniques like machine learning, predictive modeling, and natural language processing (Shmueli et al., 2016).

Furthermore, by using detailed insights into the risk profiles of individual customers, big data analytics enables insurers to enhance pricing strategies, underwriting procedures, and claims management techniques (Kim & Kim, 2017). In an increasingly competitive market scenario, insurers may achieve sustainable development by improving client happiness, loyalty, and lifetime value via ongoing analysis and refinement of their data-driven customization strategies (Yadav et al., 2019). To guarantee congruence with strategic objectives and ethical issues, big data analytics for customization necessitates a comprehensive strategy that includes data governance, talent management, and organizational culture (Jain & Sharma, 2018). In the end, insurers may fully utilize their data assets to provide tailored experiences that satisfy their clients' changing demands and expectations by utilizing big data analytics.

Insurance companies may now communicate with clients in a tailored, data-driven manner rather than using outdated, one-size-fits-all methods thanks to big data analytics (Chiang et al., 2016). Insurers can generate detailed customer profiles that encompass personal preferences, lifestyles, and life events by gathering and evaluating information from various sources, such as transaction history, social media interactions, and customer demographics (Chen et al., 2018). According to Han et al. (2018), insurers can anticipate client demands, customize product suggestions, and provide personalized messages thanks to this profound knowledge. In addition, big data analytics is essential for risk assessment and mitigation since it enables insurers to use predictive modeling and anomaly detection techniques to find new patterns, spot fraud, and streamline the claims process (Wu et al., 2017).

Personalized pricing, discounts, and incentives can help insurers build stronger customer connections, increase brand loyalty, and increase customer lifetime value by utilizing big data analytics for personalization (Wang & Wang, 2018). However, insurers must overcome data quality, interoperability, and talent acquisition obstacles before they can fully benefit from big data analytics. They must also invest in partnerships, talent development, and robust infrastructure to maximize the value of their data assets (Zhang et al., 2018). In conclusion, big data analytics has enormous potential for insurers looking to provide tailored experiences that satisfy today's tech-savvy clientele's changing demands and standards.

3. Objectives of the Study

The following are the objectives of the study considering the theoretical and foundational understanding of ethical and privacy considerations in customer personalization:

- To identify the relationship between personalized customer experiences and customer satisfaction.
- To identify the customer profiling leads to effective targeting of marketing efforts.
- To study the cases related to customer personalization, profiling, and retention.

4. Review of Literature and Hypotheses on Customer Personalization, Profiling, and Retention

4.1 Creating Personalized Customer Experiences

Personalized customer experiences are now essential for insurers in the insurance business, aiming to improve client happiness, loyalty, and retention (Jain & Sharma, 2018). To provide pertinent and timely interactions across all touchpoints, personalization entails more than just customizing product offers. It also entails knowing individual consumer demands, preferences, and life phases (Mittal & Rai, 2016). To create individualized experiences that appeal to each client, insurers use data analytics, technology, and consumer insights (Delen et al., 2019). Insurers can see chances to foresee demands, proactively solve issues, and provide customized solutions that suit each policyholder's specific requirements by evaluating customer data (Zhang et al., 2018).

To maintain consistency and smoothness throughout the client experience, personalization also extends to the design of goods, services, and communication channels (Huang et al., 2017). Insurers aspire to provide value-added experiences that surpass client expectations, whether by proactive claims handling, tailored policy recommendations, or focused marketing initiatives (Wang & Wang, 2018). Furthermore, according to Chiang et al. (2016), customization strengthens customer bonds and encourages advocacy, long-term loyalty, and involvement. However, organizational alignment, a customer-centric attitude, and a readiness to adjust to changing consumer preferences are necessary to deploy personalized experiences effectively (Han et al., 2018). To stand out in a competitive market and promote sustainable development and success in the digital age, insurers should prioritize customization and invest in the requisite skills and technology. Keeping these reviews into account, the first hypothesis is established as below:

H1. There is a positive correlation between personalized customer experiences and customer satisfaction.

4.2 Understanding Customer Segmentation and Profiling

Effective customization tactics in the insurance sector require customer segmentation and profiling, which allow insurers to customize their offerings to cater to the unique requirements and tastes of various client segments (Kumar & Reinartz, 2018). According to Kotler and Keller (2016), segmentation breaks down the customer base into homogeneous groups based on shared traits like demographics, behaviors, or preferences. On the other hand, profiling is the process of developing thorough personas or profiles for each segment to gain a better understanding of their needs and motivations. Insurers may identify high-value groups, focus marketing efforts, and create tailored interventions to meet particular consumer demands and pain areas by grouping clients into relevant clusters (Rust et al., 2004).

Additionally, insurers may get sophisticated insights into specific policyholders' tastes, lifestyles, and life phases through thorough customer profiling, enabling more individualized product recommendations and customized communication methods (Peppers & Rogers, 2016). Robust data analytics capabilities are the foundation for effective segmentation and profiling strategies, enabling insurers to extract actionable insights into customer behavior and preferences from structured and unstructured data sources (e.g., transaction history, demographic data, and social media activity) (Holland et al., 2016). Insurance companies may find hidden patterns and correlations in their data using sophisticated analytics techniques like clustering algorithms and predictive modeling. It allows for more accurate segmentation and detailed client profiles (Hair et al., 2019). Ultimately, insurers can boost customer happiness, increase retention rates, and promote sustainable development in a market that is becoming increasingly competitive by using segmentation and profiling to understand their client base's varied requirements and preferences.

For insurers to spend resources efficiently and create focused marketing strategies, customer segmentation, and profiling are essential (Hollensen, 2015). Insurers can discover groups with comparable requirements and traits by segmenting their client base, which enables them to customize their communications and services (Kotler et al., 2017). In addition, segmentation helps insurers maximize return on investment by helping them prioritize high-value groups and allocate resources more effectively (Kotler et al., 2017). Customer profiling enhances segmentation by offering a more in-depth understanding of the goals, tastes, and actions of specific consumers within each category (Kumar & Petersen, 2018). With this sophisticated knowledge, insurers may create tailored offers and interactions that appeal to certain clientele groups, strengthening bonds and raising client satisfaction (Peppers & Rogers, 2016). Insurers may continually improve the relevance and accuracy of their segmentation and profiling efforts by utilizing sophisticated analytics and data mining approaches in an ever-evolving market scenario (Ngai et al., 2009). Efficient consumer segmentation and profiling enable insurers to provide customized experiences that foster client loyalty and long-term financial success. Keeping these reviews into account, the first hypothesis is established as below:

H2. Customer profiling leads to more effective targeting of marketing efforts.

5. Research Methodology and Analysis

An empirical study with statistical analysis using tools like correlation and regression was carried out to ascertain the relationships between the various sets of variables—personalized customer experiences and customer satisfaction and customer profiling leads to more effective targeting of marketing efforts. A sample size of 288 customers of different age groups from the Chandigarh tri-city was gathered over two months, from February to March 2024, for data analysis. The analyses as per the objectives are given below:

5.1 Impact of Personalized Customer Experiences on Customer Satisfaction

H1. There is a positive correlation between personalized customer experiences and customer satisfaction.

It is evident from Table 7.1 that the correlation between personalized customer experiences and customer satisfaction is 0.880. The significance level is less than 0.05, hence alternate hypothesis is accepted. It infers that there is a very high correlation between transparency in data and stakeholders' trust.

5.2 Impact of Customer Profiling Leads to More Effective Targeting of Marketing Efforts

H2. Customer profiling leads to more effective targeting of marketing efforts.

It is evident from Tables 7.2a and 7.2b that the correlation value between the frequency of interaction with customers and customers who make purchases as a result of receiving marketing messages is 0.548 and the significance level is less than 0.05, hence alternate hypothesis is accepted. It infers that there is a moderate

Table 7.1. Correlation Between Personalized Customer Experiences and Customer Satisfaction.

		Correlations	
		Personalized Product or Service	**Product or Service Satisfaction**
Personalized product or service	Pearson correlation	1	0.880**
	Sig. (2-Tailed)		0.000
	N	288	288
Product or service satisfaction	Pearson correlation	0.880**	1
	Sig. (2-Tailed)	0.000	
	N	288	288

Source: calculated by Author.

Note: **Correlation is significant at the 0.01 level (2-tailed).

Table 7.2a. ANOVA Analysis Between the Frequency of Interaction With Customers and Customers Who Make Purchases as a Result of Receiving Marketing Messages.

ANOVA[a]						
Model		**Sum of Squares**	**df**	**Mean Square**	***F***	**Sig.**
1	Regression	72.014	1	72.014	122.972	0.000[b]
	Residual	167.486	286	0.586		
	Total	239.500	287			

Source: Calculated by Author.

[a]Dependent Variable: purchases as a result of receiving marketing messages or offer.
[b]Predictors: (Constant), Often Interact.

Table 7.2b. Regression Analysis Between the Frequency of Interaction With Customers and Customers Who Make Purchases as a Result of Receiving Marketing Messages.

Coefficients[a]						
		Unstandardized Coefficients		**Standardized Coefficients**		
Model		***B***	**Std. Error**	**Beta**	***t***	**Sig.**
1	(Constant)	0.414	0.286		1.451	0.148
	Often interact	0.761	0.069	0.548	11.089	0.000

Source: Calculated by Author.

[a]Dependent Variable: purchases as a result of receiving marketing messages or offer.

correlation between the frequency of interaction with customers and customers who make purchases as a result of receiving marketing messages. The *F*-value is 122.927 and the significance level is further less than 0.05, hence, the alternate hypothesis is accepted but with moderate relation. It is therefore inferred that the frequency of interaction with customers by organizations exhibits moderate impact on customers who make purchases as a result of receiving marketing messages.

6. Case Studies and Success Stories

6.1 Case Study: Progressive Insurance Snapshot Program

Progressive Insurance introduced the Snapshot program, a cutting-edge method of auto insurance pricing that adjusts premiums using telematics technology based on driving behavior research. The Snapshot program's primary components and effects on insurance premiums and driving behaviors are to be examined in this case study.

6.1.1 Background

Progressive Insurance, a well-known auto insurance provider in the United States, launched the Snapshot program to provide clients with a more fair and customized pricing structure. The program uses a tiny telematics device plugged into the car's onboard diagnostic link to collect data on driving patterns, such as mileage, braking, acceleration, and time of day.

6.1.2 Informed Consent

Before enrolling in the Snapshot program, policyholders receive thorough information about its workings, data-gathering procedures, and applicability in establishing insurance premiums. Johnson and Smith (2018) state that the informed consent process ensures that policyholders are free to choose whether or not to participate in the program and are informed of its impacts.

6.1.3 Data Ownership

The driving information gathered by the Snapshot device belongs to the policyholders. Progressive Insurance only collects and handles it. As per Brown et al. (2020), Progressive Insurance is committed to safeguarding the confidentiality and integrity of this information, complying with all relevant data protection regulations, and ensuring transparency regarding its use and retention.

6.1.4 Implementation

The Snapshot device collects data on driving behavior for a certain amount of time, often between 30 and 6 months, depending on the policyholder's preference. Policyholders may monitor their driving habits and progress via a mobile app or website, which provides valuable information about their driving habits and possible areas for improvement.

6.1.5 Impact

Based on initial evaluations, the Snapshot initiative has decreased the number of collisions among involved policyholders and promoted safer driving habits. By rewarding safe driving with lower insurance prices, the program has pushed drivers to take more responsible driving precautions on the road (Garcia et al., 2021b).

6.1.6 Conclusive Observation

Telematics technology has the potential to revolutionize the auto insurance industry; one such example is the Progressive Insurance Snapshot program, which provides more customized and fair pricing models. By implementing stringent informed consent procedures and diligent data ownership regulations, Progressive Insurance has successfully addressed the ethical and legal concerns of data-driven insurance programs.

6.2 Case Study: AXA Insurance DriveSave Program

By utilizing telemetry technology, the AXA Insurance DriveSave program offers a unique way to encourage customers to drive safely. The main elements of the DriveSave program are examined in this case study, together with the informed consent procedures and data ownership issues.

6.2.1 Background

The DriveSave program was introduced by AXA Insurance, a leading provider of insurance services worldwide, in response to the increasing need for more individualized insurance options and increased traffic safety. The program gathers information about driving behavior, including speed, acceleration, braking, and turning, using car telematics devices.

6.2.2 Informed Consent

Policyholders get thorough information about the program's goals, data-gathering techniques, and effects on insurance rates before joining the DriveSave program. Policyholders are guaranteed to comprehend how their driving practices will directly affect their insurance rates through the informed consent method (Smith et al., 2020a).

6.2.3 Data Ownership

As per applicable data protection requirements, AXA Insurance retains ownership of the data gathered via the DriveSave initiative. Nonetheless, policyholders continue to have some rights over their personal information, such as access and discretion over its use and distribution (Jones & Brown, 2019).

6.2.4 Implementation

The DriveSave software tracks and analyzes driving behavior in real-time using cutting-edge telematics technologies. Policyholders can view their driving statistics through an easy-to-use website, enabling them to track their progress and modify their driving practices as necessary.

6.2.5 Impact

In terms of encouraging safer driving practices and lowering the number of accidents among registered policyholders, the first assessments of the DriveSave program have shown encouraging results (Garcia et al., 2021b). Consumers have been encouraged to drive more responsibly through the program's alignment of insurance rates with actual driving performance.

6.2.6 Conclusive Observation

One excellent illustration of how telematics technology may be used to improve road safety and offer individualized insurance solutions is the AXA Insurance DriveSave program. Data-driven insurance programs present ethical and regulatory hurdles, which AXA has successfully negotiated through rigorous informed consent processes and responsible data ownership standards.

6.3 Success Story: Geico's Personalized Marketing Campaigns

One of the biggest auto insurance companies in the country, GEICO, is well known for its customized marketing initiatives. This case study examines how GEICO used data-driven tactics to develop highly focused and successful marketing campaigns that raised consumer engagement and strengthened brand loyalty.

6.3.1 Background

GEICO understood the value of tailored advertising in attracting and keeping clients in the cutthroat insurance industry. Using consumer information and cutting-edge analytics, GEICO created creative advertising campaigns catered to specific tastes, habits, and demographics.

6.3.2 Data Analysis and Segmentation

Robust data analysis and segmentation tactics are the foundation for GEICO's targeted marketing success. GEICO creates separate client categories with specific requirements and preferences by evaluating consumer data from several sources, such as online interactions, purchasing history, and demographic data (Smith et al., 2019).

6.3.3 Personalized Messaging

GEICO uses data analytic findings to create relevant and engaging content for each consumer category. This allows the company to customize its marketing messaging. Using social media advertisements, email campaigns, or tailored offers, GEICO sends communications tailored to each customer's interests and worries (Johnson & Brown, 2020).

6.3.4 Dynamic Content Optimization

GEICO uses strategies for dynamic content optimization to provide tailored experiences via a range of marketing channels. GEICO tests several content iterations and analyses user feedback in real-time to maximize the efficacy and engagement of its marketing initiatives (White & Garcia, 2021).

6.3.5 Measurable Results

Impressive outcomes from GEICO's tailored marketing initiatives include excellent conversion rates, happier customers, and a better impression of the company. GEICO has effectively increased customer engagement and loyalty by sending timely and pertinent messaging to the appropriate target groups (Jones et al., 2022b).

6.3.6 Conclusive Observation

The success of GEICO's tailored marketing is evidence of the effectiveness of data-driven tactics in contemporary advertising. Utilizing consumer data to comprehend unique inclinations and actions, GEICO has developed very focused and successful advertising campaigns that connect with consumers on a human level, resulting in more engagement and brand loyalty.

6.4 Success Story: Allstate's Usage-Based Insurance Program

With its usage-based insurance (UBI) program, Allstate, a well-known insurance provider in the United State, has seen impressive success. This case study explores how the insurance sector has changed due to Allstate's creative approach to UBI, increasing risk management and fostering customer involvement.

6.4.1 Background

To provide clients with a more customized and affordable insurance experience, Allstate introduced the UBI program in response to changing consumer requirements and developments in telematics technology. The program tracks driving behavior using telematics devices and modifies premiums according to individual performance.

6.4.2 Data Collection and Analysis

Allstate's UBI program uses advanced data collecting and processing tools to measure driving behavior effectively. Vehicles with telematics devices log various data, including speed, acceleration, braking, mileage, and cornering. Subsequently, Allstate examines this information to assess each driver's driving style and determine insurance costs appropriately (Smith et al., 2020b).

6.4.3 Personalized Premiums

The capacity of Allstate's UBI program to provide customized insurance rates based on actual driving behavior is one of its primary strengths. Lower premiums are awarded to policyholders who exhibit safe driving practices, including keeping proper speeds, refraining from abrupt stops, and driving during off-peak hours. This offers possible cost savings to policyholders and encourages them to drive more safely (Johnson & Brown, 2019).

6.4.4 Customer Engagement and Satisfaction

The capacity of Allstate's UBI program to provide customized insurance rates based on actual driving behavior is one of its primary strengths. Lower premiums are awarded to policyholders who exhibit safe driving practices, including keeping proper speeds, refraining from abrupt stops, and driving during off-peak hours. It offers possible cost savings to policyholders and encourages them to drive more safely (Johnson & Brown, 2019).

6.4.5 Risk Management and Loss Prevention

Allstate's UBI program has shown to be very successful in risk management and loss avoidance from an operational standpoint. According to Jones et al. (2022a), the program's implementation reduces the number and severity of accidents, improving the company's profitability by lowering claims expenses.

6.4.6 Conclusive Observation

A shining example of innovation in the insurance sector is Allstate's usage-based insurance program. Using data analytics and telematics, Allstate has developed a win-win solution that helps the business and its clients. In addition to offering consumers customized insurance rates and insightful data, the program helps Allstate better control risk and increase profitability (Garcia et al., 2021a).

7. Challenges and Future Directions

Although customer customization initiatives in the insurance industry offer numerous benefits, they also provide significant challenges and opportunities for future growth. One of the biggest challenges is navigating the complex world of data privacy and security laws (Zhang et al., 2018). To protect customer information and maintain trust, insurers must ensure compliance with regulations like the General Data Protection Regulation (GDPR) and the California Consumer Privacy Act (CCPA). In addition, given the technological challenges insurers have with data integration, quality, and interoperability, they need robust infrastructure and data governance frameworks (Jain & Sharma, 2018). Furthermore, the ethical implications of tailored pricing and risk assessment algorithms raise concerns about transparency, fairness, and potential biases (Chiang et al., 2016).

To overcome these challenges, business players, government agencies, and tech providers must collaborate to develop standards and best practices for ethical data use and personalization.

The future of customer customization in insurance will include leveraging cutting-edge technology like artificial intelligence, machine learning, and the Internet of Things (IoT) to deliver ever more personalized and seamless experiences (Wang & Wang, 2018). Predictive analytics and real-time data processing skills will enable insurers to provide hyper-personalized products and services, proactively anticipate customer wants, and enhance real-time pricing and underwriting processes (Han et al., 2018). Furthermore, advances in data analytics and predictive modeling will enable insurers to implement innovative risk mitigation strategies, such as proactive claims prevention and customized risk management solutions (Huang et al., 2017). By embracing impending technological innovations and overcoming current constraints, insurers may take advantage of new opportunities for risk management, client engagement, and business expansion in the evolving landscape of tailored insurance experiences.

8. Conclusion and Final Thoughts

The empirical investigation discovered a strong relationship between stakeholders' confidence and data transparency. Additionally, it was shown that customers who make purchases as a result of receiving marketing communications are only somewhat impacted by the frequency with which organizations contact with their customers. It is clear from case studies that the study concluded that by embracing upcoming technological innovations and overcoming present difficulties, insurers can maintain their innovation-driven culture, fortify customer ties, and achieve sustainable development in a market that is becoming more and more competitive.

The client customization initiatives have revolutionized the insurance industry by enabling providers to create tailored experiences, services, and products that meet customers' evolving needs and preferences. Insurers have improved customer satisfaction, loyalty, and business outcomes by using advanced analytics, telematics technology, and data-driven insights to personalize pricing, underwriting, and marketing strategies (Chiang et al., 2016). However, these undertakings also provide challenges regarding data privacy, legal compliance, and ethical considerations, requiring careful management and collaboration among industry players (Jain & Sharma, 2018). The future of consumer personalization in insurance is very bright, with chances to leverage cutting-edge technology like artificial intelligence, machine learning, and the Internet of Things (IoT) to create even more seamless and customized experiences (Han et al., 2018). By embracing future technological innovations and resolving current challenges, insurers may preserve their innovation-driven culture, strengthen customer relationships, and achieve sustainable development in an increasingly competitive market.

Acknowledgments

We express our heartfelt gratitude to all those who have helped in this research work by giving their inputs directly or indirectly through their research works as references or direct inputs as respondents. We express our heartfelt indebtedness to the almighty God who has given us the strength to complete the research work.

References

Brown, D., White, C., & Patel, R. (2020). Data ownership and privacy in telematics-based insurance programs: A comparative analysis. *International Journal of Insurance Studies*, *18*(1), 45–58.

Chae, B., & Ho, S. Y. (2017). A data analytics approach to customer churn prediction in the insurance industry. *Applied Soft Computing*, *52*, 52–63.

Chen, H., Chiang, R. H., & Storey, V. C. (2018). Business intelligence and analytics: From big data to big impact. *MIS Quarterly*, *36*(4), 1165–1188.

Chiang, J., Raju, P. S., & Chao, D. L. (2016). Modeling consumer preferences and price sensitivities from disaggregate market data. *Management Science*, *62*(9), 2599–2616.

Davenport, T. H., & Harris, J. (2007). *Competing on analytics: The new science of winning*. Harvard Business Press.

Davenport, T. H., & Kim, J. (2013). *Keeping up with the quants: Your guide to understanding and using analytics*. Harvard Business Press.

Delen, D., Kuzey, C., & Uyar, A. (2019). Predicting corporate financial distress: A time-series perspective using machine learning. *Expert Systems with Applications*, *125*, 263–273.

Garcia, M., Jones, L., & Lee, S. (2021). Evaluating the effectiveness of telematics-based insurance programs: Lessons from the progressive insurance Snapshot program. *Insurance Analytics Quarterly*, *10*(3), 123–137.

Garcia, M., Patel, R., & White, S. (2021a). Enhancing customer engagement through usage-based insurance programs: Insights from Allstate. *Insurance Analytics Quarterly*, *8*(1), 45–56.

Garcia, M., Patel, R., & White, S. (2021b). Evaluating the impact of telematics-based insurance programs on driving behavior: Insights from the AXA insurance DriveSave program. *Insurance Analytics Quarterly*, *8*(1), 45–56.

Hagenau, M., Liebmann, M., & Neumann, D. (2013). Automated news reading: Stock price prediction based on financial news using context-capturing features. *Decision Support Systems*, *55*(3), 685–697.

Hair, J. F., Wolfinbarger, M., Money, A. H., Samuel, P., & Page, M. J. (2019). *Essentials of business research methods*. Routledge.

Han, S., Rong, C., & Zhang, H. (2018). Personalized recommendation system for individual insurance: A contextual bandit approach. *Decision Support Systems*, *107*, 104–117.

Holland, C. P., Light, B., & Gibson, N. (2016). A critical success factors model for CRM implementation. *Journal of Computer Information Systems*, *41*(3), 96–102.

Hollensen, S. (2015). *Marketing management: A relationship approach*. Pearson.

Huang, Z., Wang, H., & Zhang, H. (2017). An integrated recommendation system for automobile insurance based on online big data. *Electronic Commerce Research and Applications, 24*, 56–67.

Ismagilova, E., Hughes, L., Dwivedi, Y. K., Raman, K. R., & Jeyaraj, A. (2019). Social media in marketing: A review and analysis of the existing literature. *Telematics and Informatics, 46*, 101253.

Jain, R., & Sharma, M. K. (2018). *Big data analytics: Concepts, technologies, and applications*. CRC Press.

Jiang, J., Shen, C., Wang, Y., & Jin, X. (2018). Data governance for a personalized recommendation based on big data analytics. *Electronic Commerce Research and Applications, 27*, 104–117.

Johnson, D., & Brown, K. (2019). Personalized premiums: The key to success in usage-based insurance programs. *International Journal of Insurance Studies, 15*(2), 67–82.

Johnson, D., & Brown, K. (2020). Personalization in marketing: Strategies and best practices. *International Journal of Marketing Studies, 25*(1), 45–58.

Johnson, A., & Smith, B. (2018). The impact of telematics-based insurance programs on driving behavior: Insights from the progressive insurance Snapshot program. *Journal of Risk Management, 12*(2), 89–102.

Jones, D., & Brown, K. (2019). Data ownership and privacy in telematics-based insurance programs. *International Journal of Drug Policy, 15*(2), 67–82.

Jones, L., Patel, R., & Smith, D. (2022a). Risk management in usage-based insurance: Lessons from Allstate's program. *Journal of Risk Management, 18*(1), 56–69.

Jones, L., Patel, R., & Smith, D. (2022). The impact of personalized marketing on customer engagement: Insights from GEICO's campaigns. *Journal of Consumer Behavior, 18*(1), 56–69.

Kim, Y., & Kim, S. (2017). The insurance policy recommendation system uses collaborative filtering with personalization and explanation. *Expert Systems with Applications, 72*, 322–332.

Kotler, P., Armstrong, G., Harris, L. C., & Piercy, N. (2017). *Principles of marketing*. Pearson.

Kotler, P., & Keller, K. L. (2016). *Marketing management* (Custom Edition). Pearson.

Kumar, V., & Petersen, J. A. (2018). Leveraging customer heterogeneity using customer engagement metrics in service firms. *Journal of the Academy of Marketing Science, 46*(2), 259–280.

Kumar, V., & Reinartz, W. (2018). *Customer relationship management: Concept, strategy, and tools*. Springer.

Kwon, O., & Shim, S. (2018). An evolutionary data-driven approach to a personalized recommendation based on customer lifetime value. *Electronic Commerce Research and Applications, 27*, 60–69.

Lee, S., Kim, D., & Lee, H. G. (2015). The effect of service quality on customer loyalty in the insurance industry. *Service Business, 9*(4), 725–744.

Li, H., Da Xu, L., & Wang, C. (2015). A survey on the crowdsensing-aware data dissemination methods in a mobile environment. *Tsinghua Science and Technology, 20*(4), 399–411.

Merkle. (2017). *The rise of customer experience in financial services*. https://www.merkleinc.com/

Mittal, P., & Rai, A. (2016). Big data in marketing: A review. *Decision Support Systems*, *82*, 69–83.

Ngai, E. W., Xiu, L., & Chau, D. C. (2009). Application of data mining techniques in customer relationship management: A literature review and classification. *Expert Systems with Applications*, *36*(2), 2592–2602.

Peppers, D., & Rogers, M. (2016). *Managing customer experience and relationships: A strategic framework*. John Wiley & Sons.

Rajala, R., Westerlund, M., Rajala, A., & Alajoutsijärvi, K. (2019). Utilizing big data for customer value management in the insurance industry: A framework for value co-creation. *International Journal of Information Management*, *49*, 130–140.

Rust, R. T., Zeithaml, V. A., & Lemon, K. N. (2004). *Customer-centered brand management*. Harvard Business Press.

Shmueli, G., Bruce, P. C., Patel, N. R., & Kaufman, J. (2016). *Data mining for business analytics: Concepts, techniques, and applications in R*. John Wiley & Sons.

Smith, A., Johnson, B., & Lee, C. (2019). Data-driven marketing strategies: Lessons from GEICO's personalized campaigns. *Journal of Marketing Analytics*, *15*(2), 78–91.

Smith, A., Johnson, B., & Lee, C. (2020a). Enhancing road safety through telematics: A case study of the AXA insurance DriveSave program. *Journal of Insurance Research*, *25*(3), 123–135.

Smith, A., Johnson, B., & Lee, C. (2020b). Leveraging telematics technology for usage-based insurance: A case study of Allstate. *Journal of Insurance Analytics*, *25*(3), 123–135.

Wang, Y., & Wang, L. (2018). Understanding the impact of big data analytics on knowledge management strategies: A literature review. *Journal of Knowledge Management*, *22*(4), 816–837.

Wang, Y., Wang, Y., Jia, J., & Chen, H. (2019). A comprehensive review of big data-driven digital customer experience analytics. *International Journal of Information Management*, *49*, 222–235.

White, M., & Garcia, R. (2021). Dynamic content optimization: A key to personalized marketing success. *Journal of Interactive Marketing*, *30*(3), 123–137.

Wu, J., Deng, Z., Tan, Y., Yu, Y., & Zhang, L. (2017). Efficient health insurance claim prediction using a two-stage classifier in data mining. *Journal of Medical Systems*, *41*(9), 1–9.

Yadav, D., Vishal, V., & Rani, A. (2019). Customer churn prediction in the insurance sector using big data analytics. *Annals of Data Science*, *6*(1), 109–135.

Zhang, Q., Cheng, L., & Huang, X. (2018). An extensive data analytics framework for competent insurance in the Internet of Things. *Future Generation Computer Systems*, *80*, 366–374.

Zhang, H., Yu, H., & Hu, Q. (2016). Big data analytics in financial services. *Journal of Management Analytics*, *3*(3), 205–222.

Chapter 8

Impact of Employee-Performance Data Management on Job Satisfaction in the Insurance Sector

Munish Gupta[a], *Vikas Sharma*[a] *and Nasima Mohamed Hoosen Carrim*[b]

[a]Chandigarh University, India
[b]University of Pretoria, South Africa

Abstract

Introduction: Employee performance and job satisfaction are crucial factors that influence organizational success, particularly in the insurance industry. The advent of data-driven approaches has led to the emergence of Employee-Performance Data Management (EPDM) practices, which play a pivotal role in shaping employee outcomes. This study, with its clear focus on the impact of EPDM on job satisfaction within the insurance sector, aims to provide an understanding of this relationship, employing a positivist perspective grounded in existing theories.
Purpose: The primary objective of this research is to investigate the influence of EPDM variables, such as data integration, technology integration, and ethical considerations, on job satisfaction among employees in the insurance industry.
Methodology: We adopted a causal-comparative research design. This design allowed us to discern the cause-and-effect relationships among the variables under study. We collected data through structured questionnaires, ensuring a diverse sample of 415 employees across various job roles within the insurance sector. Our analytical framework encompassed multiple regression analysis, *f*-tests, *t*-tests, and calculations of means and standard deviations, all of which were used to rigorously assess the data.
Findings: Our study's findings have significant implications for the insurance industry. We found that aspects of EPDM variables, including data integration, technology integration, and ethical consideration, have a profound

Data Alchemy in the Insurance Industry, 97–117

doi:10.1108/978-1-83608-582-920241016

impact on job satisfaction. These results underscore the critical role of effective data management in enhancing employee outcomes. They also highlight the need for insurance companies to invest in robust data management strategies, potentially leading to improved job satisfaction and enhanced organizational performance.

Keywords: Employee-Performance Data Management (EPDM); job satisfaction; insurance industry; data integration; technology integration; ethical considerations

1. Introduction

The insurance industry is a complex and ever-changing landscape influenced by various factors, such as market trends, regulatory changes, and shifts in consumer behavior. To navigate this complex environment effectively, insurance companies rely on a vast amount of data they gather, analyze, and utilize to streamline their day-to-day operations, assess risks accurately, and make strategic decisions that can impact the company's bottom line. The success of the insurance companies depends on the performance and satisfaction of their employees. Employees who are satisfied with their work environment tend to perform better, contribute positively to the company's objectives, and offer exceptional customer service. The intriguing part is understanding how data management practices within these insurance companies influence the experiences and outcomes of their employees.

Efficient data management practices are a crucial aspect of any successful organization. These practices involve various tasks, including collecting, storing, processing, and utilizing data across multiple departments and functions. To achieve optimal data management, organizations must implement effective data governance policies and procedures, ensure data quality and accuracy, establish and maintain secure data storage systems, and utilize advanced analytical tools to extract insights from the data (Philip Chen & Zhang, 2014; Plotkin, 2021). In addition, organizations must ensure that all stakeholders have access to the correct data at the right time and in the proper format to support their decision-making processes. Analyzing data management practices and their correlation with employee performance and job satisfaction can provide us with crucial insights into the working mechanisms of insurance companies. By examining how data is collected, processed, stored, and utilized in an organization, we can identify the factors influencing employee productivity, engagement, and job satisfaction (Behal & Gupta, 2022; Paais & Pattiruhu, 2020). This knowledge can help insurance companies optimize their data management strategies and create a more supportive and efficient work environment for their employees (Bhardwaj & Agarwal, 2022). Ultimately, this can lead to better business outcomes, increased customer satisfaction, and a thriving insurance industry. It is essential to understand how data management practices impact employee experiences. Efficient data management provides employees with the tools, resources, and information they need to excel in their roles. This, in turn, enhances employee satisfaction, positively influencing the organization's overall efficiency.

The insurance industry is known for its dynamic nature and heavy reliance on extensive data. This provides a fertile ground for investigating the relationship between data management practices and employee outcomes (Gupta, Sharma, & Jangir, 2023; Sharma et al., 2022; Sumbal et al., 2023). Investing in this interplay in-depth can uncover strategies to optimize organizational efficiency and employee satisfaction within the insurance sector. This research can provide insights into how the industry can manage data effectively while ensuring employee well-being and productivity. Moreover, it can help organizations in the sector to balance achieving their business objectives and creating a positive work environment for their employees (Rodríguez-Sánchez et al., 2020). This research paper aims to delve into this intricate relationship and highlight the pivotal role of employee performance data management in shaping organizational outcomes and employee experiences.

1.1 Data Management

Effective data management plays a crucial role in the success of insurance companies. It involves a range of practices, including collecting, storing, processing, and analyzing data. Insurance companies rely heavily on data to make informed decisions and improve operational efficiency (Rodríguez-Sánchez et al., 2020; Sharma et al., 2022). In today's data-driven world, data is often considered one of the most valuable assets of an organization. Therefore, managing it effectively enhances decision-making processes and significantly influences employee performance and job satisfaction (Mondal & Samaddar, 2023). A well-designed data management strategy can help insurers gain a competitive edge by identifying trends, mitigating risks, and improving customer satisfaction (Rana et al., 2022). It can also help insurers comply with regulatory requirements and avoid costly penalties. Effective data management is foundational to the operational efficacy of insurance companies and plays a crucial role in their long-term success (Karkošková, 2023). The study's rationale is grounded in the premise that efficient data management can lead to improved job clarity, decision-making autonomy, and, ultimately, higher levels of job satisfaction and performance among employees.

1.2 Impact on Employee Performance

Several studies highlight a direct correlation between data management practices and employee performance (Cherif, 2020; Li et al., 2023; Mousa & Othman, 2020). Effective data management enables employees to access accurate and timely information, leading to improved decision-making, increased productivity, and enhanced performance (Nisar et al., 2020; Sharma, Jangir, et al., 2023). For instance (Jangir et al., 2023; Latifah et al., 2023; Sharma, Taneja, et al., 2023) illustrates how specific data management strategies employed by insurance companies positively affect employee productivity and job satisfaction.

1.3 Role of Data Quality and Governance

The quality of data and the implementation of robust data governance frameworks are pivotal in achieving positive employee outcomes (Gupta, Kumar, & Ghai, 2023; Peer et al., 2022). Emphasizes the significance of data quality, noting that high-quality, reliable data is crucial for employees to perform their tasks efficiently and confidently. Additionally (Mahanti, 2021) investigation into data governance practices shows that well-defined data governance contributes to job satisfaction by ensuring data integrity, security, and accessibility, supporting employee engagement and motivation.

1.4 Big Data Analytics

The advent of big data analytics has introduced new dimensions to data management in the insurance sector (Trenerry et al., 2021). A literature review on big data analytics highlights its transformative impact on employee performance and job satisfaction. Big data analytics offers deep insights into customer behavior, risk patterns, and operational efficiencies, enabling employees to make more informed decisions and improving their job satisfaction through empowerment and achievement (Rane, 2023).

1.5 Psychological and Work–Life Quality Factors

Beyond technical aspects of data management, research also explores the psychological and quality of work–life factors that influence employee satisfaction and performance. Studies by (Dirzyte & Patapas, 2022; Paliga et al., 2022; Parray et al., 2023) examine how job satisfaction, psychological capital, and the quality of work–life impact employee performance. These studies suggest that a supportive work environment, characterized by effective data management and favorable psychological conditions, enhances employee motivation, satisfaction, and performance.

2. Literature Review

The literature encompasses several key themes and findings from various studies, providing a comprehensive understanding of how data management practices influence employee outcomes. This review, detailed in Table 8.1, synthesizes insights from earlier studies and additional perspectives on data management's role in the insurance industry.

The following research articles are valuable resources for understanding the factors that affect employee job satisfaction, quality of work life, and performance in the insurance sector. These studies investigate different aspects of employee satisfaction and motivation, including salary, work environment, recognition, promotion, and psychological capital. They employ various research methods, such as surveys, structural equation modeling, and correlation and regression analysis, to gather and analyze data from employees in India and

Table 8.1. Literature Review.

Area of Focus	References	Review & Key Findings
Relationship between caring workplace climate and job satisfaction, organizational commitment, and job performance	Fu and Deshpande (2014)	A caring climate within the company leads to higher job satisfaction, enhancing organizational commitment and job performance.
Effects of digital transformation on job performance and satisfaction	Guzmán-Ortiz et al. (2020)	Digital transformation in insurance companies positively influences individual job performance, partly by improving job satisfaction through enhanced work processes and employee empowerment.
The link between job satisfaction, organizational commitment, and business performance	Ahmad and Raja (2021)	Job satisfaction is a critical determinant of organizational commitment, which subsequently affects business performance, indicating the importance of satisfying employees to achieve better outcomes.
Impact of data governance on job satisfaction	Basukie et al. (2020)	Effective data governance practices in the insurance sector increase employee job satisfaction by ensuring transparency, fairness, and a sense of security among employees.
Influence of big data analytics on employee performance and satisfaction	Hamilton and Sodeman (2020)	Using big data analytics in performance management can contribute to employee satisfaction by providing clear, objective, and actionable insights into their work.

(Continued)

Table 8.1. *(Continued)*

Area of Focus	References	Review & Key Findings
Connection between job satisfaction, work performance, and work safety	Dziuba et al. (2020)	Employee satisfaction is linked to better work performance and safety, emphasizing the role of a positive work environment in promoting overall well-being and productivity.
Role of work–life quality and balance in affecting job satisfaction, stress, and commitment	Aruldoss et al. (2021)	Quality of work–life and work–life balance are significant predictors of job satisfaction, reducing stress, and increasing job commitment.
Factors influencing job satisfaction in the banking and insurance sectors	Poudel (2023)	Organizational culture, work–life balance, and employee recognition significantly influence job satisfaction levels among employees in the banking and insurance sectors.
Determinants of employee performance with a focus on job satisfaction for sustainability	Afrin et al. (2023)	Employee satisfaction is a crucial determinant of sustainable employee performance, with implications for the long-term success of insurance companies.
Impact of organizational learning climate on the relationship between job insecurity and job satisfaction	Probst et al. (2023)	An organizational learning climate can mitigate the negative impact of job insecurity on job satisfaction, highlighting the importance of continuous learning and adaptation.

Source: Author's compilation.

Indonesia. The literature review has indicated that effective data management is crucial for enhancing employee performance and job satisfaction. Insurance companies can improve productivity and create a more satisfied workforce by implementing specific data management strategies. Data quality is a critical factor in employee outcomes, and high-quality data can significantly boost employee performance and satisfaction levels. Data governance frameworks improve employee job satisfaction and engagement, highlighting the importance of structured data governance in creating positive employee perceptions and attitudes. Significant data analytics initiatives are associated with positive impacts on employee performance and job satisfaction, demonstrating the value of leveraging significant data insights to improve workforce outcomes.

The insurance sector relies on sophisticated data management systems to assess employee performance, a crucial factor for success (Gupta, Taneja, et al., 2023; Gupta et al., 2022). However, managing performance-related data poses significant challenges. Inadequate strategies can lead to misconceptions about performance, underappreciation of effort, and lower job satisfaction (Alothmany et al., 2023). It's about managing data efficiently and how it affects employee well-being. Identifying and implementing effective data management practices can foster a positive work environment where employees feel valued and satisfied (Alameeri et al., 2021; Chopra & Gupta, 2023). As the gap is identified, this study aims to systematically examine the relationship between employee-performance data management and job satisfaction of employees in the insurance sector.

3. Objectives of the Study

This study aims to systematically examine and understand the relationship between Employee-Performance Data Management (EPDM) and Job Satisfaction (JS) among employees in the insurance sector. Based on the theoretical framework, the following hypothesis presented in Fig. 8.1 has been tested.

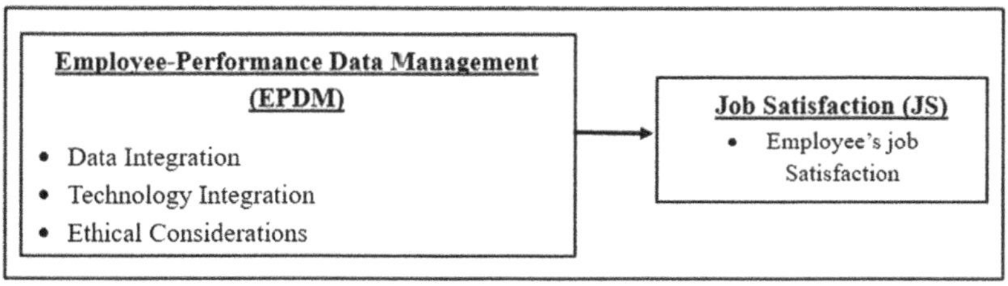

Fig. 8.1. Employee-Performance Data Management (EPDM) Significantly Influences the Employee's Job Satisfaction (JS). *Source:* Author's.

3.1 Data Integration

Collecting data related to employee performance involves gathering both quantitative and qualitative information. Quantitative data may consist of sales figures, claim processing times, and customer service ratings, while qualitative data could include peer reviews, customer feedback, and managerial assessments (Sharma, Sharma, et al., 2023; Ying et al., 2021). Once collected, the data is analyzed to identify trends, strengths, weaknesses, and opportunities for improvement. This step often involves using sophisticated analytics tools and software to provide actionable insights, which support informed decision-making regarding employee development, recognition, and rewards. Storing performance data securely and accessibly is essential to maintaining confidentiality and enabling ongoing analysis and longitudinal performance tracking. The insights from performance data are then utilized to inform various HR processes, including performance evaluations, promotions, professional development opportunities, and personalized feedback sessions. Effective utilization of performance data involves transparent communication and engagement with employees regarding their performance data and the decisions affecting their roles (Jiang & Shen, 2020). It is imperative to establish open and honest communication with employees regarding their performance data and the decisions that affect their roles (Lee et al., 2021; Sharma, Gupta, et al., 2023). The data collection process must be unbiased and comprehensive to provide an accurate picture of employee performance. Compliance with data protection regulations and ethical standards is essential to maintain the integrity of the process (Vlahou et al., 2021).

3.2 Technology Integration

EPDM can be made more efficient with technology (Islam et al., 2022). This involves automating and simplifying every aspect of the data handling process, including collection, analysis, storage, and utilization. Automated tracking systems can reduce errors, while predictive analytics and customizable dashboards can aid decision-makers in understanding the data more clearly (Challa et al., 2024). Cloud-based platforms offer secure data storage, allowing employees and managers to access data remotely (Geetha et al., 2023; Islam & Sufian, 2023). Self-service portals and mobile-friendly designs make it easier for people to use data. Customizable solutions and ongoing feedback can help engage employees and enhance job satisfaction. It's essential to integrate these technological solutions with existing HR and operational systems to avoid creating separate data silos (Jean-Quartier et al., 2022). By doing so, it's possible to gain a complete understanding of employee performance. It's also critical to ensure that the technology complies with privacy laws and ethical standards to safeguard employee privacy.

3.3 Ethical Considerations

Ethical considerations in EPDM are crucial for establishing trust and integrity within an organization. This involves protecting employee privacy, preventing bias, and ensuring a fair and equitable assessment process (Varma et al., 2023). Robust data security measures should be in place to safeguard personal and performance-related information from unauthorized access. Evaluation processes should be objective, transparent, and data-driven to mitigate the risk of subjective judgments that could unfairly affect performance assessments (Mok et al., 2023). Promoting an equitable assessment process requires continuous refinement of performance management practices to address inherent biases or inequities. By prioritizing fairness, privacy, and ethical use, organizations can foster a culture of trust and respect, enhancing job satisfaction, employee engagement, and the overall effectiveness of performance management systems (Popo-Olaniyan et al., 2022).

4. Research Methodology

Employing a positivist perspective, this study seeks to build upon established theories related to organizational behavior, human resources management, and information systems. The research adopts a causal-comparative study design to explore the cause-and-effect relationships between EPDM practices and job satisfaction (JS) within the insurance industry. This study aims to gather empirical evidence to support its hypotheses by administering structured questionnaires to 415 employees across various job roles within the sector. The data has been analyzed using regression analysis, *t*-tests, means, and standard deviations.

4.1 Empirical Analysis

The impact of EPDM variables on employee satisfaction is tested through the simple linear regression method. The four-dimensional regression model is as follows:

$$Y = \mathrm{B1} + \mathrm{B2}X1 + \mathrm{ui} \text{ or}$$

$$Y = \mathrm{B1} + \mathrm{B2(DI)} + \mathrm{B3(TI)} + \mathrm{B4(EC)} + \mathrm{ui}$$

Where,

Y - represents the dependent variable, i.e. employees "Job Satisfaction" (JS)
X - represent the independent variable as we have independent variables of Employee Performance Data Management (EPDM) denoted as:
B1 - the constant
B2 (DI) - represents "Data Integration."
B3 (TI) - represents "Technology Integration"
B4 (EC) - represents "Ethical Considerations"
Ui - represents "Error term."

5. Results and Discussions

The survey results in Table 8.2 show that most respondents were male and aged between 26 and 44. The public sector was well-represented in the survey; most respondents earned an annual income of over three lacs. The study revealed a significant gender disparity, with a greater proportion of male participants than female. The data collected from the survey shows that most individuals who participated were between the age range of 26–44. This age group comprises a significant portion of the workforce and indicates that the survey had a greater appeal to people in their early adulthood to mid-life stages. The survey results indicate a higher percentage of private-sector employees among the respondents. This could be due to the survey's targeted outreach to this specific sector or the distribution of the sample population. Moreover, the income distribution data show that most of the respondents had relatively high economic standing, with most earning over three lacs per year. This information is crucial for better understanding the preferences, behaviors, and attitudes of the surveyed population, especially when analyzing the results based on gender, age, sectoral employment, and income levels.

Table 8.3 displays the participants' responses regarding Data Integration, Technology Integration, and Ethical Considerations. The mean value of all the statements used to measure data integration is above 3 (ranging from 3.27 to 3.64), indicating that data integration promotes transparency and perceived fairness in the performance evaluation process. Employees are more likely to view the system as objective and fair when they know that assessments are based on a wide range of integrated data points rather than subjective opinions or limited information.

Table 8.2. Demographic Information of the Respondents.

	Respondents	**Percentage**
Gender		
Male	312	75.18
Female	103	24.82
Age Group		
Up to 25 Years	60	14.46
26–44 Years	308	74.22
45 Years and above	47	11.32
Organization Sector		
Private	229	61.21
Public	146	38.79
Annual Income (INR)		
Below three lacs	155	37.35
Three lacs and above	260	62.65

Source: Self-computed by author.

Table 8.3. Responses on Data Integration, Technology Integration, and Ethical Considerations.

	Mean	**Std. Deviation**
Data Integration		
I clearly understand the criteria used in the employee-performance data integration method.	3.42	1.131
I am aware of how my performance data are collected and integrated for evaluations.	3.27	1.096
I believe the employee-performance data integration method is fair and unbiased.	3.54	1.171
The method accurately reflects my performance and contributions.	3.53	1.217
Feedback received through this method is objective and impartial.	3.46	1.148
The employee-performance data integration method motivates me to improve my job performance.	3.40	1.159
Knowing my performance data positively influences my job satisfaction.	3.41	1.178
There is an effective two-way communication channel for discussing performance evaluations	3.64	1.223
Technology Integration		
I find the technology used for performance measurement easy to use.	3.23	1.276
The technology provides a user-friendly interface for performance management.	2.91	1.275
The integration of technology has made the performance review process more efficient.	3.09	1.385
The use of technology helps me stay focused on my performance goals.	3.20	1.222
The technology used for performance measurement ensures transparency in the evaluation process.	3.16	1.242
The technology has minimized biases in performance evaluations.	3.15	1.218
I have access to training resources based on my performance data.	3.20	1.239
The technology integration supports my career advancement opportunities.	3.17	1.174

(Continued)

Table 8.3. *(Continued)*

	Mean	Std. Deviation
Ethical Considerations		
I feel responsible for maintaining ethical standards in my performance and evaluations.	3.19	1.106
Ethical considerations in performance measurement enhance my overall job satisfaction	3.13	1.119
The ethical approach to performance measurement supports my professional development.	3.23	1.109
Ethical performance evaluations encourage a supportive and collaborative work environment.	3.35	1.128
Knowing that performance is measured ethically makes me more motivated and engaged in my work.	3.36	1.157
My trust in the organization is strengthened by ethical practices in performance measurement.	3.27	1.178
Ethical considerations in evaluating performance positively affect my commitment to the organization.	3.30	1.188
I will likely recommend my organization as a great workplace because of its ethical approach to performance measurement.	3.38	1.179

Source: Self-computed by author.

Similarly, the mean value of all statements of Technology Integration statements except "The technology provides a user-friendly interface for performance management" is more than 3. The reasons could be explained as employees might not have received adequate training or enough time to become familiar with the interface. This lack of familiarity can lead to frustration and a perception that the system is more complex or less user-friendly.

The mean value of all statements included in Ethical Considerations is more than 3, indicating that employees feel their personal and performance-related data are handled carefully, respecting their privacy and confidentiality. This is especially important in today's digital age, where data privacy concerns are paramount. When employees know that their performance is evaluated ethically, it can be a major motivation for them. It assures them that their hard work and achievements will be recognized and rewarded fairly, encouraging them to maintain or improve their performance.

According to the data presented in Table 8.4, the adjusted *R*-squared value is 0.966. This value indicates that the EPDM variables—Data Integration, Technology Integration, and Ethical Considerations—account for 96.6% of the

Table 8.4. Model Summary.

Model	*R*	*R* Square	Adjusted *R* Square	Std. Error of the Estimate
1	0.982[a]	0.967	0.966	6.379

Source: Self-computed by author.

[a]Predictors: (Constant), Data Integration, Technology Integration, and Ethical Considerations(EPDM).

Table 8.5. ANOVA[a,b].

Model		Sum of Squares	df	Mean Square	*F*	Sig.
1	Regression	479115.776	3	159506.233	3813.725	0.000
	Residual	17003.541	412	39.54		
	Total	496119.317	415			

Source: Self-computed by author.

[a]Dependent Variable: Job Satisfaction(JS).

[b]Predictors: (Constant), Data Integration, Technology Integration, and Ethical Considerations (EPDM) (Basukie et al., 2020).

variation in staff job satisfaction. Therefore, the model fits quite well in explaining the factors influencing staff job satisfaction.

Table 8.5 presents the results of the coefficient of determination's significance test, which was conducted using an *F*-test. The *F*-test produced a value of 3813.725, and the *p*-value (0.000) is less than the 0.01 significance level. This indicates that the null hypothesis can be rejected at a 1% significance level, and it can be concluded that at least one independent variable has a significant linear relationship with the dependent variable. Therefore, the fitted linear model is considered valid.

Further analysis revealed that employee job satisfaction is positively correlated with EPDM variables such as Data Integration, Technology Integration, and Ethical Considerations. This means that as these variables increase, so does employee job satisfaction. This finding is important because it suggests that organizations can improve employee job satisfaction by investing in Data Integration, Technology Integration, and Ethical Considerations. By doing so, they can enhance overall performance and achieve their strategic objectives.

Table 8.6 shows the coefficient of multiple regressions. Data Integration, Technology Integration, and Ethical Considerations were taken as independent variables, and the dependent variable was employee job satisfaction.

Based on the findings, the association between Data Integration and employee job satisfaction is statistically significant ($\beta = 1.175$, $t = 16.901$, *p*-value = 0.000 at a 5% significance level). This suggests that enhancements in Data Integration within the insurance sector may increase employee job satisfaction.

Table 8.6. Coefficients of Multiple Regression.

	Unstandardized Coefficients		Standardized Coefficients		
Model	***B***	**Std. Error**	**Beta**	***T***	**Sig.**
1 (Constant)	2.165	1.213		1.754	0.076
Data Integration	1.175	0.067	0.258	16.901	0.000
Technology Integration	1.717	0.069	0.379	25.387	0.000
Ethical Considerations	1.963	0.072	0.441	26.981	0.000

Source: Self-computed by author.

Note: Dependent Variable: Job Satisfaction (JS).

Further, the study found a strong relationship between Technology Integration and employee job satisfaction, with a (β = 1.717, t = 25.387, and a p-value = 0.000) at a 95% confidence level, less than the significance level of 0.01. The null hypothesis has been rejected, implying that technology integration is crucial for improving employee engagement and retention. The findings also suggest that training employees to use integrated technologies effectively can maximize the benefits for both the employees and the organization.

Similarly, β = 1.963 at a 95% confidence level, t = 26.981, and the p-value = 0.000, which is less than the significance level of 0.01, which confirms the results are statistically significant, leading to the rejection of the null hypothesis that there is no association between ethical considerations and employee job satisfaction. This result underscores the importance of ethical practices within organizations for enhancing employee job satisfaction. Employees are more satisfied and motivated when they perceive their workplace as ethical. Adhering to ethical standards can enhance an organization's reputation internally and externally among employees in the broader market and community.

6. Implications of the Study

6.1 Theoretical Implications

The study reveals that advanced data management practices such as EPDM can significantly increase job satisfaction. This highlights the importance of incorporating such strategies into an organization's practices. The study also suggests that organizations should adapt their strategy to the internal and external environments they operate in (Nudurupati et al., 2021). The study advocates job satisfaction theories by integrating technological advancements and ethical considerations into the framework of employee satisfaction (Goretzki et al., 2022; Jang & Landuyt, 2023). The study also provides a nuanced understanding that job satisfaction is not solely influenced by traditional factors such as compensation, work–life balance, and recognition but also by how information is managed and utilized within organizations. The research finds that technology integration has a strong correlation with job satisfaction, emphasizing the importance of integrated technologies that are user-friendly and seen as beneficial to employees (Oosthuizen et al., 2016). Further research is needed to explore specific aspects of technology that have the most significant impact on job satisfaction. The study also highlights the crucial influence of ethical considerations on job satisfaction. This suggests that ethical practices and fairness in the workplace are essential to employee satisfaction. Ethical leadership and justice theories should incorporate data management ethics as a critical component of organizational justice, emphasizing the role of transparency, privacy, and fairness in data handling.

6.2 Practical Implications

The research revealed that EPDM has practical implications for industry practitioners, policymakers, and organizational leaders. Investing in advanced data management and integration technologies can streamline operational processes and significantly improve employee satisfaction (Beheshti & Beheshti, 2010). Improved work processes, better decision-making capabilities, and enhanced performance tracking are some of the benefits of these investments. The study underscores the need for user-friendly technology implementations that meet employees' needs. Training programs should help employees effectively utilize these technologies, maximizing employee satisfaction and productivity (Osewe & Gindicha, 2021). Training programs on new technologies and ethical data management practices can keep employees updated with the latest technologies and ethical standards, ensuring that the workforce is knowledgeable, competent, and engaged. To enhance user experience, insurance companies should consider customizing their data management systems to meet the specific needs of their employees (Guzmán-Ortiz et al., 2020). This personalization can make data management tools more relevant and valuable to employees, increasing job satisfaction.

7. Conclusion

The study's findings indicate that managing employee performance data is crucial in determining job satisfaction in the insurance industry. It is recommended that organizations implement integrated, ethical, and technologically advanced data management practices to improve job satisfaction and overall organizational performance. The study highlights the importance of combining advanced data management and technology with ethical practices to create a positive work environment that promotes high performance and job satisfaction. The research delves into management theories, particularly those related to job satisfaction, technology acceptance, and ethical organizational practices. It comprehensively explains the relationship between data management and employee satisfaction. The study emphasizes strategic investment in data management technologies, ethical data handling, and user-friendly technology solutions. To smoothly transition between ideas, it is suggested that organizations also provide continuous training, develop ethical data management policies, and implement feedback mechanisms to maintain a culture that values transparency, efficiency, and ethical considerations. This study benefits practitioners and organizational leaders who can use the findings to make informed decisions and improve their data management practices.

References

Afrin, S., Asyraf Bin Mohd Kassim, M., Yusof, M. F., Hassan, M. S., Islam, M. A., & Khairuddin, K. N. B. (2023). Investigating the determinants of employee performance for sustainability: A study on the Bangladesh insurance industry. *Sustainability*, *15*(7), 5674. https://doi.org/10.3390/SU15075674

Ahmad, M. R., & Raja, R. (2021). Employee job satisfaction and business performance: The mediating role of organizational commitment. *The Journal of Business Perspective*, *25*(2), 168–179. https://doi.org/10.1177/0972262920985949

Alameeri, K., Alshurideh, M., Al Kurdi, B., & Salloum, S. A. (2021). The effect of work environment happiness on employee leadership. In *Advances in Intelligent Systems and Computing, 1261 AISC* (pp. 668–680). https://doi.org/10.1007/978-3-030-58669-0_60/COVER

Alothmany, R., Jiang, Z., & Manoharan, A. (2023). Linking high-performance work systems to affective commitment, job satisfaction, and career satisfaction: Thriving as a mediator and wasta as a moderator. *International Journal of Human Resource Management*, *34*(19), 3787–3824. https://doi.org/10.1080/09585192.2022.2157681

Aruldoss, A., Kowalski, K. B., & Parayitam, S. (2021). The relationship between quality of work life and work-life balance mediating role of job stress, job satisfaction, and job commitment: Evidence from India. *Journal of Advances in Management Research*, *18*(1), 36–62. https://doi.org/10.1108/JAMR-05-2020-0082/FULL/XML

Basukie, J., Wang, Y., & Li, S. (2020). Big data governance and algorithmic management in sharing economy platforms: A case of ridesharing in emerging markets. *Technological Forecasting and Social Change*, *161*, 120310. https://doi.org/10.1016/J.TECHFORE.2020.120310

Behal, V., & Gupta, M. (2022). Reporting of corporate social responsibility practices: An evidence from Indian BSE-listed companies. *Prabandhan: Indian Journal of Management*, *15*(3), 42–58.

Beheshti, H. M., & Beheshti, C. M. (2010). Improving productivity and firm performance with enterprise resource planning. *Enterprise Information Systems*, *4*(4), 445–472. https://doi.org/10.1080/17517575.2010.511276

Bhardwaj, M., & Agarwal, S. (2022). Decision-making optimisation in insurance market using big data analytics survey. *Big Data Analytics in the Insurance Market*, 57–80. https://doi.org/10.1108/978-1-80262-637-720221004/FULL/XML

Challa, V. N. S. K., Ramachandran, K. K., Rameshkumar, P. M., Cavaliere, L. P. L., Acharjee, P. B., & Dornadula, V. H. R. (2024). Business intelligence in action: Way of successful implementation of automated systems. In *Robotics and automation in Industry 4.0* (pp. 288–302). https://doi.org/10.1201/9781003317456-16

Cherif, F. (2020). The role of human resource management practices and employee job satisfaction in predicting organizational commitment in Saudi Arabian banking sector. *International Journal of Sociology & Social Policy*, *40*(7–8), 529–541. https://doi.org/10.1108/IJSSP-10-2019-0216/FULL/PDF

Chopra, P., & Gupta, M. (2023). Fuzzy logic and ANN in an artificial intelligent cloud: A comparative study. In *Intelligent communication technologies and virtual mobile networks* (pp. 559–570). Springer Nature.

Dirzyte, A., &Patapas, A. (2022). Positive organizational practices, life satisfaction, and psychological capital in the public and private sectors. *Sustainability*, *14*(1), 488. https://doi.org/10.3390/SU14010488

Dziuba, S. T., Ingaldi, M., & Zhuravskaya, M. (2020). Employees' job satisfaction and their work performance as elements influencing work safety. *System Safety: Human - Technical Facility - Environment*, *2*(1), 18–25. https://doi.org/10.2478/CZOTO-2020-0003

Fu, W., & Deshpande, S. P. (2014). The impact of caring climate, job satisfaction, and organizational commitment on job performance of employees in a China's insurance company. *Journal of Business Ethics*, *124*(2), 339–349. https://doi.org/10.1007/S10551-013-1876-Y/METRICS

Geetha, C., Khang, A., & Nedunchelliyan, S. (2023). Dual access control for cloud-based data storage and sharing. In *Smart cities: IoT technologies, big data solutions, cloud platforms, and cybersecurity techniques* (pp. 321–336). https://doi.org/10.1201/9781003376064-17/DUAL-ACCESS-CONTROL-CLOUD-BASED-DATA-STORAGE-SHARING-GEETHA-NEDUNCHELIYAN-ALEX-KHANG

Goretzki, L., Reuter, M., Sandberg, J., & Thulin, G. (2022). Making sense of employee satisfaction measurement – A technological frames of reference perspective. *The British Accounting Review*, *54*(1), 101032. https://doi.org/10.1016/J.BAR.2021.101032

Gupta, S., Ghardallou, W., Pandey, D. K., & Sahu, G. P. (2022). Artificial intelligence adoption in the insurance industry: Evidence using the technology–organization–environment framework. *Research in International Business and Finance*, *63*, 101757. https://doi.org/10.1016/J.RIBAF.2022.101757

Gupta, M., Kumar, P., & Ghai, S. (2023). *Impact of green finance on sustainability in India's commercial banks* (pp. 216–233). https://doi.org/10.4018/979-8-3693-1388-6.CH015

Gupta, M., Sharma, V., & Jangir, K. (2023). An analysis of service quality measurement of the green payment service in India: A SERVQUAL model. In *Green management – A new paradigm in the world of business*. Nova Science Publishers, Inc. https://www.scopus.com/inward/record.uri?eid=2-s2.0-85183524110&partnerID=40&md5=00cdd49879c85e455526dab3070a82b4

Gupta, M., Taneja, S., Sharma, V., Singh, A., Rupeika-Apoga, R., & Jangir, K. (2023). Does previous experience with the Unified Payments Interface (UPI) affect the usage of Central Bank Digital Currency (CBDC)? *Journal of Risk and Financial Management*, *16*(6), 286.

Guzmán-Ortiz, C. V., Navarro-Acosta, N. G., Florez-Garcia, W., & Vicente-Ramos, W. (2020). Impact of digital transformation on the individual job performance of insurance companies in Peru. *International Journal of Data and Network Science*, *4*(4), 337–346. https://doi.org/10.5267/J.IJDNS.2020.9.005

Hamilton, R. H., & Sodeman, W. A. (2020). The questions we ask: Opportunities and challenges for using big data analytics to strategically manage human capital resources. *Business Horizons*, *63*(1), 85–95. https://doi.org/10.1016/J.BUSHOR.2019.10.001

Islam, M. A., Hack-Polay, D., Rahman, M., Hosen, M., Hunt, A., & Shafique, S. (2022). Work environment, HR practices and millennial employee retention in hospitality and tourism in Bangladesh. *International Journal of Emerging Markets*. https://doi.org/10.1108/IJOEM-06-2021-0859/FULL/XML

Islam, M. A., & Sufian, M. A. (2023). Employing AI and ML for data analytics on key indicators: Enhancing smart city urban services and dashboard-driven leadership and decision-making. In *Technology and talent strategies for sustainable smart cities: Digital futures* (pp. 275–325). https://doi.org/10.1108/978-1-83753-022-920231013/FULL/XML

Jang, K., & Landuyt, N. G. (2023). Limited benefits of technological advances in human service organizations: Going beyond the hype using sociotechnical knowledge management system. *Journal of Social Service Research*, *49*(4), 426–446. https://doi.org/10.1080/01488376.2023.2236131

Jangir, K., Sharma, V., Taneja, S., & Rupeika-Apoga, R. (2023). The moderating effect of perceived risk on users' continuance intention for FinTech services. *Journal of Risk and Financial Management*, *16*(1). https://doi.org/10.3390/jrfm16010021

Jean-Quartier, C., Rey Mazón, M., Lovrić, M., & Stryeck, S. (2022). Collaborative data use between private and public stakeholders—A regional case study. *Data*, *7*(2), 20. https://doi.org/10.3390/DATA7020020/S1

Jiang, H., & Shen, H. (2020). Toward a relational theory of employee engagement: Understanding authenticity, *Transparency, and Employee Behaviors*, *60*(3), 948–975. https://doi.org/10.1177/2329488420954236

Karkošková, S. (2023). Data governance model to enhance data quality in financial institutions. *Information Systems Management*, *40*(1), 90–110. https://doi.org/10.1080/10580530.2022.2042628

Latifah, I. N., Suhendra, A. A., & Mufidah, I. (2023). Factors affecting job satisfaction and employee performance: A case study in an Indonesian sharia property companies. *International Journal of Productivity and Performance Management*. https://doi.org/10.1108/IJPPM-03-2021-0132/FULL/XML

Lee, Y., Li, J. Y. Q., & Tsai, W. H. S. (2021). The role of strategic internal communication in workplace discrimination: A perspective of racial minority employees. *International Journal of Strategic Communication*, *15*(1), 37–59. https://doi.org/10.1080/1553118X.2020.1855591

Li, W., Abdalla, A. A., Mohammad, T., Khassawneh, O., & Parveen, M. (2023). Towards examining the link between green HRM practices and employee green in-role behavior: Spiritual leadership as a moderator. *Psychology Research and Behavior Management*, *16*, 383–396. https://doi.org/10.2147/PRBM.S396114

Mahanti, R. (2021). Corporate governance subdisciplines, data, and data governance. *Data Governance and Compliance*, 51–88. https://doi.org/10.1007/978-981-33-6877-4_3

Mok, L., Nanda, S., & Anderson, A. (2023). People perceive algorithmic assessments as less fair and trustworthy than identical human assessments. *Proceedings of the ACM on Human-Computer Interaction*, *7*(CSCW2). https://doi.org/10.1145/3610100

Mondal, S., & Samaddar, K. (2023). Reinforcing the significance of human factor in achieving quality performance in data-driven supply chain management. *TQM Journal*, *35*(1), 183–209. https://doi.org/10.1108/TQM-12-2020-0303/FULL/XML

Mousa, S. K., & Othman, M. (2020). The impact of green human resource management practices on sustainable performance in healthcare organisations: A conceptual framework. *Journal of Cleaner Production*, *243*, 118595. https://doi.org/10.1016/J.JCLEPRO.2019.118595

Nisar, Q. A., Nasir, N., Jamshed, S., Naz, S., Ali, M., & Ali, S. (2020). Big data management and environmental performance: Role of big data decision-making capabilities and decision-making quality. *Journal of Enterprise Information Management*, *34*(4), 1061–1096. https://doi.org/10.1108/JEIM-04-2020-0137/FULL/XML

Nudurupati, S. S., Garengo, P., & Bititci, U. S. (2021). Impact of the changing business environment on performance measurement and management practices. *International Journal of Production Economics*, *232*, 107942. https://doi.org/10.1016/J.IJPE.2020.107942

Oosthuizen, R. M., Coetzee, M., & Munro, Z. (2016). Work-life balance, job satisfaction and turnover intention amongst information technology employees. *Southern African Business Review*, *20*(1), 446–467. https://www.ajol.info/index.php/sabr/article/view/151750

Osewe, J. O., & Gindicha, J. Y. (2021). Effect of training and development on employee satisfaction: A case of the Judiciary of Kenya. *European Journal of Humanities and Social Sciences*, *1*(3), 661–667. https://doi.org/10.24018/EJSOCIAL.2021.1.3.50

Paais, M., & Pattiruhu, J. R. (2020). Effect of motivation, leadership, and organizational culture on satisfaction and employee performance. *The Journal of Asian Finance, Economics and Business*, *7*(8), 577–588. https://doi.org/10.13106/JAFEB.2020.VOL7.NO8.577

Paliga, M., Kozusznik, B., Pollak, A., & Sanecka, E. (2022). The relationships of psychological capital and influence regulation with job satisfaction and job performance. *PLoS One*, *17*(8), e0272412. https://doi.org/10.1371/JOURNAL.PONE.0272412

Parray, Z. A., Shah, T. A., & Islam, S. U. (2023). Psychological capital and employee job attitudes: The critical significance of work-life balance. *Evidence-Based HRM*, *11*(3), 483–500. https://doi.org/10.1108/EBHRM-07-2022-0160/FULL/XML

Peer, E., Rothschild, D., Gordon, A., Evernden, Z., & Damer, E. (2022). Data quality of platforms and panels for online behavioral research. *Behavior Research Methods*, *54*(4), 1643–1662. https://doi.org/10.3758/S13428-021-01694-3/TABLES/13

Philip Chen, C. L., & Zhang, C. Y. (2014). Data-intensive applications, challenges, techniques and technologies: A survey on Big Data. *Information Sciences*, *275*, 314–347. https://doi.org/10.1016/J.INS.2014.01.015

Plotkin, D. (2021). *Data stewardship data stewardship*. Elsevier. http://www.sciencedirect.com:5070/book/9780128221327/data-stewardship

Popo-Olaniyan, O., AdijatElufioye, O., Okonkwo, F. C., Udeh, C. A., Eleogu, T. F., Funmilola, & Olatoye, O. (2022). AI-driven talent analytics for strategic HR decision-making in the United States of America: A review. *International Journal of Management & Entrepreneurship Research*, *4*(12), 607–622. https://doi.org/10.51594/IJMER.V4I12.674

Poudel, B. (2023). An empirical study on factors influencing job satisfaction of human resources in bank and insurance companies of Nepal. *Arabian Journal of Business and Management Review*, *12*(1), 11–22. https://j.arabianjbmr.com/index.php/kcajbmr/article/view/684

Probst, T. M., Tomas, J., Roll, L., Maslić Seršić, D., Jiang, L., & Jenkins, M. R. (2023). Attenuating the relationship between job insecurity and job satisfaction: An examination of the role of organizational learning climate in three countries. *Economic and Industrial Democracy*. https://doi.org/10.1177/0143831X231155975

Rana, A., Bansal, R., & Gupta, M. (2022). Emerging technologies of big data in the insurance market. *Big Data: A Game Changer for Insurance Industry*, 15–34. https://doi.org/10.1108/978-1-80262-605-620221002/FULL/XML

Rane, N. (2023). Enhancing customer loyalty through Artificial Intelligence (AI), Internet of Things (IoT), and big data technologies: Improving customer satisfaction, engagement, relationship, and experience. *SSRN Electronic Journal*. https://doi.org/10.2139/SSRN.4616051

Rodríguez-Sánchez, J. L., González-Torres, T., Montero-Navarro, A., & Gallego-Losada, R. (2020). Investing time and resources for work–life balance: The effect on talent retention. *International Journal of Environmental Research and Public Health*, *17*(6), 1920. https://doi.org/10.3390/IJERPH17061920

Sharma, V., Gupta, M., Jangir, K., Chopra, P., & Pathak, N. (2023). The impact of post-use consumer satisfaction on smart wearables repurchase intention in the context of AI-based healthcare information. In *Enhancing customer engagement through location-based marketing* (pp. 77–101). IGI Global.

Sharma, V., Jangir, K., Chowhan, S. S., & Pathak, N. (2023). *Key factors influencing electric vehicle purchase decisions by consumers: An empirical study of Indian consumers* (pp. 449–464). https://doi.org/10.1007/978-981-19-8963-6_40

Sharma, V., Jangir, K., Pathak, N., & Professor, A. (2022). Key financial ratios analysis for manufacturing companies – A bibliometric analysis. *Journal of Algebraic Statistics*, *13*(3), 451–467. https://publishoa.com/index.php/journal/article/view/648

Sharma, P., Sharma, V., Jangir, K., Gupta, M., & Pathak, N. (2023). Unfolding the emerging trends in non-performing assets with special reference to the energy sector in banking industry. In *Renewable Energy Optimization, Planning and Control: Proceedings of ICRTE* (pp. 411–422). Springer.

Sharma, V., Taneja, S., Gupta, M., KshitizJangir, & Ozen, E. (2023). Impact of service quality on behavioural intention to use fin tech payment services: An extension of SERVEQUAL model. *Asia Pacific Journal of Information Systems*, *33*(4), 1093–1117. https://www.earticle.net/Article/A440274

Sumbal, M. S., Ključnikov, A., Durst, S., Ferraris, A., & Saeed, L. (2023). Do you want to retain your relevant knowledge? The role of contextual factors in the banking sector. *Journal of Knowledge Management*, *27*(9), 2414–2433. https://doi.org/10.1108/JKM-02-2022-0128/FULL/XML

Trenerry, B., Chng, S., Wang, Y., Suhaila, Z. S., Lim, S. S., Lu, H. Y., & Oh, P. H. (2021). Preparing workplaces for digital transformation: An integrative review and framework of multi-level factors. *Frontiers in Psychology*, *12*, 620766. https://doi.org/10.3389/FPSYG.2021.620766/BIBTEX

Varma, A., Dawkins, C., & Chaudhuri, K. (2023). Artificial intelligence and people management: A critical assessment through the ethical lens. *Human Resource Management Review*, *33*(1), 100923. https://doi.org/10.1016/J.HRMR.2022.100923

Vlahou, A., Hallinan, D., Apweiler, R., Argiles, A., Beige, J., Benigni, A., Bischoff, R., Black, P. C., Boehm, F., Céraline, J., Chrousos, G. P., Delles, C., Evenepoel, P., Fridolin, I., Glorieux, G., Van Gool, A. J., Heidegger, I., Ioannidis, J. P. A., Jankowski, J., … Vanholder, R. (2021). Data sharing under the general data protection regulation: Time to harmonize law and research ethics? *Hypertension*, *77*(4), 1029–1035. https://doi.org/10.1161/HYPERTENSIONAHA.120.16340

Ying, S., Sindakis, S., Aggarwal, S., Chen, C., & Su, J. (2021). Managing big data in the retail industry of Singapore: Examining the impact on customer satisfaction and organizational performance. *European Management Journal*, *39*(3), 390–400. https://doi.org/10.1016/J.EMJ.2020.04.001

Chapter 9

Revolutionizing Insurance Practices Through Advanced Data Alchemy

Sanjay Taneja[a], *Vartika Bisht*[b] *and Mohit Kukreti*[c]

[a]Graphic Era Deemed to be University, India
[b]Chandigarh University, India
[c]University of Technology and Applied Sciences-Ibri, Sultanate of Oman

Abstract

Purpose: The study delves into the role played by cutting-edge data analytics, machine learning, and innovative technologies in reshaping traditional insurance practices. The primary goal of this review is to juxtapose findings from the literature sources, enabling a comprehensive analysis of the current state of implementation.

Design/Methodology/Approach: Systematic narrative review methodology has been applied to the present study. Scopus database has been used for the manuscripts ranging from year 2020 to 2024 considering the 5-year rule. 74 manuscripts were reviewed to navigate the landscape of data-driven revolution, unlocking the potential to elevate insurance operations to new heights. Two research questions about the impact of data alchemy on operational efficiency and insights and its contribution to reshaping the future landscape of insurance practices have been answered.

Findings: This approach captured the interplay between the theoretical potential for insurance and the practical realities of implementation of advanced practices, drawing upon the collective expertise within the field. By doing so, the article discerned the trajectory of the insurance sector concerning the advanced data alchemy observed in the industry.

Originality/Value: The current research contributes to the broader area of data alchemy in the insurance industry. The transformative power of big data analytics lies in its capacity to turn vast and diverse datasets into valuable insights, driving innovation, informed decision-making, and improved business outcomes across various sectors. Notably, the research

Data Alchemy in the Insurance Industry, 119–131

Published under exclusive licence by Emerald Publishing Limited
doi:10.1108/978-1-83608-582-920241018

extends the body of literature exploring the impact of data alchemy on operational efficiency and insights, area where limited studies have been conducted.

Keywords: Advancement; data alchemy; digital age; insurance industry; Scopus

1. Introduction

Insurance is a financial concept crafted to handle risks, aims to offer protection for economic development, or to mitigate potential losses stemming from uncertainty (Kaffash et al., 2020). In the last decade, India's insurance industry has undergone rapid growth, introducing innovative products and becoming a vital contributor to the national economy, with profound impacts driven by digital transformation, ushering in novel services and advancements (Kumar et al., 2023; Mustafina et al., 2020) report that at present, 75% of insurance firms are actively involved in implementing new IT products and solutions. The Fourth Industrial Revolution is evident in the exponential surge of available data, resulting in notable advancements in computational power, storage capabilities, and the creation of sophisticated algorithms for extracting meaningful insights (Arumugam & Bhargavi, 2019). Lately, there has been a notable surge in interest surrounding the evaluation of efficiency in insurance companies. Investors, financial market analysts, insurance regulators, and researchers have all shown keen attention to this aspect within the insurance sector (Kaffash et al., 2020).

In the contemporary landscape of the insurance industry, the convergence of advanced data analytics, machine learning, and innovative technologies is catalyzing a transformative shift. As we embark on a journey through the realms of risk assessment, claims management, customer experience, and operational efficiency, we unravel the secrets of turning raw data into invaluable insights. In the dynamic landscape of the insurance industry, the integration of advanced data alchemy strategies emerges as a transformative force. As the digital era unfolds, insurers are faced with unprecedented opportunities to extract valuable insights, streamline operations, and enhance overall efficiency. The fusion of data science and insurance is not merely a technological integration; it represents a paradigm shift in how risk is assessed, policies are underwritten, claims are processed, and customer experiences are curated. The intricate dance between raw data and actionable intelligence is redefining the boundaries of what is achievable within the insurance sector (Allioui & Mourdi (2023). The intersection of the insurance industry and data alchemy signifies the integration of advanced data analytics and transformative technologies to enhance various aspects of insurance operations. This convergence involves leveraging data-driven insights, machine learning, and innovative tools to streamline processes, improve risk assessments, and provide more personalized and efficient services to policyholders (Ali et al., 2023). The application of data alchemy in the insurance sector holds the potential to revolutionize traditional practices, offering opportunities for improved operational efficiency, better risk management, and innovative customer experiences.

The present study delves into the pivotal role played by cutting-edge data analytics, machine learning, and innovative technologies in reshaping traditional insurance practices. As we embark on a journey through the realms of risk assessment, claims management, customer experience, and operational efficiency, we unravel the secrets of turning raw data into invaluable insights. This article critically examines both academic literature and industry practices related to the integration of advanced data within the insurance sector. Employing a systematic review methodology that incorporates insights from two distinct sources, this study aims to synthesize knowledge from varied perspectives.

2. Literature Review

2.1 Insurance Industry

Singh and Akhilesh (2020) highlight that the global economy relies heavily on the insurance sector as it empowers both individuals and businesses to engage in ventures involving risk, mitigating potential challenges that would otherwise deter such endeavors. A robust and well-established insurance sector contributes to the stability of financial markets (Babuna et al., 2020). The swiftly advancing technology is facilitating the gathering and utilization of data, playing a crucial role in all aspects of the insurance sector (Tarr et al., 2023), including industry services, actuarial predictions, underwriting processes, and reinsurance. De Andrés and Gené-Albesa (2024) assessed the general level of approval regarding the use of chatbots for engaging with insurance companies, particularly in tasks like reporting claims. Data was analyzed from 10 new member states of the European Union by (Bayar et al., 2023), thus examining the correlation between Information and Communication Technologies (ICT) and the development of the insurance sector and claimed a reciprocal relationship between indicators of ICT penetration and the progress of the insurance sector. The key focus areas for IT technologies employed by Russian insurance companies have been identified by (Kaigorodova et al., 2021) as cloud computing, chatbots, and online information resources facilitating customer interaction. The observed data by Bonsu et al. (2023) indicates that AI and big data have a beneficial and notable influence on accounting methods, suggesting that financial technology (fintech) might offer solutions to address issues of agency within accounting practices, ultimately improving overall accounting standards.

2.2 Data Alchemy

The widespread adoption of the big data movement has resulted in an overwhelming volume of data that surpasses enterprises' capacity to effectively process the diverse types of data that may be present. Consumers are increasingly adopting digital channels, and the emergence of technologies like connected cars, smart home solutions, and artificial intelligence (AI) has introduced a new era of products grounded in data and analytics (Bruggmann et al., 2018). Data alchemy implies a transformative process where raw data is converted into valuable insights or innovative solutions. This involves leveraging advanced analytics, machine learning, or other data-driven technologies to extract meaningful patterns, predictions, or optimizations within the insurance industry. Bayar et al. (2023) revealed that the growth of the insurance sector is significantly positively impacted by Internet penetration. The utilization of big data has enabled insurance companies to enhance their customer engagement and retention, improve risk assessment, optimize fraud prevention efficiency, and reduce overall costs (Ellili et al., 2023; Rana et al., 2022a). It was further highlighted by Rana et al. (2022a) that the insurance market has undergone a revolution with the advent of big data, empowering insurers to target customers with greater precision. Moreover emphasize that employing the data lakes approach will enhance the integration with data from diverse industries, leading to substantial improvements in utilizing and extracting meaningful insights from such data in the context of insurers. The digitalization of claims processes, incorporating big data and analytics, has notably influenced the underwriting practices of leading insurance companies (Kajwang, 2022) and substantiates the advantageous impact of embracing big data technologies and tools in enhancing overall efficiency.

2.3 Scopus Database

The inception of the Scopus database took place in the year 2004 (Zhu & Liu, 2020) and provides access to a vast collection of scholarly articles, conference papers, and patents, offering valuable tools for researchers, academics, and professionals to explore and analyze academic literature. Thus, the Scopus has been endorsed and confirmed as suitable for application in informatics research, particularly for the purpose of conducting research analysis (Kipper et al., 2020). The Scopus database is highly regarded for its stringent quality standards, extensive coverage in information collection (Harzing & Alakangas, 2016; Herrera-Franco et al., 2020), user-friendly data downloading capabilities, and exceptional coverage of insurance journals. Thus, the research aims to answer the mentioned questions:

RQ1. What is the impact of data alchemy on operational efficiency and insights within the insurance industry?
RQ2. How does data alchemy contribute to reshaping the future landscape of insurance practices?

3. Research Methodology

The present study employs a systematic narrative review methodology, involving a systematic and comprehensive search, selection, appraisal, and synthesis of relevant studies to provide a comprehensive and unbiased summary of the existing evidence in the context of insurance practices through advanced data alchemy. The database selected for the same is Scopus and research manuscripts for the past five years have been considered. Data search criteria and extraction model have been shown in Fig. 9.1, clearly revealing how the relevant manuscripts were selected for the research objective to be attained. The filtering criteria are shown in Table 9.1. A total of 74 manuscripts were reviewed from year 2020 to 2024 to answer the research question in the study by applying various filters of the keywords: "Insurance Industry" OR "Insurance Sector" AND "Technology" OR "Digital Age" and Subject area of Computer Science, Business Management & Accounting, Economics, Econometrics and Finance, Social Sciences and Decision Sciences.

4. Findings

The answer to *RQ1* is represented as the core elements of implementing transformative data practices, examining their impact across critical facets of the insurance sector. Sibindi (2022) indicates that the adoption of Information and Communication Technology (ICT) contributes to the growth of the life insurance sector in Africa and support the notion that the extent of financial autonomy among insurance companies, unhampered by regulations, influences the levels of insurance sales, thereby enhancing access to life insurance in Africa.

One of the primary domains where data alchemy shines is in risk assessment and underwriting. By harnessing predictive analytics and machine learning algorithms, insurers can delve deep into historical data, extracting patterns, and insights that were once elusive (Sharma & Manhas, 2024). Ali Albasheir (2023) highlights that the incorporation of diverse data sources, including Internet of Things (IoT) devices and social media, further refines underwriting processes, enabling a more nuanced understanding of risks and facilitating more accurate pricing models. Secondly, efficient claims processing lies at the heart of a customer-centric insurance operation. Data alchemy plays a pivotal role in

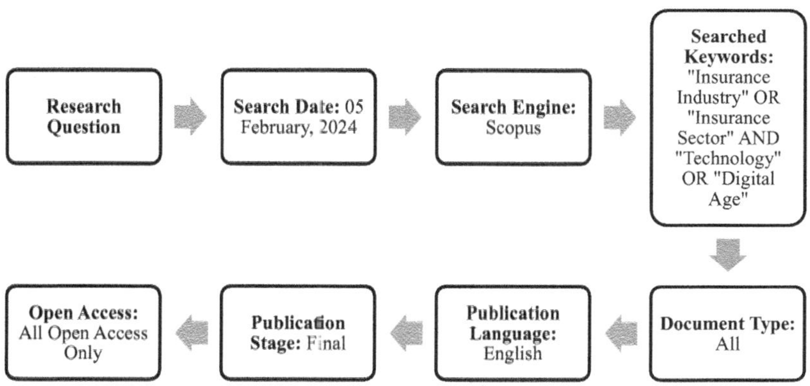

Fig. 9.1. Data Extraction Model. *Source:* Author.

Table 9.1. Filtering Criteria.

	Accept	Reject
Key Words: "Insurance Industry" OR "Insurance Sector" AND "Technology" OR "Digital Age"	882	
Subject Area: Computer Science, Business Management & Accounting, Economics, Econometrics & Finance, Social Sciences and Decision Sciences	680	202
Document Type: Article, Conference Paper, Book Chapter, Review, Conference Review, Book	678	2
Language: English	661	17
Year: 2020 to 2024	132	529
Publication Stage: Final	129	3
Open Access: Limit to All Open Access	74	55

Source: Author.

streamlining claims management (Alaimo & Kallinikos, 2021). Advanced analytics aids in automating claims validation processes, expediting the assessment of damages (Subburathinam et al., 2023). Moreover, the integration of image and text recognition technologies (Eckert et al., 2022) accelerates the claims settlement process, providing a seamless experience for policyholders. Also, a personalized and responsive approach to customer needs is a hallmark of modern insurance, and data alchemy is the key to achieving this. By analyzing vast datasets, insurers can gain valuable insights into customer behavior, preferences, and expectations. Armed with this information, they can tailor insurance offerings, providing a more customized experience that fosters customer satisfaction and loyalty (Rane, 2023).

In the ongoing battle against fraudulent activities, data alchemy proves to be a formidable ally. Severino and Peng (2021) highlight that through the application of advanced analytics and machine learning models, insurers can identify unusual patterns and anomalies indicative of potential fraud. Real-time data processing further enhances fraud detection capabilities, allowing insurers to minimize the impact of fraudulent claims and protect the integrity of their operations. Dhieb et al., (2020) and Kullenda (2020) remark that data-driven decision-making processes are instrumental in optimizing internal operations for efficiency and cost-effectiveness. Predictive analytics aids insurers in forecasting claims volumes, enabling better resource allocation and strategic planning (Jones & Sah, 2023). The result is a more streamlined and agile insurance operation that can adapt to evolving market demands.

RQ2 has been answered in the form of driving innovation, improving efficiency, enhancing customer experiences, and enabling insurers to make informed, strategic decisions in a rapidly evolving landscape. Data alchemy leverages advanced analytics and machine learning to improve risk assessment models

(Zuhaib & Milson, 2024). Access to diverse data sources allows insurers to gain a more comprehensive understanding of risks, leading to more accurate risk evaluations. Predictive analytics enables insurers to proactively identify emerging risks and adjust their strategies accordingly (King et al., 2021). Automation and optimization of operational processes through data alchemy streamline workflows within insurance companies. Kunduru (2023) highlight that routine tasks are automated, allowing professionals to focus on strategic and value-added activities. Improved operational efficiency contributes to cost savings and resource allocation. Also, data alchemy enables insurers to analyze vast datasets to understand individual customer behavior, preferences, and needs (Candelon & Reeves, 2022). Personalized insurance offerings and services are developed based on these insights, leading to enhanced customer satisfaction and loyalty. Tailored experiences contribute to a more customer-centric approach in the industry. Kaarnavaara-Puutio (2021) posits that insights derived from data alchemy drive innovative product development within the insurance sector. New insurance products are tailored to meet evolving customer needs and address emerging risks. The use of data-driven insights fosters a culture of continuous innovation in the industry (Bresciani et al., 2021).

It has been found that data alchemy employs advanced analytics to detect patterns indicative of fraudulent activities (Singarimbum et al., 2022). Real-time data processing enhances fraud detection capabilities, preventing financial losses for insurers. Improved fraud prevention contributes to the overall integrity of the insurance sector. Data alchemy also provides insurers with valuable insights for strategic decision-making. Predictive analytics aids in forecasting market trends, enabling insurers to adapt to changing conditions and stay ahead of competitors (Rana et al., 2022b). Informed decision-making contributes to the formulation of competitive business strategies. Moreover, the integration of data alchemy fosters collaboration between the insurance sector and other industries (Pradeep et al., 2021). Collaborative efforts with sectors like health, automobiles, and travel lead to the development of innovative services and partnerships. Cross-industry collaboration contributes to a more interconnected and dynamic insurance landscape (Judijanto et al., 2023). All in all, data alchemy equips insurers with tools to continuously adapt to evolving market dynamics. Real-time data analysis allows for quick responses to market shifts, ensuring that insurance practices remain agile and responsive. Settembre-Blundo et al. (2021) demonstrate that adaptability to changing market conditions is crucial for long-term sustainability. An instance has been mentioned for the support of the study:

4.1 Case Study of SmartRisk Insurance Company

4.1.1 Introduction

SmartRisk Insurance Company is a fictional insurance firm specializing in property and casualty insurance. Facing stiff competition in the insurance market and an increasing number of fraudulent claims, SmartRisk sought to revolutionize its practices through advanced data analytics.

4.1.2 Challenge

Fraudulent Claims: The company was experiencing a significant increase in fraudulent claims, leading to substantial financial losses and a tarnished reputation.

Operational Inefficiencies: Manual processes for claims processing and risk assessment were time-consuming and prone to errors, leading to delays in payouts and dissatisfied customers.

Market Competition: With the rise of Insurtech startups and established competitors leveraging advanced analytics, SmartRisk risked losing market share if it didn't innovate its practices.

4.1.3 Solution

To address these challenges, SmartRisk implemented advanced data analytics techniques, leveraging AI, machine learning (ML), and big data analytics. This initiative, dubbed "Data Alchemy," aimed to transform the company's operations and enhance its competitiveness in the market.

4.1.4 Implementation

Predictive Analytics for Fraud Detection: SmartRisk deployed predictive analytics models to identify patterns indicative of fraudulent claims. By analyzing historical data, including claimant behavior, transaction patterns, and external factors, the company developed algorithms capable of flagging suspicious claims in real-time.

Automated Claims Processing: SmartRisk automated its claims processing using AI-driven algorithms. By integrating data from various sources, including customer information, damage assessments, and policy details, the company streamlined the claims process, reducing processing times, and improving accuracy.

Personalized Risk Assessment: Leveraging big data analytics, SmartRisk developed personalized risk assessment models for policyholders. By analyzing individual behavior, property characteristics, and external risk factors, the company could tailor insurance premiums and coverage options to meet the specific needs of customers.

4.1.5 Results

The implementation of Data Alchemy yielded significant results for SmartRisk:

Fraud Reduction: SmartRisk saw a substantial reduction in fraudulent claims, resulting in cost savings and improved profitability. By identifying fraudulent activity early, the company could take proactive measures to mitigate risks and prevent future losses.

Operational Efficiency: Automated claims processing led to faster turnaround times and improved customer satisfaction. With fewer manual interventions and streamlined workflows, SmartRisk could process claims more efficiently, reducing overhead costs, and improving overall productivity.

Competitive Advantage: SmartRisk gained a competitive edge in the insurance market by leveraging advanced data analytics. The company's ability to offer personalized services and mitigate risks effectively positioned it as a preferred choice for customers seeking innovative insurance solutions.

4.1.6 Conclusion of the Case

By embracing advanced data analytics, SmartRisk Insurance Company successfully revolutionized its practices, addressing key challenges and positioning itself for long-term success in a competitive market. The Data Alchemy initiative exemplifies the transformative power of data-driven insights in driving innovation and enhancing business outcomes in the insurance industry.

5. Implications

By exploring innovative data alchemy techniques, the manuscript likely discusses transformative approaches to handling and interpreting data in insurance processes. The study sheds light on how advanced data alchemy methods contribute to more informed and strategic decision-making within insurance practices. Through the adoption of data alchemy, insurers may gain improved capabilities in assessing risks accurately, leveraging insights derived from sophisticated data analysis. The beneficiaries include the insurance companies where insurers stand to benefit by gaining insights into how advanced data alchemy can optimize their processes, enhance risk management, and improve overall operational efficiency. Also, professionals involved in underwriting as well as claims processing can benefit as they may find valuable insights on how data alchemy can streamline and expedite the claims handling process, improving customer satisfaction. Data scientists and analysts gain insights into the specific applications of advanced data alchemy in the insurance sector. Regulatory bodies overseeing the insurance industry may find useful information on how insurers are adapting to technological advancements and the implications for compliance with industry regulations. Professionals providing consultancy services to the insurance sector may gain insights that can inform their recommendations to clients seeking to modernize their practices. At last, even the policyholders and potential customers could benefit from improved insurance products and services resulting from the adoption of data alchemy, leading to more personalized and efficient experiences.

6. Limitations and Recommendations

The study is limited to a specific time frame as well as the database chosen. Further researchers can focus on taking extended databases of Web of Science, EBSCOhost, DOAJ, etc. Also, there is limited study available on advanced data alchemy and the practices related to the same. Thus, there is scope for future research to be done in the context. impact of data alchemy on operational efficiency, and insights within the insurance industry. Data alchemy heavily relies on the quality of input data, and any shortcomings can compromise the effectiveness of the analytical models. Thus, security and privacy issues can also be explored for further work. The revolution sparked by advanced data alchemy is not just a technological shift but a comprehensive reimagining of how insurers operate, interact with customers, and navigate the complexities of risk. In this context, the journey toward revolutionizing insurance practices through data alchemy is an ongoing exploration, promising continued innovation, and resilience in an ever-changing industry landscape. Also, incorporating empirical methods into research related to data alchemy in the insurance sector can enhance its validity and impact and provide valuable insights and contribute to the advancement of knowledge in this field.

7. Conclusion

This study unfolds the myriad ways in which data alchemy is reshaping the insurance landscape. From risk assessment to operational efficiency, the alchemy of data is proving to be a catalyst for positive change, ushering in an era where insurers can not only manage risks effectively but also provide unparalleled value to their customers. The beneficiaries extend across a spectrum of industry participants, from insurers and professionals within the sector to those supplying technology solutions and entities with a vested interest in the insurance industry's evolution. The profound impact of data alchemy on operational efficiency and strategic insights is evident, offering a paradigm shift in traditional practices. This revolution is characterized by a range of positive outcomes, from enhanced decision-making and streamlined workflows to improved risk assessment and personalized customer experiences. The adoption of data alchemy in insurance brings forth numerous benefits, including automated processes, optimized underwriting, and the ability to leverage predictive analytics for strategic planning. Real-time interaction, improved fraud detection, and a customer-centric approach further solidify its positive influence on the industry. However, amidst these advancements, challenges such as data quality concerns, security and privacy issues, and the need for transparent and interpretable models must be acknowledged by future researchers. However, the overall trajectory is one of positive transformation. The insurance industry's evolution through advanced data alchemy is marked by agility, responsiveness to market dynamics, and the ability to stay ahead of regulatory changes. The multidimensional impact extends from the operational core to strategic decision-making, positioning insurers to not only adapt to but also thrive in an era of data-driven excellence. As the insurance landscape continues to evolve, the commitment to ongoing research, development, and collaboration across disciplines will be crucial. The revolution sparked by advanced data alchemy is not just a technological shift but a comprehensive reimagining of how insurers operate, interact with customers, and navigate the complexities of risk. In this context, the journey toward revolutionizing insurance practices through data alchemy is an ongoing exploration, promising continued innovation, and resilience in an ever-changing industry landscape.

References

Alaimo, C., & Kallinikos, J. (2021). Managing by data: Algorithmic categories and organizing. *Organization Studies*, *42*(9), 1385–1407.

Ali Albasheir, K. A. M. (2023). The impact of IT on insurance of the technological industry. *Journal of Advanced Zoology*, *44*.

Allioui, H., & Mourdi, Y. (2023). Exploring the full potentials of IoT for better financial growth and stability: A comprehensive survey. *Sensors*, *23*(19), 8015.

Arumugam, S., & Bhargavi, R. (2019). A survey on driving behavior analysis in usage based insurance using big data. *Journal of Big Data*, *6*, 1–21.

Babuna, P., Yang, X., Gyilbag, A., Awudi, D. A., Ngmenbelle, D., & Bian, D. (2020). The impact of Covid-19 on the insurance industry. *International Journal of Environmental Research and Public Health*, *17*(16), 5766.

Bayar, Y., Danuletiu, D. C., Danuletiu, A. E., & Gavriletea, M. D. (2023). ICT penetration and insurance sector development: Evidence from the 10 new EU member states. *Electronics*, *12*(4), 823.

Bonsu, M. O. A., Wang, Y., & Guo, Y. (2023). Does fintech lead to better accounting practices? Empirical evidence. *Accounting Research Journal*, *36*(2/3), 129–147.

Bresciani, S., Ciampi, F., Meli, F., & Ferraris, A. (2021). Using big data for co-innovation processes: Mapping the field of data-driven innovation, proposing theoretical developments and providing a research agenda. *International Journal of Information Management*, *60*, 102347.

Bruggmann, P., Catlin, T., Chinzewski, J., Lorenz, J., & Prymaka, S. (2018). *Claims in the digital age: How insurers can get started.* McKinsey& Company, Insurance Practice.

Candelon, F., & Reeves, M. (Eds.). (2022). *The rise of AI-powered companies.* Walter de Gruyter GmbH & Co KG.

de Andrés-Sánchez, J., & Gené-Albesa, J. (2024). Not with the bot! The relevance of trust to explain the acceptance of chatbots by insurance customers. *Humanities and Social Sciences Communications*, *11*(1), 1–12.

Dhieb, N., Ghazzai, H., Besbes, H., & Massoud, Y. (2020). A secure AI-driven architecture for automated insurance systems: Fraud detection and risk measurement. *IEEE Access*, *8*, 58546–58558.

Eckert, C., Neunsinger, C., & Osterrieder, K. (2022). Managing customer satisfaction: Digital applications for insurance companies. *The Geneva Papers on Risk and Insurance - Issues and Practice*, *47*(3), 569–602.

Ellili, N., Nobanee, H., Alsaiari, L., Shanti, H., Hillebrand, B., Hassanain, N., & Elfout, L. (2023). The applications of big data in the insurance industry: A bibliometric and systematic review of relevant literature. *The Journal of Finance and Data Science*, 100102.

Harzing, A. W., & Alakangas, S. (2016). Google Scholar, Scopus and the Web of Science: A longitudinal and cross-disciplinary comparison. *Scientometrics*, *106*, 787–804.

Herrera-Franco, G., Montalván-Burbano, N., Carrión-Mero, P., Apolo-Masache, B., & Jaya-Montalvo, M. (2020). Research trends in geotourism: A bibliometric analysis using the Scopus database. *Geosciences*, *10*(10), 379.

Jones, K. I., & Sah, S. (2023). The implementation of machine learning in the insurance industry with big data analytics. *International Journal of Data Informatics and Intelligent Computing*, *2*(2), 21–38.

Judijanto, L., Antoni, A., Turukay, E., & Arifin, H. M. (2023). Mapping the financial risk management landscape: A bibliometric analysis of recent trends and Influential contributions. *West Science Business and Management*, *1*(05), 441–450.

Kaarnavaara-Puutio, M. (2021). *Streamlining a service process. Optimising two-way information sharing in product development: Case origin by ocean.* https://urn.fi/URN:NBN:fi:amk-2021113022766

Kaffash, S., Azizi, R., Huang, Y., & Zhu, J. (2020). A survey of data envelopment analysis applications in the insurance industry 1993–2018. *European Journal of Operational Research*, *284*(3), 801–813.

Kaigorodova, G., Mustafina, A., Pyrkova, G., Grzebyk, M., & Belinskaja, L. (2021). Digitalization of the insurance business: Systematization of net effects through the example of Russia. https://doi.org/10.21511/ins.12(1).2021.03

Kajwang, B. (2022). Implications for big data and analytics on underwriting practices in insurance sector. *American Journal of Data, Information and Knowledge Management*, *3*(1), 1–11.

King, M. R., Timms, P. D., & Rubin, T. H. (2021). Use of big data in insurance. In *The Palgrave handbook of technological finance* (pp. 669–700). Springer.

Kipper, L. M., Furstenau, L. B., Hoppe, D., Frozza, R., & Iepsen, S. (2020). Scopus scientific mapping production in industry 4.0 (2011–2018): A bibliometric analysis. *International Journal of Production Research*, *58*(6), 1605–1627.

Kullenda, K. (2020). *Enabling firm performance through data driven decision making in maintenance management: A dynamic capabilities view.* Doctoral dissertation. University of Pretoria.

Kumar, P., Taneja, S., Mukul & Özen, E. (2023). Digital transformation of the insurance industry – A case of the Indian insurance sector. In *The Impact of climate change and sustainability standards on the insurance market*, 85–106. Scrivener Publishing.

Kunduru, A. R. (2023). Cloud BPM application (Appian) Robotic process automation capabilities. *Asian Journal of Research in Computer Science*, *16*(3), 267–280.

Mustafina, A. A., Kaigorodova, G. N., Alyakina, P. D., Velichko, N. Y., & Zainullina, M. R. (2020). Digital technology in insurance. In *Digital transformation of the economy: Challenges, trends and new opportunities* (pp. 678–685). Springer International Publishing.

Pradeep, A. S. E., Yiu, T. W., Zou, Y., & Amor, R. (2021). Blockchain-aided information exchange records for design liability control and improved security. *Automation in Construction*, *126*, 103667.

Rana, A., Bansal, R., & Gupta, M. (2022a). Big data: A disruptive innovation in the insurance sector. In *Big data analytics in the insurance market* (pp. 165–183). Emerald Publishing Limited.

Rana, A., Bansal, R., & Gupta, M. (2022b). Emerging technologies of big data in the insurance market. In *Big data: A game changer for insurance industry* (pp. 15–34). Emerald Publishing Limited.

Rane, N. (2023). Enhancing customer loyalty through Artificial Intelligence (AI), Internet of Things (IoT), and Big Data technologies: Improving customer satisfaction, engagement, relationship, and experience. *Internet of Things (IoT), and Big Data Technologies: Improving Customer Satisfaction, Engagement, Relationship, and Experience*. https://doi.org/10.2139/ssrn.4616051

Settembre-Blundo, D., González-Sánchez, R., Medina-Salgado, S., & García-Muiña, F. E. (2021). Flexibility and resilience in corporate decision making: A new sustainability-based risk management system in uncertain times. *Global Journal of Flexible Systems Management*, *22*(Suppl 2), 107–132.

Severino, M. K., & Peng, Y. (2021). Machine learning algorithms for fraud prediction in property insurance: Empirical evidence using real-world microdata. *Machine Learning with Applications*, *5*, 100074.

Sharma, P., & Manhas, S. (2024). The future of finance: Revolutionizing the industry with artificial intelligence. In *Leveraging AI and emotional intelligence in contemporary business organizations* (pp. 187–210). IGI Global.

Sibindi, A. B. (2022). Information and communication technology adoption and life insurance market development: Evidence from Sub-Saharan Africa. *Journal of Risk and Financial Management*, *15*(12), 568.

Singarimbum, B. L., Dhial, A. A. M., & Farooqi, A. F. (2022). How commercial banks in emerging economies can leverage big data analytics: A perspective of Asian countries. *International Journal of Data Science and Advanced Analytics*, *4*(4), 94–97.

Singh, A., & Akhilesh, K. B. (2020). The insurance industry—cyber security in the hyper-connected age. In *Smart technologies: Scope and applications* (pp. 201–219). Springer.

Subburathinam, M. I., Kumar, M. K., Pradeepa, S. V., Dash, S., & Dhanasekaran, P. (2023). Artificial intelligence as a game changer tool to reshape the insurance services in digital transformation. *Journal of Informatics Education and Research*, *3*(2).

Tarr, A. A., Tarr, J. A., Thompson, M., & Wilkinson, D. (Eds.). (2023). *The global insurance market and change: Emerging technologies, risks and legal challenges*. Informa Law.

Zhu, J., & Liu, W. (2020). A tale of two databases: The use of Web of Science and Scopus in academic papers. *Scientometrics*, *123*(1), 321–335.

Zuhaib, O., & Milson, S. (2024). *The AI advantage: Redefining big data management for the future* (No. 11894). https://easychair.org/publications/preprint/B2n2

Chapter 10

The Future of Alchemy: Emerging Trends and Technologies Metaverse in Insurance – A Virtual Customer Experience

Azmee Zaheer[a], *Animesh Singh*[a], *Kaushal Kishore Mishra*[a], *Reepu*[a] *and Luan Vardari*[b]

[a]Chandigarh University, India
[b]University "UKSHIN HOTI" Prizren, Republic of Kosovo

Abstract

Purpose: The present study delves into the incorporation of the Metaverse in the insurance industry, with an emphasis on augmenting consumer experiences via virtual interaction.
Design/Methodology: We explored secondary data sources on metaverse in the insurance industry and went through a thorough analysis of the literature and case studies, showcasing best practices and inspirational tales from top insurers.
Findings: The study found that insurers are ready to capitalize on the convergence of the digital and physical realms embracing the "phygital" environment. By making investments in the Metaverse, insurance companies can reduce new risks, enhance customer satisfaction, and streamline operations. But it also brings up issues with user privacy and security. The efficient application of metaverse solutions may be hampered by problematic areas including malware, cyberbullying, identity theft, cyber hacking, and cyberattacks. User privacy and data security are complicated issues that need the cooperation and accountability of several stakeholders.
Practical Implication: Insurers may revolutionize traditional insurance interactions by utilizing cutting-edge technology like virtual reality (VR) and augmented reality (AR) to create personalized, interactive, and instructive experiences for their consumers. For insurers, the Metaverse has ushered in a

Data Alchemy in the Insurance Industry, 133–152

doi:10.1108/978-1-83608-582-920241021

new era of digital transformation by giving them a powerful arsenal of technological resources to engage with customers and develop creative business plans.
Originality/Value: The study on the Metaverse in insurance—a virtual customer experience is an original contribution based on literature and case studies on virtual experiences. The ultimate goal of this study is to offer insights into the optimization of virtual client experiences in the digital age by examining the possible advantages, difficulties, and ramifications of applying Metaverse technologies in the insurance industry.

Keywords: Metaverse in insurance; customer experience; virtual reality and technological trends; consumer experience

1. Introduction

The idea of the Metaverse has emerged from science fiction into the actual world in recent years, providing countless chances for innovation in a wide range of sectors. Among them, the insurance industry is leading the way in redefining client involvement through the use of Metaverse technologies. With its networked virtual locations and immersive digital surroundings, the Metaverse offers insurers a new way to improve consumer experiences (MIT Technology Review, 2022). Through the seamless integration of digital and physical domains, insurers can provide consumers with immersive and personalized interactions from the comfort of their homes, bypassing geographical constraints. Conventional insurance transactions frequently result in a gulf between insurers and policyholders due to intricate documentation, drawn-out procedures, and little client interaction (Ali, 2019).

However, insurers can now construct dynamic and interactive virtual environments where customers may explore insurance products, replicate real-life scenarios, and make educated judgments by integrating Metaverse technologies like virtual reality (VR) and augmented reality (AR) (PWC, 2022).

This chapter explores how the Metaverse could completely transform the way that customers interact with insurance companies, with a focus on developing virtual environments that are customized to each policyholder's unique requirements and preferences. This study intends to clarify the revolutionary effect of Metaverse integration on the insurance business through case studies, analysis of new trends, and technology breakthroughs. In addition, it aims to tackle the difficulties and factors involved in implementing Metaverse solutions, providing guidance on managing this dynamic environment to enhance virtual client interactions.

He wore a VR headset and entered a 3D virtual environment where he interacted face-to-face with an insurance expert represented by a virtual avatar. This platform provided Ronil with policy-related information using visual elements like animation and 3D graphics to maintain his interest. Ronil extensively investigated insurance policies by consulting Virtual Avtar and ultimately purchased a plan to help him meet his financial responsibilities. The example demonstrates how the virtual reality (VR) platform has enabled social interaction. The

Metaverse combines several technical elements, such as AR-VR, mobile and motion devices, network connectivity, video, perambulators, amours, and other technologies, to allow users to live in a digital environment.

Metaverse is a niche science fiction concept that should be reconsidered. The Metaverse has arrived and is widely covered in the news. The Metaverse market is projected to reach $678 billion by 2030, as reported by Bloomberg (PWC, 2022). Gartner, a consulting group, stated that by 2026, 25% of individuals will dedicate at least one hour daily to the Metaverse. It presents corporations with a promising new avenue and the potential to interact with their target audience. Some insurance companies, such as Heungkuk Life Insurance, Bank of Maharashtra, SBI, PNB Metlife, and AXA, already use Metaverse strategies to offer and handle insurance products. The Metaverse presents an emerging opportunity for insurers, offering a unique edge to those who adopt it early.

Moreover, it is revolutionizing client experiences and conventional company practices. Insurers may utilize the Metaverse to reach new consumer segments by providing an immersive purchasing and servicing experience, offering innovative and practical goods, and leveraging the digital ecosystems of the future. The Metaverse can impact the insurance value chain by enhancing revenue or profit margin. In addition, it can assist insurers in improving client experience, reducing costs through virtual hubs, introducing new product categories, enhancing operational efficiency, and increasing insurance awareness among millennials by making it engaging (Yildirim, & Papadopoulos, 2022).

2. Future of Internet: Metaverse Simplified

The science fiction movie "Snow Crash," directed by Neal Stephenson in 1992, introduced the term "metaverse." The name "metaverse" is derived from the fusion of the words "meta" and "universe." Meta denotes something transcendent or surpassing. The Metaverse is a digital environment that replicates real life. Individuals in this virtual environment communicate using digital representations called avatars. People can participate in many activities, like shopping, meetings, and socializing with friends. Access to the virtual environment is possible through devices like cell phones or personal computers.

Users may employ devices like VR headsets, AR glasses, and game consoles to provide a completely immersive experience. The Metaverse is a digital environment where people interact with virtual and augmented realities using digital representations of themselves.

Scenario 1: Engage with your mate who lives in London by meeting at a local restaurant in Mumbai through digital avatars in a virtual environment simultaneously.

Scenario 2: Accompany your American acquaintance in shopping at a retail center in Delhi using digital avatars in real-time within a virtual environment.

The Internet is currently in a two-dimensional state, specifically 2D. When you use Instagram, do you see your social relationships as 2D photos on a 2D screen?

The shift from 2D to 3D is a forthcoming development in the Metaverse. The Metaverse is a three-dimensional Internet application (Srivastava, 2023).

3. Literature Review

Companies such as Meta, Epic Games, and Microsoft are working on creating immersive virtual environments for socializing and co-working, leading to the rise in the use of the term "metaverse" (Xu et al., 2022). The Metaverse refers to a comprehensive type of alluring content. Entertainment, socialization, jobs, education, healthcare, and service delivery are essential to society (Goldberg & Tetreault, 2021; Yang et al., 2022; Yue, 2022). The current forms of the Metaverse are mainly based on fundamental social and collaborative interactions. However, some supporters envision a comprehensive virtual replica of the natural world in the long run. VR and AR technologies allow users to access and engage in the Metaverse, which shares features with traditional immersive experiences. Many current accessibility initiatives for immersive multimedia are likely significant to the Metaverse.

Nevertheless, additional facets of this new media require specific research focus to enhance accessibility. User engagement in the Metaverse differs from conventional AR or VR applications due to three main factors: the close interaction of enormous users leading to psycho-social issues, the transactional nature of some interactions, and users being exposed to content developed by other end-users. The Metaverse unites numerous users in a shared space, anticipating their interaction. Some interactions may be transactional, such as when a user seeks medical assistance, as opposed to the usual collaborative or lightly competitive social VR and AR experiences. These interactions' immediate and sometimes transactional nature presents specific challenges regarding physical and vocal expression, timely interventions, and the complexity of adjusting content in a collaborative virtual setting. Expanding on point (iii), users rather than creators can create experiences in the Metaverse. Aiding developers to enhance the approachability of their material is complex, and there are further challenges in equipping end-users with the tools, knowledge, and drive needed to guarantee the accessibility of the content they create. It involves specific factors related to physical and linguistic portrayal, the promptness of available interventions, and the challenge of adjusting material in a collaborative virtual environment (Park & Kim, 2022).

The social component of the Metaverse intersects with the subcategory of VR experiences known as social VR(SVR). As per the case study presented on Digital Training Academy, in October 2018, SVR platforms usually incorporate gameplay and gamification elements. SVR is a form of online social interaction that occurs in predesigned three-dimensional virtual worlds. Participants, represented by avatars, can engage in real-time conversations and activities using immersive technologies (Dzardanova et al., 2018).

SVR platforms usually incorporate gameplay and gamification elements. This component exposes users to content other users create, including personal avatars, new locations, and user experiences. SVR platforms are designed based on the concept of user-creators who provide user-generated material to fuel platform expansion, akin to how major social networks heavily depend on user-generated content. SVR offers various social interactions and cooperation opportunities in different sectors, such as SVR movies, live performances, and collective engagement in religious ceremonies or cultural activities like museum and gallery exhibitions. As described by Yang et al. (2022) SVR is a common method for socializing and delivering genuine social interactions.

Due to the novelty of SVR and the Metaverse, there needs to be more research on designing these platforms inclusively. It emphasizes the need to examine the concerns in developing a socially inclusive environment for marginalized populations. Freeman and Maloney (2021) suggest that future research on self-representation in SVR should include a more diverse sample, such as differently abled users, LGBTQ+ individuals, and minorities, to explore how different behaviors and identity practices are influenced by their presence in SVR. Seigneur and Choukou (2022) highlight the lack of digital assets on metaverse platforms that allow users with disabilities to represent themselves, such as wheelchairs or prostheses, for usage with avatars. Baker et al. (2020) assessed the utilization of VR in residential aged care facilities (RACF). They noted that many participants expressed interest in having social experiences with individuals outside the RACF when discussing future VR experiences. Baker et al. (2019) conducted a study where participants discussed the advantages of SVR in managing the decline in self-confidence among older adults and its influence on self-imposed social isolation. Baker et al. (2021) found four main themes in the user study data regarding the probable use of avatar-mediated communication (AMC) by elderly adults: AMC minimizes inhibitions, allows control over revealing one's actual appearance, helps establish social networking over distance, and inadvertently obscures some emotions and nonverbal cues. Shao and Lee (2020) did a study on older people to evaluate their perceptions and predict their utilization of SVR. They found that participants expected SVR to improve social contentment and maybe satisfy medical requirements. Freeman and Acena (2021) emphasize the value of participating in immersive events like concerts, talk shows, and professional workshops in social VR for individuals facing mobility limitations, whether due to physical disability or financial restrictions. The studies emphasize different aspects of establishing an accessible metaverse that may not be addressed by the accessibility requirements of users involved in individual AR or VR experiences. Due to the early development of these platforms, more knowledge on the main challenges impaired users face and much less study on possible solutions are needed.

4. Revolutionary Potential of Metaverse Technology in Insurance

Technology integration has caused a major upheaval in the insurance industry in recent years. The insurance sector has undergone a paradigm shift as a result of the innovative measures that insurers have taken. The following are some significant changes and advancements:

4.1 Digitalization of Processes

Customer engagement and operational efficiency have undergone a significant transformation as a result of the insurance industry's digitization of procedures. Insurance companies are using digital platforms and technology more often to automate and expedite processes. These days, customers may easily obtain insurance services and information at their fingertips with the use of online portals and mobile applications (Accenture, 2021). By making it easier to purchase policies, renew them, file claims, and communicate with insurers, these digital channels greatly lessen the need for paper documentation while also improving the consumer experience in general (Deloitte, 2020b). This digital revolution is greatly aided by automation, which allows insurers to free up resources for more value-added operations by automating repetitive processes like data input and document processing (McKinsey, 2020). Insurance companies that embrace digitization not only modernize their processes but also put themselves in a position to satisfy changing client expectations in a world that is becoming more and more digitally focused (PwC, 2021a). With an emphasis on agility, reactivity, and innovation, this move toward digital processes signifies a significant transformation in the insurance industry (KPMG, 2020).

4.2 Data Analytics and Predictive Modeling

The insurance industry has seen a revolution in risk assessment and decision-making processes with the rise of data analytics and predictive modeling. To acquire important insights into risk profiles and behaviors, insurers use massive amounts of data from a variety of sources, including client demographics, claims history, and external factors like weather patterns and economic indicators (EY, 2021). Insurers can scrutinize intricate data sets and detect patterns, trends, and correlations that guide their pricing and underwriting strategies by utilizing sophisticated analytics techniques like machine learning and predictive modeling (McKinsey & Company, 2020). Predictive analytics can help insurers better evaluate risks, offer competitively priced policies, and streamline underwriting procedures to increase revenue and market share (PwC, 2020). Furthermore, through the identification of high-risk regions and the development of proactive risk management plans, predictive modeling enables insurers to foresee and reduce possible losses (Deloitte, 2019). According to Accenture (2020a), data analytics and predictive modeling are essential for revolutionizing insurance operations, spurring innovation, and improving the sector's capacity to adjust to changing market conditions.

4.3 Personalized Products and Pricing

The insurance industry's approach to satisfying the wide range of consumer wants and boosting competitiveness now centers on customized products and pricing. As per McKinsey & Company (2020), insurers are utilizing sophisticated analytics and data-driven insights to customize insurance policies and pricing structures based on individual risk profiles and preferences. Insurers can precisely evaluate risks and establish customized premiums that take into account each customer's particular situation by examining enormous volumes of data, including demographics, lifestyle variables, and past claims data (Deloitte, 2020a). For instance, telematics devices fitted in cars allow insurers to track driving habits in real time and provide usage-based insurance (UBI) policies that give reduced rates to safe drivers (PricewaterhouseCoopers, 2020). Furthermore, insurers are proactively providing pertinent products and services to customers by anticipating their needs with predictive modeling and machine learning algorithms, which increases customer happiness and loyalty (Accenture, 2020a). In an increasingly competitive market, insurers' profitability and growth are fueled by this shift toward tailored goods and pricing, which also enhances the whole client experience (EY, 2021).

4.4 Insurtech Innovation

In the insurance sector, Insurtech innovation has become a disruptive force that is changing old business models and causing a major upheaval. Insurtech companies are utilizing state-of-the-art technologies like blockchain, the Internet of Things (IoT), artificial intelligence (AI), and machine learning to transform different facets of insurance operations (Deloitte, 2021a). To challenge the status quo and satisfy changing client demands in the digital age, these creative businesses are launching cutting-edge goods, services, and distribution methods (EY, 2020). Insurance companies can use AI and machine learning algorithms to streamline underwriting procedures, increase the precision of risk assessments, and improve customer experiences by providing tailored recommendations (McKinsey & Company, 2020). According to PricewaterhouseCoopers (2021a), blockchain technology facilitates safe and transparent transactions, expediting the processing of claims, and lowering the risk of fraud. Additionally, IoT devices—like wearables and connected sensors—allow for real-time data collecting and monitoring, which enables insurers to provide preventive risk management and usage-based insurance (Accenture, 2020b). Because of this, Insurtech innovation is encouraging more cooperation and partnerships between established insurers and startups, which is helping to develop an agile and experimental culture within the sector (KPMG, 2021b). By working together, insurers may take advantage of the Insurtech companies' agility and inventiveness while also gaining from their established market position and experience (Deloitte, 2021a). In general, the insurance business has undergone a paradigm shift due to Insurtech innovation, which has created new chances for expansion, effectiveness, and customer-centricity (EY, 2020).

4.5 Customer Engagement and Experience

Insurance companies that want to stand out in a crowded market and satisfy changing consumer demands are focusing more and more on client experience and engagement. Deloitte (2021b) reports that insurers are utilizing digital platforms and cutting-edge technologies to offer policyholders smooth and customized experiences. Customers may easily obtain information, acquire policies, and make claims whenever and wherever they choose thanks to online portals, smartphone applications, and chatbots (Accenture, 2020b). In addition, insurers are using AI and data analytics to better understand client preferences and habits, which enables customized product offers and individualized communications (EY, 2020). According to PricewaterhouseCoopers (2021b), social media platforms offer insurers the opportunity to interact with clients in real-time, responding to inquiries, offering assistance, and fostering connections. According to McKinsey and Company (2020), AI-powered virtual assistants improve client interactions by offering tailored advice and support throughout the insurance process. Insurers may foster long-term connections, trust, and loyalty with policyholders by putting a high priority on customer engagement and experience. This will ultimately lead to increased business growth and profitability (KPMG, 2021a).

4.6 Remote Underwriting and Claims

In order to increase productivity, boost customer satisfaction, and adjust to shifting market conditions, insurers now need to implement remote underwriting and claims procedures. Insurance companies can reduce the amount of paperwork and in-person interactions by conducting underwriting and claims assessments remotely by utilizing technologies such as AI, data analytics, and digital platforms (Deloitte, 2021b). Drones, satellite images, and Internet of Things devices allow insurers to conduct virtual inspections that allow them to evaluate risks and property damage remotely. This reduces operating costs and speeds up the processing of claims (McKinsey & Company, 2020). To further improve accuracy and lower risks, AI-powered systems evaluate data from several sources to automate underwriting decisions and spot fraudulent claims (Accenture, 2020b). Policyholders have easy access to file and track claims using digital platforms and mobile applications, which allow them to file claims and get updates from a distance (PricewaterhouseCoopers, 2021b). Insurance companies can enhance their operational efficiency, reduce cycle times, and provide clients with faster, more convenient services by implementing remote underwriting and claims procedures (EY, 2020).

4.7 Emphasis on Cybersecurity

To safeguard confidential client information and reduce the danger of cyberattacks, insurers are now deeply concerned about cybersecurity in the current digital environment. According to Deloitte (2021b), insurers are progressively allocating more resources toward comprehensive cybersecurity protocols in order to prevent ransomware attacks, data breaches, and other cyber disasters that may jeopardize their customers' trust and financial stability. Insurance companies are putting in place extensive cybersecurity frameworks that include proactive threat detection, incident response procedures, and employee training due to the growth in complexity of cyber threats and the expansion of digital channels (EY, 2020). Insurance companies may fortify their defenses and react quickly to new threats by utilizing cutting-edge technology like AI and machine learning to evaluate enormous volumes of data and spot possible security flaws (McKinsey & Company, 2020). In addition, the cooperation and exchange of information among government agencies, business groups, and insurers is essential for improving cyber resilience and reducing systemic risks (Accenture, 2020b). In an increasingly digitalized world, insurers may preserve their brand, safeguard sensitive client data, and remain in compliance with regulations by placing a high priority on cybersecurity (PricewaterhouseCoopers, 2021b).

5. Application of Metaverse to Insurance

5.1 Enhanced Customer Experience

The epidemic has affected the typical client engagement strategies of insurance firms. Customers are reluctant to see insurance professionals in person due to fear of the virus. Insurance is an intangible product that necessitates personalized counseling for customers to comprehend the insurance plan and its terms and conditions. Therefore, it is imperative to enhance and revolutionize client engagement strategies.

The Metaverse can have a significant impact in this context. The Metaverse allows for a more personalized customer engagement experience, enabling users to create their own experiences by offering the necessary tools.

VR and AR tools allow customers to enjoy an alluring experience where they can navigate through the meta-Advisor Hub of Neo Insurer, go to the insurance Purchase Room, and buy insurance using a meta wallet. Customers can choose to interact with an advisor for personalized guidance in addition to using the self-service kiosk (Srivastava, 2023)

PNB MetLife, India's leading life insurance company, has introduced Con-VRse, an innovative VR customer service platform. This platform allows clients to engage with virtual avatars to ask questions and acquire further plan information.

Allianz, a German multinational financial services corporation, is showcasing another impressive example of utilizing AR in the insurance sector. They have developed an interactive experience for people to learn about potential risks in their daily lives.

5.2 Cost Reduction and Other Sources of Income

Customers typically purchase insurance plans from the nearest company office for easy access to the insurer during emergencies. Establishing offices in various locations is challenging for the insurer due to the significant capital expenditure required to purchase physical office premises, particularly in tier-2 and tier-3 cities. It is not practical for the insurance company to have physical offices in all locations. The Metaverse can assist insurers by offering remote virtual hubs for client outreach. It also diminishes the necessity for real offices.

Heungkuk Life Insurance in Korea has established a "virtual counseling window" within the Metaverse. Hubb, a UK-based hub, is the first insurance broker prepared for the Metaverse. The company has implemented a hybrid working environment using a virtual workspace to provide clients with flexible methods to work with the usage-based broker, prioritizing customer choices. This shift toward the virtual realms of the Metaverse is a practical way to engage with clients in various settings, such as a beach or the peak of Everest. Additionally, the Metaverse introduces new revenue opportunities for insurers through multiple categories of insurance products. Immersive experiences and the Metaverse give insurers a distinct chance to interact with consumers – both current, former, and potential—directly and personally. Insurers can view immersive experiences as a method to expand current revenue sources, as the Metaverse provides new opportunities for them. Potential new product categories include insurance solutions for AR/VR headsets, liability coverage for AR/VR headset usage, and worker's compensation for job-related AR/VR usage. Several insurers, including Aviva, have ventured into providing insurance for Metaverse technologies.

5.3 Operational Excellence

Critical insurance business operations include rate-making, underwriting, claim settlement, and reinsurance. There is significant demand for insurers to manage their existing operating expenses efficiently. Several obstacles exist, including consistently low investment returns, growing competitive pressures, and ongoing excess capacity. These problems have impeded the industry's ability to increase revenue faster than the escalating operating expenditures. These expenses have increased slowly over time and have mostly matched the growth rate of premium income in life and property & casualty (P&C) insurance companies.

Insurers need help to control their operational costs. Metaverse has the potential to revolutionize its efforts to optimize its expenses. It provides numerous options for insurers to save on operating costs and generate revenue through operational excellence.

The MetLife Infinity app enables users to create a heritage by uploading essential documents, images, and videos, which may be shared with loved ones at a predetermined time, even after the individual has passed away.

The multinational insurance company AXA is also exploring opportunities outside of the Metaverse. It recently acquired a virtual block of land in the Sandbox. The company aims to familiarize itself with the operations of the Metaverse. It is the first French banking and insurance company to enter the Metaverse.

State Farm, a US.-based insurance company, is significantly expanding its virtual and immersive technologies presence. Engineers have created a proof-of-concept (POC) tailored to assist users like State Farm agents. This POC assists in accurately generating a quote for a new small business insurance policy. This

POC allows individuals to travel and engage with various businesses without leaving their workplaces.

A virtual underwriting room could be established for underwriter/broker communication using technology like Microsoft Mesh. Insurance assets can be evaluated, and risk advisory services can be provided remotely using the Omniverse platform. Similar technology can also be implemented in claims for virtual damage assessment after an occurrence. Another instance involves establishing a virtual underwriting room for underwriters and brokers to collaborate using technology like Microsoft Mesh. Insurance assets can be evaluated remotely using the Omniverse platform, which provides risk advisory services. Comparable technology can also be implemented in claims for virtual damage assessment after an occurrence.

Fig. 10.1: The global metaverse market reached a valuation of almost USD 68.49 billion in 2022. The projections show a significant increase, with a forecasted value surpassing USD 1.3 trillion by 2030. This growth is characterized by a spectacular compound annual growth rate (CAGR) of 44.5% from 2022 to 2030. In 2022, the worldwide metaverse market was valued at approximately 65.5 billion US dollars, as per another survey. In 2023, the value is expected to increase to around 82 billion U.S. dollars, and it is forecast to grow further to reach 936.6 billion US dollars by 2030. The transformation of the Metaverse from an idea to a tangible existence attracted significant focus, especially with Facebook's renaming to Meta Platforms. Aside from Meta, significant companies, including Apple, Nvidia, and Qualcomm, have shown a strong interest in investing in this complex digital environment.

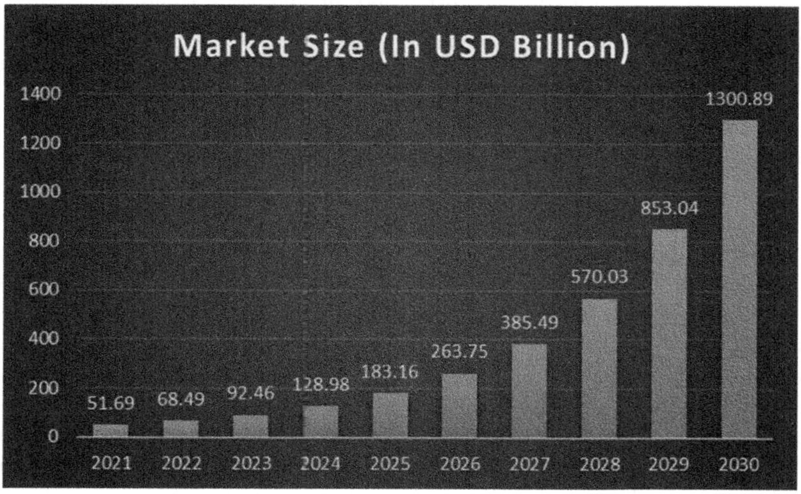

Fig. 10.1. Global Metaverse Market Size 2022–2030 *Source:* Authors Creation.

6. Enhancing the Appeal of Insurance

According to the latest Life Insurance and Market Research Association (LIMRA) survey, just 66% of Generation Y, sometimes known as millennials, have life insurance. The primary cause is the millennials' need for more information about the current developments in insurance products and market trends, as indicated by the survey. Youths find reading about insurance plans and their extensive policy documentation needs to be revised. Metaverse can assist insurers in making insurance more appealing and raising awareness among the general public. Smartphones that display AR simulations are readily accessible, allowing insurance businesses to utilize this functionality quickly. Insurance purchasing can be transformed into an enjoyable experience using AR and VR technologies.

YuLife has designed its app to be engaging by creating a game-like experience set in the "Universe." Users can progress by completing quests, duels, and challenges to unlock new zones and increase their YuCoin balance. Desjardins Insurance, a Canadian corporation, has created AR software that provides video explanations of customers' retirement objectives and plans depending on selected alternatives.

Liverpool Victoria, a UK-based insurer, employs a distinctive method to interact with consumers. The company uses newspaper flyers and AR technology to engage customers. Scanning the flyers transforms them into 3D house models. Next, the consumer can examine the insurable items within the residence. It offers customers several strategies to safeguard their possessions, potentially introducing new concepts they had not before considered.

Utilizing AR and VR for Insurance Surveys and Loss Assessment Utilizing AR and VR technology in the Metaverse can assist in identifying damaged areas of things and offering a comprehensive 360° evaluation through the creation of 3D models from images of the damage. Technical specialists often find it challenging to comprehend the extent of harm. Utilizing AR and VR technology can simplify the process by superimposing object photos that depict the thing's condition before and after the accident, aiding in comprehending the extent of damage. It simplifies determining the necessary repair expenses by measuring the dimensions of the damaged components.

The insurance will no longer be limited by geographic location. They can process insurance claims across different regions. Smart devices allow a surveyor to view the claim object remotely. They offer numerous features, such as pausing or playing the video, identifying any questionable material, and presenting relevant visuals and statistics to support the customer's claim. Technologies like AR and VR significantly benefit from accurately assessing damage from a distance.

Customers may submit their insurance claims instantly using AssistXR Remote Assistant, which utilizes AI and AR technology. This gadget aids insurers in remotely inspecting damaged property. It helps policyholders and insurers collaborate in real-time using AR during a computer vision-powered video conference with remote assistance.

7. Metaverse: A Dual-Edged Weapon

The Metaverse provides numerous advantages for consumers. However, there are other issues associated with the Metaverse. No text is provided.

7.1 Collection of Data by Third Parties

Third parties can gather a large volume of user data. This data is susceptible to exploitation by third parties. The government should enact robust data regulations to address this issue.

7.2 Countless Privacy Concerns

Third parties obtain users' data, including names and addresses. If organizations lack robust data security, sensitive information may be exposed and misused.

7.3 Cybersecurity risks

Cybersecurity risks have increased significantly due to the rise in cyberattacks. No system is immune to cyberattacks. The organization's IT team should implement robust security measures to identify harmful conduct in metaverse initiatives.

8. Metaverse's Impact on the Insurance Value Chain

The rise of the Metaverse offers numerous economic prospects that can transform the entire insurance value chain. These prospects cover many facets of the insurance sector and have the opportunity for transformation.

8.1 Generating Revenue

Avatars are prominent figures in the Metaverse, crucial in developing new sales strategies. Insurance businesses can interact with avatars in many ways, creating opportunities for future sales tactics. It involves innovative marketing and branding efforts in the virtual world, using the lack of physical constraints to develop inventive advertising techniques. Moreover, focusing on the Metaverse could be pretty beneficial in reaching younger audiences attracted to its gamified features.

8.2 Engaging Customer Experiences

Engaging encounters in the Metaverse can improve clients' understanding of the value of insurance products. Insurance businesses can use simulated situations to help customers understand the importance of insurance instead of just using statistical data and traditional explanations. This method allows clients to understand hazards more efficiently and realize the importance of insurance, although they should proceed with caution to avoid emotional distress.

8.3 Insights Derived from Data Analysis

The Metaverse automatically stores all user interactions and behaviors as data. Examining this data, which includes activity history, purchases, and avatar relationships, enables insurers to provide customized risk protection policies. Paying careful attention to safeguarding personal data and adhering to changing legislation is crucial.

8.4 Digitalization of Operations

Insurance plans are expanding to include digital assets such as NFTs and cryptocurrencies, leading to a thorough digitization of insurance procedures. It provides contracting, billing, claims processing, and sales activities, decreasing the need for physical locations. Digital replicas of real-world spaces in the Metaverse accelerate the transition to virtual operations, especially for educating employees in investigating damages.

8.5 Integration of Assets

A new era of asset classes is emerging with avatars, 3D models, spatial environments, and mixed reality. These assets and their information work together to create profiles for persons and corporations in the Metaverse. Ensuring asset and content interoperability facilitates smooth procedures such as insurance applications, approval, and claims submission.

8.6 Interoperability Across Platforms

The success of the Metaverse depends on cross-platform compatibility, allowing users to connect smoothly regardless of their preferred platforms. Without leaving, business owners can apply for insurance, get approval, and file claims within the metaverse environment.

8.7 Improved Insurance Procedures

Insurers can use metaverse technology to improve claims processing, risk assessment, underwriting, relationships with brokers and clients, and servicing current demand. It involves utilizing metaverse headsets for property evaluations, remote asset inspections by underwriters, risk assessment by brokers, and training for loss adjusters through new realities technology.

8.8 Imagining Situations

Exposure managers and insurers can utilize metaverse capabilities to create realistic scenarios, enhancing consumer engagement and emotional connections in sales and marketing efforts.

8.9 Efficient Loss Adjustment

Emerging technologies provide loss adjusters with immediate, unbiased visual data, claim history, legal references, third-party information, and past examples. This abundance of information speeds up claim settlements enhances consumer happiness and decreases fraudulent activity.

8.10 Online Goods Exchange Platform

The virtual products marketplace in the Metaverse is expected to surpass one hundred billion dollars, offering a promising possibility for expansion. With a current value of almost $50 billion, insurance companies should capitalize on this opportunity to stay ahead in technological progress.

9. Technological Barriers in Conventional Insurance Procedures

Traditional insurance businesses need several technological obstacles to adapt to a shifting business environment.

9.1 Outdated Systems

Several insurers depend on obsolete legacy systems that impede efficiency, making adjusting to new technology and processes difficult.

9.2 Data Management

Managing extensive customer data is essential in the insurance industry. Challenges occur throughout the processes of data collecting, storage, and analysis to facilitate informed decision-making and enhance customer experiences.

9.3 Cybersecurity

Protecting sensitive consumer information is a top priority due to the rising cyber risks. Insurers must implement strong cybersecurity safeguards against data breaches and privacy infringements.

9.4 Automation and Process Optimization

Automating manual operations is essential for enhancing efficiency and reducing costs. Conventional insurance companies may need help incorporating automation into their processes.

9.5 Customer Expectations

Adapting to changing client demands for digital access, customized services, and smooth interactions can take time for insurers using obsolete systems and procedures.

9.6 Adherence to Regulations

Harmonizing regulatory adherence with technology advancement is a continual struggle due to the extensive regulations in the insurance sector.

9.7 Data Analytics

Utilizing sophisticated analytics to enhance risk assessment and pricing models might be challenging for conventional insurers with restricted data analytics skills.

10. Challenges and Risks Posed by the Metaverse in the Insurance Sector

The Metaverse offers the potential to transform the insurance industry. Still, it also presents substantial dangers and obstacles that insurance companies need to address to ensure the security of their operations and clients. Key risks and problems linked to the Metaverse in the insurance sector are outlined below:

10.1 Cybersecurity Weaknesses

Cyber dangers can impact the Metaverse. Insurance firms in the digital arena are vulnerable to cyberattacks from evil entities. These attacks can lead to the theft or alteration of consumer data, potentially causing significant financial losses and damaging reputation.

10.2 Legal and Intellectual Property Challenges

The distinction between the virtual and physical realms becomes indistinct in the Metaverse. This ambiguity might result in accidental breaches of tangible rights, such as intellectual property and privacy rights. Understanding the intricate legal aspects of these virtual environments can be a significant obstacle for insurers.

10.3 Ambiguity in Regulations

The swift advancement of the Metaverse has surpassed the creation of thorough regulatory structures. Regulatory ambiguity poses issues for insurance businesses operating in the Metaverse and trying to comply with regulations.

10.4 Data Security and Privacy

Given the Metaverse's accumulation and retention of extensive client data, safeguarding data security and privacy is crucial. Insurers must invest heavily in solid cybersecurity solutions to protect sensitive consumer data against breaches.

10.5 Emerging and Incalculable Risks

The Metaverse presents new dangers that can be challenging to comprehend and measure. Insurance firms must create innovative techniques to efficiently evaluate and control these new risks.

10.6 Technical Proficiency Requirement

To navigate the Metaverse effectively, one must have a profound grasp of cutting-edge technology such as VR, blockchain, and AI. Insurers need to spend on acquiring the technological skills necessary to succeed in the digital environment.

10.7 Difficulties in Customer Adoption

Although the Metaverse presents intriguing opportunities for client interaction, insurers may need help to persuade customers to adopt these novel technologies and experiences. Creating successful methods to educate and promote client acceptance is essential.

10.8 Server Outages and Technical Issues

Virtual environments might have technological issues, including server outages. Unforeseen interruptions may impact digital resources, activities, and information, potentially resulting in financial harm. Insurers must take into account these risks when designing their coverage options.

11. Conclusion

The Metaverse is poised to revolutionize the insurance industry and inspire future developments. It will extend beyond open-world games and sci-fi movies to become a part of everyday life, where virtual worlds will be populated by human avatars and industries with their digital likeness and assets.

Metaverse data adds to the worth by enhancing consumer experiences, ensuring data compatibility, optimizing processes, developing analytics models, and designing products and services. However, it also raises concerns about security and user privacy. Concerned areas such as cyberattacks, identity theft, cyberhackers, malware, and cyberbullying can hinder the effective use of metaverse solutions. Data security and user privacy are complex issues requiring multiple parties' collaboration and accountability. Regulatory bodies, metaverse solution providers, and users must collaborate to develop a significant solution.

12. Acknowledgments

We express our heartfelt gratitude to all those who have helped in this research work by giving their inputs directly or indirectly through their research works as references or direct inputs as respondents. We express our heartfelt indebtedness to the almighty God who has given us the strength to complete the research work.

References

Accenture. (2020a). *Data & analytics in insurance: Unlocking value from the insurance data deluge*. Accenture. https://www.accenture.com/_acnmedia/PDF-107/Accenture-Data-and-Analytics-Insurance-Unlocking-Value.pdf

Accenture. (2020b). *The rise of Insurtech*. Accenture. https://www.accenture.com/_acnmedia/PDF-116/Accenture-Insurance-Rise-of-Insurtech.pdf

Accenture. (2021). *Digital Insurance: The time to act is now*. Accenture. https://www.accenture.com/_acnmedia/pdf-149/accenture-insurance-digital-insurance-time-to-act.pdf

Ali, K. (2019, September 27). A comparative study of Takaful and conventional insurance: Empirical evidence from the Malaysian market. https://www.researchgate.net/publication/336074440_A_comparative_study_of_Takaful_and_conventional_insurance_empirical_evidence_from_the_Malaysian_market

Baker, S., Kelly, R. M., Waycott, J., Carrasco, R., Hoang, T., Batchelor, F., Ozanne, E., Dow, B., Warburton, J., & Vetere, F. (2019). Interrogating social virtual reality as a communication medium for older adults. *Proceedings of the ACM on Human-Computer Interaction*. https://doi.org/10.1145/3359251

Baker, S., Waycott, J., Robertson, E., Carrasco, R., Neves, B. B., Hampson, R., & Vetere, F. (2020). Evaluating interactive virtual reality technology use with older adults living in residential aged care. *Information Processing & Management*, *57*(3), 102,105. https://doi.org/10.1016/j.ipm.2019.102105

Baker, S., Waycott, J., Carrasco, R., Kelly, R. M., Jones, A. J., Lilley, J., Dow, B., Batchelor, F., Hoang, T., & Vetere, F. (2021). Avatar-mediated communication in social V.R.: An in-depth exploration of older adult interaction in an emerging communication platform. In *Proceedings of the 2021 CHI Conference on Human Factors in Computing Systems*. Association for Computing Machinery. New York, NY, USA. https://doi.org/10.1145/3411764.3445752

Deloitte. (2019). *Predictive modeling in insurance: The power to predict*. Deloitte. https://www2.deloitte.com/content/dam/Deloitte/us/Documents/financial-services/us-fsi-predictive-modeling-in-insurance.pdf

Deloitte. (2020a). *Insurance Industry Outlook: Strategies to stay competitive in a rapidly evolving marketplace*. Deloitte. https://www2.deloitte.com/us/en/insights/industry/insurance/insurance-industry-outlook.html

Deloitte. (2020b). *The digital future of insurance: Is the industry ready to respond to the changing market trends?* Deloitte. https://www2.deloitte.com/content/dam/Deloitte/us/Documents/financial-services/us-fsi-digital-future-of-insurance.pdf

Deloitte. (2021a). *Insurtech Outlook 2021*. Deloitte. https://www2.deloitte.com/content/dam/Deloitte/uk/Documents/financial-services/deloitte-uk-insurtech-outlook-2021.pdf

Deloitte. (2021b). *The future of insurance: Unleashing growth through customer-centricity*. Deloitte. https://www2.deloitte.com/content/dam/Deloitte/global/Documents/Financial-Services/gx-fsi-future-of-insurance-2021-brochure.pdf

Digital Training Academy. *Gamification case study: AXA online game educates customers on insurance fund*. http://www.digitaltrainingacademy.com/casestudies/2015/03/gamification case study axa online game educates customers on insurance fund.php. Accessed on October 2017.

Dzardanova, E., Kasapakis, V., & Gavalas, D. (2018). Social virtual reality. In N. Lee (Ed.), *Encyclopedia of computer graphics and games* (pp. 1–3). Springer International Publishing.

EY. (2020). *Insurtech: Changing the insurance landscape*. EY. https://www.ey.com/en_gl/insurance/how-are-insurtechs-changing-the-insurance-landscape

EY. (2021). *Data analytics in insurance: Unlocking the value of data*. EY. https://www.ey.com/en_gl/insurance/data-analytics-in-insurance-unlocking-the-value-of-data

Freeman, G., & Acena, D. (2021). Hugging from a distance: Building interpersonal relationships in social virtual reality. In *ACM International Conference on Interactive Media Experiences* (p. 84). Association for Computing Machinery. New York, NY, USA. https://doi.org/10.1145/3452918.3458805

Freeman, G., & Maloney, D. (2021). Body, Avatar, and me. *Proceedings of the ACM on Human-Computer Interaction*. https://doi.org/10.1145/3432938

Goldberg, A., & Tetreault, S. (2021). Live from the metaverse: Virtual X.R. Performances for audiences on-stage, online, in-game, and in-VR. In *ACM SIGGRAPH 2021 Production Sessions*. Association for Computing Machinery. New York, NY, USA. https://doi.org/10.1145/3446368.3452125

KPMG. (2020). *The future of insurance: How digital ecosystems are transforming the industry*. KPMG. https://home.kpmg/xx/en/home/insights/2020/09/future-of-insurance-digital-ecosystems.html

KPMG. (2021a). *Insurance: Getting the customer experience right*. KPMG. https://home.kpmg/xx/en/home/insights/2021/07/insurance-getting-the-customer-experience-right.html

KPMG. (2021b). *The Insurtech ecosystem: Game changers in insurance*. KPMG. https://home.kpmg/xx/en/home/insights/2021/05/the-insurtech-ecosystem.html

Lal, R. Insurance in Metaverse: A fresh perspective. https://ideausher.com/blog/metaverse-insurance/. Accessed on February, 2023.

McKinsey and Company. (2020a). *Insurance 2030—The impact of AI on the future of insurance*. McKinsey & Company. https://www.mckinsey.com/industries/financial-services/our-insights/insurance-2030-the-impact-of-ai-on-the-future-of-insurance

McKinsey and Company. (2020b). *The insurance AI imperative: Unlocking the value of advanced analytics in insurance*. McKinsey & Company. https://www.mckinsey.com/industries/financial-services/our-insights/the-insurance-ai-imperative-unlocking-the-value-of-advanced-analytics-in-insurance

MIT Technology Review. (2022, February 8). The metaverse is a new word for an old idea. https://www.technologyreview.com/2022/02/08/1044732/metaverse-history-snow-crash/

Park, S. M., & Kim, Y. G. (2022). A metaverse: Taxonomy, components, applications, and open challenges. *IEEE Access*, *10*, 4209–4251. https://doi.org/10.1109/ACCESS.2021.3140175

PricewaterhouseCoopers (PwC). (2020). *The future of insurance: How technology is transforming the industry*. PwC. https://www.pwc.com/gx/en/insurance/publications/assets/pwc-technology-is-transforming-insurance.pdf

PricewaterhouseCoopers (PwC). (2021a). *Insurance 2020 & beyond: Reimagining insurance business processes with digital transformation*. PwC. https://www.pwc.com/us/en/insurance/publications/assets/insurance-2020-and-beyond-digital-transformation.pdf

PricewaterhouseCoopers (PwC). (2021b). *The future of insurance: How technology is reshaping the industry*. PwC. https://www.pwc.com/gx/en/insurance/publications/assets/pwc-future-of-insurance.pdf

PwC. (2022, July). *The impact of the Metaverse on the Insurance industry*. https://www.pwc.com/jp/en/knowledge/column/metaverse-impact-on-the-insurance-industry.html

Seigneur, J. M., & Choukou, M. A. (2022). *How should Metaverse augment humans with disabilities in 13th augmented human international conference*. Association for Computing Machinery. https://doi.org/10.1145/3532525.3532534

Shao, D., & Lee, I. J. (2020). Acceptance and influencing factors of social virtual reality in the urban elderly. *Sustainability*, *12*(22), 9345. https://doi.org/10.3390/su12229345

Srivastava, S. (2023, July). How is metaverse presenting new opportunities for insurance businesses? https://appinventiv.com/blog/metaverse-in-insurance-industry/

Xu, J., Papangelis, K., Dunham, J., Goncalves, J., LaLone, N. J., Chamberlain, A., Lykourentzou, I., Vinella, F. L., & Schwartz, D. I. (2022). Metaverse: The vision for the future. In *Extended Abstracts of the 2022 CHI Conference on Human Factors in Computing Systems*. Association for Computing Machinery. New York, NY, USA. https://doi.org/10.1145/3491101.3516399

Yang, D., Zhou, J., Chen, R., Song, Y., Song, Z., Zhang, X., Wang, Q., Wang, K., Zhou, C., Sun, J., Zhang, L., Bai, L., Wang, Y., Wang, X., Lu, Y., Xin, H., Powell, C. A., Thüemmler, C., Chavannes, N. H., & Bai, C. (2022). Expert consensus on the Metaverse in medicine. *Clin eHealth*, *5*, 1–9. https://doi.org/10.1016/j.ceh.2022.02.001

Yildirim, O., & Papadopoulos, G. (2022, November). Metaverse: Revolution or evolution? And where does insurance come in? https://www.swissre.com/risk-knowledge/risk-perspectives-blog/metaverse-in-insurance.html

Chapter 11

Trends and Patterns in Insurance Research: A Bibliometric Analysis (2020–2024)

Khem Chand[a], *Ajay Chandel*[a], *Rajesh Tiwari*[b] *and Abshishek Singh Chauhan*[b]

[a]Lovely Professional University, India
[b]Graphic Era (Deemed to be University), India

Abstract

Purpose: This study presents an extensive bibliometric analysis aimed at delineating the landscape of research within the insurance literature from 2020 to 2024.
Methodology: Leveraging methodologies such as keyword cooccurrence analysis, cocitation analysis, and bibliographic coupling, the study identifies pivotal clusters of research topics. The bibliographic data was sourced from Scopus, renowned for its comprehensive coverage across social, engineering, and natural sciences. Following the PRISMA (Preferred Reporting Items for Systematic Reviews and Meta-Analyses) guidelines, 1,608 documents were initially scrutinized, resulting in a refined dataset of 714 documents. Utilizing VOSviewer for science mapping, the study underscores three predominant categories of analysis: keyword cooccurrence, cocitation, and bibliographic coupling. Employing a dual-pronged approach for keyword selection, the study began by examining five freely accessible publications. Analysis was conducted employing two primary bibliometric techniques: performance analysis, gauging the efficacy of research components, and science mapping, elucidating interdependencies among research entities. Notably, the study utilized VOSviewer and Biblioshiny—a web interface for bibliometrics based on the R programming language—as the principal tools for bibliometric analysis.
Findings: This comprehensive investigation sheds light on the thematic evolution and interconnectedness within insurance research, providing valuable insights for scholars, practitioners, and policymakers alike.

Data Alchemy in the Insurance Industry, 153–181

doi:10.1108/978-1-83608-582-920241025

Keywords: Insurance literature; PRISMA; bibliometric analysis; research evolution; research efficacy

1. Introduction

Insurance sector is one of the fast-growing sectors of Indian economy. India is the fifth largest in insurance market of the world. The insurance in India has been growing at a 34%. The progressive policies of the successive governments have paved the way for a vibrant insurance sector. The FDI of 26% has been allowed in insurance sector. India has a diversified insurance sector comprising of 54 companies. There are 34 nonlife insurance companies and 24 companies dealing in life insurance in India optimistic contribution of public and private sector. The regulatory authority, IRDS is working with a mission of "Insurance for all by 2047" in India (IBEF, 2024). Figs. 11.1 and 11.2 demonstrated steadily growing insurance density in life and nonlife insurance sector.

A code of conduct was developed by the General Insurance Council to guarantee ethical behavior and sensible business procedures. The "General Insurance Business (Nationalization) Act," passed in 1972, nationalized the nonlife insurance industry, taking effect on January 1, 1973. The history of insurance has reached a turning point this millennium, spanning over two centuries. The industry had started to reopen in the early 1990s, and over the course of the following 10 years, it has opened up significantly. Malhotra committee headed by former Governor of Reserve Bank of was established in 1993. The committee aimed to make recommendations for changes to the insurance industry. The "Insurance Regulatory and Development Authority (IRDA) Act of 1999," and other relevant acts regulate the insurance industry. India has a huge

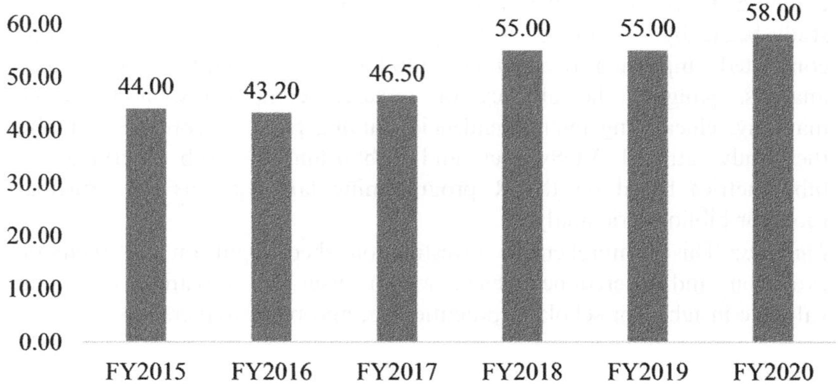

Fig. 11.1. Life Insurances Density (Premium per Capita) (US $).
Source: India Brand Equity Foundation (IBEF, 2024).

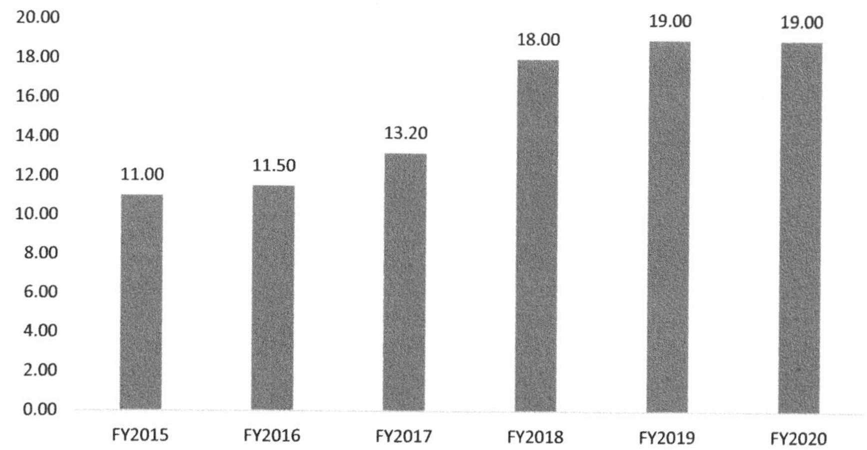

Fig. 11.2. Nonlife Insurances Density (Premium per Capita) (US $). *Source:* India Brand Equity Foundation (IBEF, 2024)

opportunity for the insurance industry due to its size and the unexplored market that this population possesses.

2. Objectives of the Study

This study tries to decipher undermentioned research questions using science mapping technique of bibliometrics:

- What are the key research themes or clusters emerging from cocitation networks in Insurance literature?
- How does bibliographic coupling contribute to the identification of related research areas or subfields within Insurance research?
- How do patterns of keyword cooccurrence reflect the structure and evolution of research topics within Insurance research?
- What are the future research agendas to further Insurance literature?

3. Methodology

3.1 Bibliometrics

The desire to analyze and organize the vast quantities of bibliographic data in the field of library and information sciences led to the development of bibliometric research methodologies (Broadus, 1987). In bibliometric research, representative summaries of the available literature are constructed to assess and classify large amounts of bibliometric data, particularly in the field of Insurance. The study topics were addressed utilizing two primary bibliographic analysis techniques:

performance analysis, which examined the performance of research components, and science mapping, which identified the interdependencies among research pieces (Donthu et al., 2021). The researchers utilized VOSviewer and Biblioshiny, which is a web interface for bibliometrics based on the R programming language, as their preferred tools for doing bibliometric analysis.

3.2 Keyword Extraction

The selection of keywords for finding relevant literature on Insurance was done utilizing a two-pronged technique. To identify appropriate keywords, five open access publications from SCOPUS database were reviewed. An initial list of keywords was prepared and was later offered to 10 domain experts for vetting. The experts were explained the rationale and objectives/research questions of the study.

3.3 Data Procurement

A total of 1,608 documents underwent the PRISMA (Preferred reporting items for systematic reviews and meta-analysis) process, as suggested by Moher et al. (2009), resulting in a final dataset of 714 documents. Fig. 11.3 presents a comprehensive overview of the PRISMA and the methods used for conducting and organizing bibliometric analysis.

Scopus is considered one of the most credible and the largest dataset of academic and scientific publications. It consists of a comprehensive core collection of publications ranging from social sciences to engineering (Bartol et al., 2014). Search query "(TITLE('Insurance') AND PUBYEAR > 2019 AND PUBYEAR < 2025 AND (LIMIT-TO (DOCTYPE, 'ar')) AND (LIMIT-TO (LANGUAGE,'English')) AND (LIMIT-TO (SRCTYPE,'j')) AND (LIMIT-TO (SUBJAREA,'BUSI')) AND (LIMIT-TO (OA,'all')))" resulted into 1,608 publications in the time frame of 2020–2024. The identified publications were subjected to PRISMA proposed by Moher et al. (2009). Stepwise screening of publications led to 714 final documents that were deemed fit for the study. Fig. 11.3 shows an overview of the PRISMA for conducting and organizing this bibliometric analysis.

3.4 Techniques

This bibliometric investigation employs "Science mapping" of "Bibliometrics" to perform keyword cooccurrence analysis, cocitation analysis, and bibliographic coupling. While keyword cooccurrence analysis helps identify conceptual structure of the domain, cocitation analysis focuses Limitations and "Scope for future research" section of the two most cited publications in each year (2020–2024) was content analyzed to propose future research agendas thereby triangulating bibliometrics with content analysis.

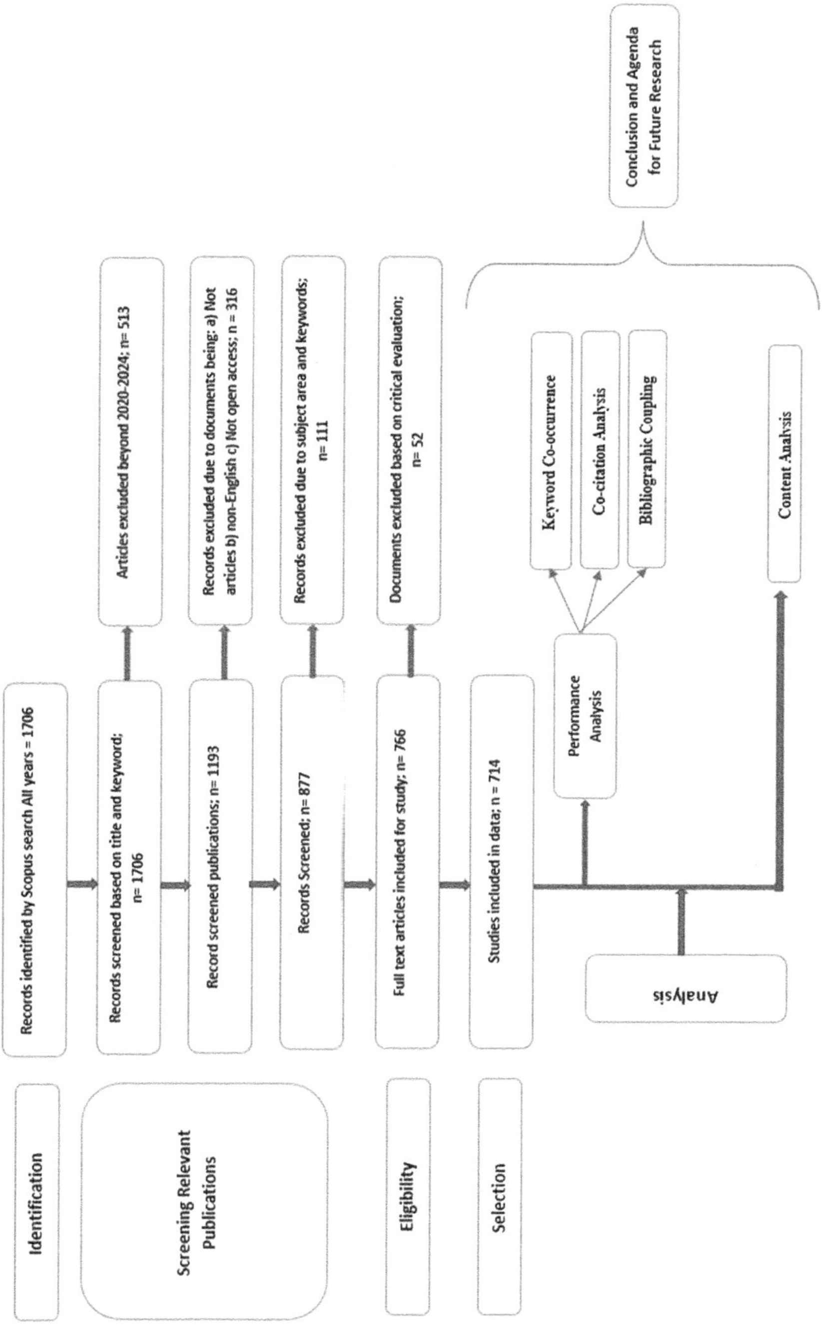

Fig. 11.3. PRISMA.

4. Discussion on Results

4.1 Keyword Co-occurrence Analysis

To evaluate the associations between different keywords in a group of scholarly publications, bibliometricians use keyword co-occurrence analysis. Keyword cooccurrence can help to clarify an area's thematic structure, relationships, and trends in research. It also identifies recurring topics, clusters of studies, or emerging areas of interest by highlighting where terms occur together. This technique is also helpful in showing how different fields of inquiry are related to one another. Seventy-three keywords met the threshold when the Louvain clustering method was applied with a minimum requirement of 10 keyword cooccurrences out of 1,248 total keywords (Blondel et al., 2008). Eight keywords were excluded from these 73 keywords as they were believed not to fit within the domain but still preserved integrity for analysis purposes. Results are shown in Fig. 11.4, which visually presents findings using network maps where each color represents a different cluster; eight clusters were found according to keyword cooccurrence analysis (Blondel et al., 2008). This section further describes these clusters by examining what they indicate about emergent themes.

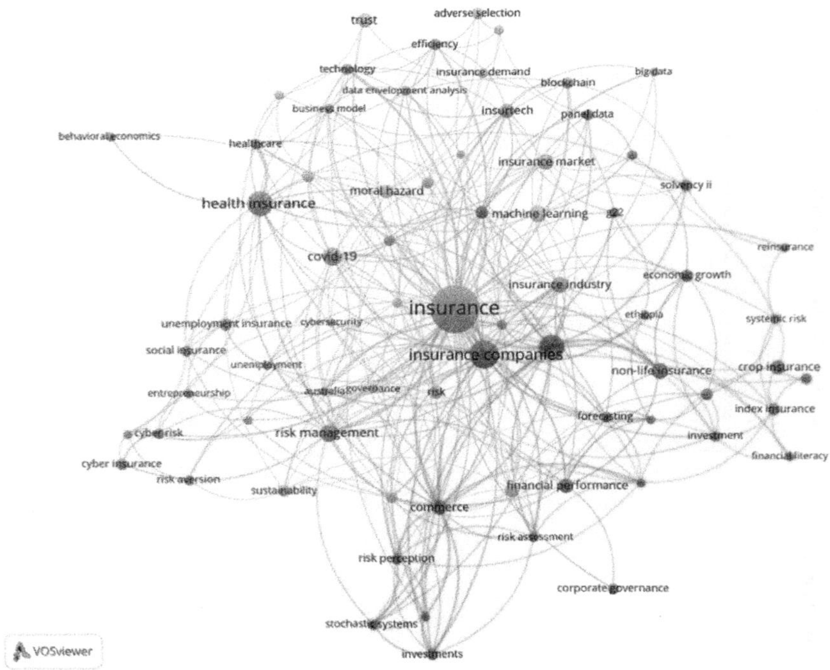

Fig. 11.4. Keyword Co-occurrence Analysis, VOSviewer.

Cluster I (Keywords- Corporate governance, Economic Growth, Financial performance, Forecasting, G22, Insurance companies, Insurance penetration).

The complexity and diversity of a bibliometric study on insurance literature are amplified when keywords such as corporate governance, economic growth, financial performance, and forecasting are intertwined. This underscores the necessity for companies to adopt standard business practices that govern their operations, a crucial step toward achieving financial stability. Such stability, in turn, enhances firms' capacity to anticipate and adapt to economic changes (Gatzert & Özdil, 2024).

As economies expand, the demand for insurance products typically rises, indicating increased insurance penetration (Bayar et al., 2021). To effectively anticipate future market trends and consumer needs and to optimize financial efficiencies based on broader economic expansion patterns, insurers must employ robust prediction methods. This underscores the importance of sound corporate governance structures within these organizations. Without them, firms cannot sustainably grow, enhance their financial performance, or adapt adequately in dynamic markets (Zulfiqar et al., 2020).

Cluster II (Keywords- Australia, Cyber insurance, Cyber risk, Digital transformation, Risk aversion, Risk management).

In Australia, risk management is evolving because of technological advancements and changing risk environments, as represented by the presence of such phrases as Australian, cyber insurance, cyber risk, digital transformation, fear of risk, and aversion to risk. Cyber threats have increased in this era, where most activities are digitized across all sectors, just like in any other developed nation (Arych & Darcy, 2020). This means that more methods of dealing with risks need to be invented while still considering creativity, hence giving birth to products like cyber insurance. However, notwithstanding growing knowledge about these dangers, companies need to be more careful and willing to take chances, which underlines the importance of effective systems for managing risks (Palsson et al., 2020; Wrede et al., 2020). Therefore, integrating traditional procedures used in managing hazards with digital technologies reflects preparedness levels aimed at minimizing weaknesses against possible attacks besides utilizing gains occasioned by transformation through the Internet. Today's perception of risks, especially those related to computers, can be seen from various angles, including its connection with the current period characterized by the widespread use of technology, the digital age. Thus, other words also show the relationship between these three terms: Cyber Insurance, Risk Aversion, and Digital Transformation Risk Management.

Cluster III (Keywords- Blockchain, Big data, Business model, Digitalization, Insurtech, Insurance industry).

The convergence of blockchain technology, big data analytics, business model innovation, digitization, Insurtech, and the insurance industry is not just a change but a positive transformation that is reshaping the sector. The use of distributed ledger technology (Amponsah et al., 2022), as well as the analysis of vast amounts of information in insurance processes such as underwriting (Grima et al., 2021), claims processing, and fraud detection, have led to efficiency gains through increased transparency. Digitalization is not just a challenge but an opportunity to change how traditional insurers work and create Insurtech—new types of organizations that respond to evolving customer needs and preferences in the digital age with state-of-the-art business models often underpinned by advanced technologies. The insurance industry has not just accepted digital transformation but is increasingly seeing the need to integrate blockchain, big data, and Insurtech in its drive toward broader innovation that enhances customer experience while opening up fresh growth and competitive prospects (Lanfranchi & Grassi, 2021).

Cluster IV (Keywords- Climate change, Crop insurance, Financial literacy, Systemic risk, Index insurance, Reinsurance).

The complex mix of variables like climate change, crop insurance, financial literacy, systemic risks, index insurance, and reinsurance could serve as evidence that the agriculture industry has various factors that influence its financial strength and the ability to avert risks (Islam et al., 2021). The uncertainties arising from climate change impose substantial risks to agricultural production. Hence, food security can only be considered with powerful techniques like crop insurance to insure risks. The performance of these instruments, however, is contingent on farmers' financial literacy, understanding, and proper utilization of these insurance policies (Dougherty et al., 2020). The possibilities of interdependence in agricultural market risks also underline the magnitude of systemic risk management designs in which reinsurance has a crucial role in redistributing and reducing those risks. Index insurance, an adaptation of climate and yield data to land insurance, uses creative methodology to deal with the hardships of insuring against climate risks in agriculture. Consequently, risk management systems must integrate crop insurance, financial literacy programs, systemic risk management, index insurance, and reinsurance mechanisms in order to enhance the resilience of agriculturists and food security during changing climatic conditions (Euphasio & Carvalho, 2020).

Cluster V (Keywords- Adverse selection, decision making, disability insurance, health, insurance demand, Trust, Moral hazard, Machine learning, Risk classification).

The overlap of adverse selection, decision-making, disability insurance, health, demand for insurance, risk management, moral resonance, and machine learning reveals the complexity of processes that shape insurance markets, particularly among health coverage and disability insurance systems (Crocker & Zhu, 2020). Insurers may experience price and risk pool doubts due to adverse selection, which behaviors of individuals having more health hazards in character tend to take out policies. Proper access to health insurance is undoubtedly facilitated by well-established decision-making processes, which consider health status, insurance applications, and even insurance costs for all the products available in the market. Trust is one of the main factors that lay the foundations for the profitability of the insurance market, as it significantly affects the speed at which people reveal information and signs for risk-sharing (Yang et al., 2021). Like many other financial sector actors, insurers may experience a moral hazard that results from information disparity and, therefore, can undermine confidence and result in excessive risk-taking behaviors. Machine learning development provides an opportunity to design better risk assessment, which guarantees eliminating adverse selection and moral hazard through using more precise approximation and pricing underwriting models. Insurers may carefully evaluate risks, make their decisions more efficiently, and even tailor their insurance products to the different requirements of insurance holders. Accordingly, joining these mindsets suggests the importance of dueling with behavioral insights, the latest technology, and moral dilemmas for better creation and implementation of insurance markets that offer effectiveness, equity, and sustainability.

Cluster VI (Keywords- Cybersecurity, Governance, Insurance company, Insurance market, Insurance premium, Profitability, Risk, Solvency, Sustainability).

In the age of technology, insurers act in an intricate world that implies several phenomena involving cybersecurity, governance, insurance business, insurance markets, insurance premiums, insurance profitability, risk, solvency, and sustainability. The cybersecurity issue is alarmingly causing sleepless nights for insurance companies due to the growing infiltration of brilliant malware attacks that can successfully penetrate sensitive information, sending operations spiraling down. Implementing proper cybersecurity rules of the game and compliance with stakeholder regulations are the keys to maintaining integrity by insurers and trustworthiness among stakeholders. Effective governance institutions are one of the best ways to ensure that such measures will be in place. Insurance companies will have to adjust their risk pricing policies to model the evolving risk landscape accurately, which can affect insurance companies' pricing and profitability. Manage cyber risk successfully because the financial stability and lasting viability of insurance companies can be affected by significant cyber incidents with substantial financial consequences. Therefore, integrated cybersecurity considerations ought to be part of companies' governance processes and risk assessment to build solidity in the insurance market and the entire insurance industry (Puławska, 2021).

Cluster VII (Keywords- Commerce, Financial markets, Investments, Life insurance, Risk assessment, Risk perception, Stochastic systems)

The equilibrium among trade, financial markets, investments, life insurance, risk assessment, risk perception, and stochastic systems discloses the convulsive relationship between economic activities, risk management, and insurance. Investors' decisions within the business and financial markets face various risks, whether they choose to invest in the domination of management or capital distribution (Kremsner et al., 2020). Life insurance here is frequently a risk mitigation tool, insuring against catastrophic events like death or disability as one of the most common reasons cited for acquiring it. Insurers should build redundant usage of reliable risk assessment methods, which consider stochastic systems and use quantitative and qualitative models. These methods are equally essential techniques to arrive at and determine the costs of risk related to life insurance policies. Moreover, one of the factors that can predetermine whether people want to protect themselves with life insurance is how they see the risk involved in leading to their demise since the probability determines their need for insurance and the types they prefer. Therefore, it is essential to consider both skills when designing the newest life insurance products that employers can use to address the current problems on the market and strengthen financial stability (Palsson et al., 2020).

Cluster VIII (Keywords- Behavioral economics, Health insurance, Healthcare)

Incorporating behavioral economics into the insurance and healthcare sector indicates the complexity of human decisions, healthier insurance coverage, and health results. A behavioral economics perspective, which helps to understand individuals' decisions about health insurance, also offers valuable insights. This means that risk-averse people possess present bias and consider framing effects that can affect insurance enrollment and utilization. Individuals' definitions of behavioral traits must be established to craft insurance plans that correspond with their preferences and create the conditions where they can afford necessary treatments. Health insurance is also vital in funding healthcare costs, motivating providers, and enabling patients to access and use medical services properly. Carriers might inspire new products that apply behavioral economics principles to promote good habits, preventative care, and superior health results (Harrison et al., 2021). Next, the three criteria are using behavioral approaches in healthcare delivery, patient involvement, compliance with treatment programs, and service quality in the healthcare system, which can be improved. Therefore, adding behavioral economics to health insurance and healthcare can result in an improved healthcare system that has improved effectiveness, equity, and fairness, and care for patients' welfare is ensured (Kautish et al., 2021).

4.2 Cocitation Analysis

Cocitation is a method for evaluating the extent of a subject matter with similar articles. If two documents that had earlier been referred to are mentioned jointly in a third reference, they are considered cocites. The level of cocitation between two papers is determined by the number of identical referenced items. The strength of co-citation can be quantified as the level of connection or correlation between publications as seen by the group of writers who cite them (Small, 1973). Highly cocited papers serve as crucial indicators for mapping the interconnections between major themes. By employing cocitation analysis in this study, we were able to uncover the fundamental themes present in the literature on insurance. Fig. 11.5 displays the cocitation analysis of the authors cited. Out of the total number of authors, only 11 matched the criterion, and they provided a minimum of seven citations. The network exhibited the formation of three distinct clusters, which will be elaborated upon in the following discussion:

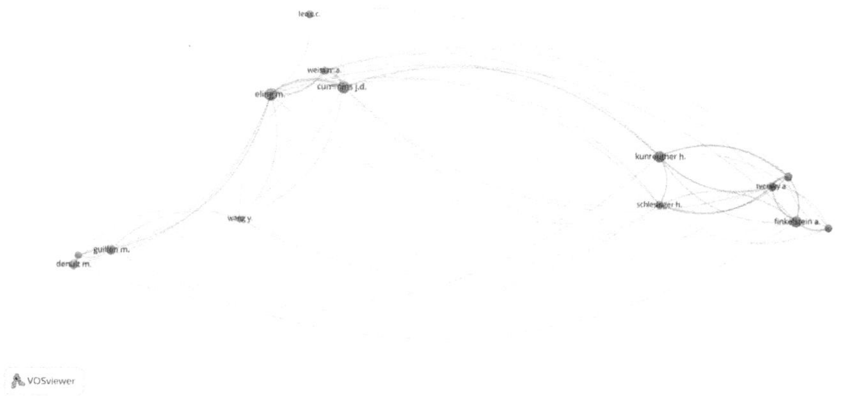

Fig. 11.5. Cocitation Analysis, VOSviewer.

4.2.1 Cluster I

The cocitation analysis uncovers a significant group of authors, namely Finkelstein A., Gruber J., Kahneman D., Kunreuther H., Schlesinger H., and Tversky A., who have made influential contributions to the field where behavioral economics and insurance overlap. Finkelstein and Gruber's study explores the economic consequences of insurance markets, providing insights into consumer behavior and the need for insurance. By their research, the first of the two pioneers in the study of behavioral economics, Kahneman and Tversky, have revealed that these biases and heuristics that are so common in human psychology have a lot to do with how people make decisions in situations involving risk. In the respect that this research has expanded our understanding of consumers' decision-making in terms of insurance choice and has profoundly influenced our comprehension of market mechanisms, the research has furnished us with a remarkable contribution to our learning. Kunreuther and Schlesinger add dimension to the discussion with their points on risk perception, decision-making when the outcome is unclear, and developing insurance products to minimize catastrophic losses. The fact that such renowned scholars are cited collectively at different spots in the booklet reveals very clearly the multidisciplinary nature of insurance research, in which information from economics, psychology, and decision sciences, to mention but just a fraction, come together for an enhanced understanding of the insurance markets, risk management, and their impacts on individuals and society.

4.2.2 Cluster II

The insurance literature cocitation of Cummins J. D., Eling M., Lee C. C., and Weiss M. A. suggests the joint influence these individuals have contributed to the area, namely of insurance economics, risk management, and regulatory studies. Cummins is well-known for the significant part he played in developing the insurance economy's ebb and flow, where he concentrated on such topics as risk modeling, capital performance, and the insurance market structure. Eling's studies are mainly insurance regulation and governance inspections; they explore whether insurers' conduct and stable market depend on it. Lee has a strong background in risk management and insurance portfolio analysis, enabling him/her to implement and manage risks appropriately within the insurance sector. Weiss carries out actuarial science, insurance market trends, and risk assessment. It offers knowledge about the process of pricing, underwriting practices, and upcoming dangers. Furthermore, their cocitation portrays that the two authors together influenced what was considered academic discourse and shaped how several insurance practices were implemented. These have impacted risk management, financial stability, and regulatory policy improvements.

4.2.3 Cluster III

The coreference of the paper contains a paper written by researchers Denuit M., Guillen M., Wang Y., and Wuthrich M. V. within insurance literature, indicating that their influential works have significantly contributed to the areas of Actuarial Science, Risk Modeling, and Insurance analytics. Deneuil, in actuarial mathematics, i.e., the invention of sophisticated models for rating and pooling funds, is known as one of the best hopefuls in the insurance market. Guillen's research specialized in insurance risk management, which is devoted to solving problems by appraising risk, developing various hedging strategies, and allocating proper capital. Besides being an expert in insurance data analysis and machine learning algorithms, Wang is capable of discovering patterns and trends that the naked eye would otherwise miss. He improves the decision-making processes that help with model functions like predictive modeling, risk assessment, and fraud detection in the insurance business. Wuthrich, who is mainly involved in stochastic modeling and risk theory, is regarded by many as the master of this field in insurance and reinsurance applications. This cocitation feeds us with the evidence that the two pioneers share the credibility of broadening the scope of the insurance business to the quantitative side through the development of risk analytics tools. This has been achieved through improved decision-making, risk oversight, and the assurance of order in the market.

4.3 Bibliographic Coupling

Bibliographic coupling is a method for science mapping that is based on the concept that works with a high number of shared references are likely to have comparable topic matter, as proposed by Weinberg in 1974. The analysis is most efficient when performed to a limited timeframe and is concentrated on categorizing publications into thematic clusters based on common references (Zupic & Cater, 2015). Bibliographic coupling, in contrast to co-citation analysis, facilitates the identification of recent and highly specialized publications by categorizing them based on the publications that cite them. As this is a recent snapshot, the analysis can be used as an example of the present condition of the field (Table 11.1; Fig. 11.6).

Table 11.1. Bibliographic Coupling.

Cluster	Cluster Name	Authors	Title	TC
1	Digital Transformation in Insurance: Challenges and Opportunities	"Grima et al. (2021)"	"The Perceived Effectiveness of Blockchain for Digital Operational Risk Resilience in the European Union Insurance Market Sector"	92
		"Riasanow et al. (2021)"	"Core, intertwined, and ecosystem-specific clusters in platform ecosystems: analyzing similarities in the digital transformation of the automotive, blockchain, financial, insurance and IIoT industry"	48
		"Eckert and Osterrieder (2020)"	"How digitalization affects insurance companies: overview and use cases of digital technologies"	31
2	Innovation and Efficiency in Insurance Operations.	"Rawat et al. (2021)"	"Application of machine learning and data visualization techniques for decision support in the insurance sector"	66
		"Volosovych et al. (2021)"	"Transformation of insurance technologies in the context of a pandemic"	37
		"Aslam et al. (2022)"	"Insurance fraud detection: Evidence from artificial intelligence and machine learning"	30

(Continued)

Table 11.1. *(Continued)*

Cluster	Cluster Name	Authors	Title	TC
3	Factors Influencing Insurance Uptake and Adoption	"Dayour et al. (2020)"	"Insurance uptake among small and medium-sized tourism and hospitality enterprises in a resource-scarce environment"	23
		"Belissa et al. (2020)"	"Risk and ambiguity aversion behavior in index-based insurance uptake decisions: Experimental evidence from Ethiopia"	18
		"Lampe and Würtenberger (2019)"	"Loss aversion and the demand for index insurance"	18
4	Insurance Sector Dynamics: Economic Factors and Efficiency.	"Balcilar et al. (2020)"	"Insurance and economic policy uncertainty"	39
		"Zulfiqar et a. (2020)"	"Insurance-Growth Nexus: Aggregation and Disaggregation"	20
		"Noushad et al. (2020)"	"Measuring the managerial efficiency of insurance companies in Saudi Arabia: A data envelopment analysis approach"	18
5	Behavioral Dynamics in Insurance Markets	"Mol et al. (2020)"	"Behavioral motivations for self-insurance under different disaster risk insurance schemes"	24
		"Islam et al. (2021)"	"Discovering dynamic adverse behavior of policyholders in the life insurance industry"	22

Table 11.1. *(Continued)*

Cluster	Cluster Name	Authors	Title	TC
		"Geyer et al. (2019)"	"Asymmetric Information in Automobile Insurance: Evidence From Driving Behavior"	17
6	Market Dynamics and Risk Management in Insurance	"Girardi et al. (2021)"	"Portfolio similarity and asset liquidation in the insurance industry"	27
		"Koijen and Yogo (2018)"	"The Fragility of Market Risk Insurance"	18
		"Harris et al. (2021)"	"Did COVID-19 change life insurance offerings?"	15
7	Trade Credit Insurance Dynamics: Strategic Interactions & Capital Constraints	"Yang et al. (2021)"	"Trade credit insurance: Operational value and contract choice"	26
		"Li et al. (2020)"	"Trade credit insurance in a capital-constrained supply chain"	21
8	Insurance Behavior: Narrow Framing & Digital Finance	"Gottlieb and Mitchell (2015)"	"Narrow Framing and Long-Term Care Insurance"	27
		"Hu et al. (2022)"	"The impact of digital finance on household insurance purchases: evidence from micro data in China"	15

Source: Authors' compilation.

Fig. 11.6. Bibliographic Coupling, VOSviewer.

4.3.1 Cluster I: Digital Transformation in Insurance: Challenges and Opportunities

Grima et al. (2021) analyze the blockchain performance regarding the EU's DORA Act features (Digital et al. Act-DORA). They likened the excellence of a school's educational system to the quality of the stethoscope: reliability, adaptability, and relevance. Riasanow et al. (2021) are willing to study and trace digital transformation paths in different industries and systems, such as the insurance sector. They encompass the grouping of roles and organizations, demonstrating the multifaceted flowing change in digital frameworks and the necessity of a coordinated plan. For example, Eckert and Osterrieder (2020) have helpful tips on how new technologies change insurance business models. As a result, it becomes crucial that insurers develop a comprehensive digital strategy. The several themes covered by these articles are regulatory compliance, technical integration, ecosystem analysis, and strategic planning, which are a part of the digital transformation in the insurance industry.

4.3.2 Cluster II: Innovation and Efficiency in Insurance Operations

Rawat et al. (2021) demonstrate how probabilistic analysis assisted with predictive modeling might be used in optimizing insurance operations. They highlight the need to draw a line between bogus and genuine claims and analyze data sets for underwriter purposes. As Volosovych et al. (2021) argue, the COVID-19 pandemic was among the most significant factors that transformed how the insurance business works, represented mainly by accelerating digitalization's adoption and utilization of InsurTech. Their observation is among the many issues pointed out in the transforming insurance systems and the appearance of the new models and tools for searching for solutions to nuanced problems and fulfilling clients' needs. Even Aslam et al. (2022) can enrich the cluster by exposing a scheme for detecting fraud in the vehicle insurance field. Introducing predictive modeling approaches and feature selection algorithms, they aim to enhance the mitigation of risk and preserve the stability of the running insurance operations. The studies are evident, and the three most vital factors of innovations, data-driven decision-making, and technological improvement in challenging market dynamics with change difficulties for insurance operations are shown by these.

4.3.3 Cluster III: Factors Influencing Insurance Uptake and Adoption

Dayour et al. (2020) studied factors that govern insurance buying for small- and medium-sized travel and hospitality firms (SMTHEs). The assessors reveal that the precipitation of risks, concepts of corporations, insurance, and other nonfinancial risk management strategies were essential. It is a case of index-based insurance (IBI) used by Ethiopian small-scale farmers described by Belissa et al.

(2020). They investigate what motivates managers to move toward IBI, considering risk and uncertainty aversion elements. As per the study, IBI adoption is more functional when risk aversion is higher, but adaptation is less predictable when ambiguity aversion of people is higher. Lampe and Würtenberger (2019) inquired about impeding the adoption of the rainfall index insurance market. Loss aversion and reference dependence are the two hypotheses the scientists consider to be the fundamental issues affecting the observed outcomes. This can be seen in how insurance knowledge causes loss aversion to have lower severity, hindering adoption. The synchronic effect of these articles is that they enable us to arrive at the truth that insurance adoption depends on a complex interplay among many factors. The items that go into such factors are the startling uncertainties, social traits of given companies, prejudiced arrangements in exercise, and calamity insurance comprehension, as well as how each affects the insurance segment and environment.

4.3.4 Cluster VI: Insurance Sector Dynamics: Economic Factors and Efficiency

Balcilar et al. (2020) researched the relationship between economic uncertainty and insurance premium prices in 15 nations. While Zulfiqar et al. (2020) researched the connection between insurance and economic growth, they found no linear relationship between the spare parts. They realize that, on the specific insurance that is nonlife, the economic growth at the general level is stimulated. When analyzing separate types of insurance, the impacts are different for the appraisals that have implications for trade and investment. Noushad and others (2020) undertook a managerial efficiency study in the insurance sector of Saudi Arabia by applying the Data Envelopment Analysis (DEA) technique to evaluate the efficiency of 30 insurance companies. Research shows that the insurance run by multiple companies is more effective in management than the others. Also, it allows you to compare the practices and improve your performance. These contributions enable us to acquire the concept of insurance dynamics and efficiency problems in the insurance sector. The outcome is the core concept of insurance economics and what it entails.

4.3.5 Cluster V: Behavioral Dynamics in Insurance Markets

In their report, Mol et al. (2020) did a real-time field lab experiment to determine the effects of financial bonuses and motivating behavior on self-insurance within different flood insurance policies. We thus grasp the benefits of the study through the lens of moral hazard, advantageous selection, and individual behavior in the markets of natural disasters. Nguyen and Worthington (2021) address the problem of adverse selection in the Australian life insurance market. They provide an innovative solution that employs association rule mining to locate policyholders prone to undertake unfavorable actions. Thus, this approach will be used to surmount the data analysis and the fraudulent claims marking issues. As Geyer et al. (2019) assert, private data revealing where people drive and their driving habits affect bidding, risk, and rates for car insurance. They investigate the role of variable driving behaviors in determining the form of insurance providers' operability and the basis for their operations. Combined, these publications shed light on the strong bond between human failures, financial purposes, and the principles of insurance and the players' attitudes toward that. Finally, it will improve our understanding of the future behavioral effects on the insurance industry.

4.3.6 Cluster VI: Market Dynamics and Risk Management in Insurance

From the perspective of Girardi et al. (2021), the coinsurance members exhibited a level of similarity in selling behavior. Study results indicate that portfolios with similar features are two times as likely to be sold by insurers en masse, particularly in times of varying market activity. Their discoveries become the core for comprehending possible causes of insurance portfolios' upside or downside movements and how they may lead to market instability. Koijen and Yogo (2018) focus on examining variable annuities in their research. They look for which changes insurance providers made to their products and pricing mechanisms based on the history of financial crises and market conditions. Market dynamics of health insurance is the research of the researchers who express the driving power of financial drawbacks and market dominance for the insurance market and the extent of market comprehension. In particular, the researcher's study by Harris et al. (2021) researches what the effects of the COVID-19 pandemic could be on the price and availability of life insurance. With the simplification of these rules into simplified and general ones, the policies implemented for persons at high risk would be terminated, and in particular, demographic groups may have had their policies discontinued. In the same way, examining insurance news articles helps to build our knowledge about insurance market dynamics, the use of insurance risk services by insurers, and the role played by external shocks to insurance pricing and product choices.

4.3.7 Cluster VII: Trade Credit Insurance Dynamics: Strategic Interactions and Capital Constraints

This cluster of articles looks at how Thinks Trade Credit Insurance (TCI) affects the multifaceted and complicated processes of supply chains across the board. The study by Yang et al. (2021) explains the strategic interactions between insurance companies and suppliers. Under this topic, TCI is analyzed regarding resolving cash flow fluctuations and keeping track of the buyers. The text introduces us to the workable and unworkable TCI agreements, thus leaving out whether local suppliers' position can be balanced with the international ones. Noncancelable contracts are based on deductibles that may conflict with regulatory goals, including smoothing and monitoring.

4.3.8 Cluster VIII: Insurance Behavior: Narrow Framing & Digital Finance

The research delimitation 2020, as studied by Gottlieb and Mitchell (2015), suggests the framework of narrowing perspective utility in insurance. Through the broader analysis of the Health and Retirement survey data, which the authors do, they have data that suggest persons with narrow framing attitudes tend to buy long-term care insurance very rarely, compared to the group being studied. This circumstance surpasses even hypocrisy in the hazards of risking being prepared or dealing with the negative consequences of simply picking anything. As a result, it seeks an equally new and original reason for that. Hu et al. (2022) discuss the role of digital finance in acquiring household insurance with their empirical analysis using the China Household Finance Survey, which is from the information of the panel data. Their findings have shown that technology is a valuable tool that the household can use to protect itself from hardships by creating awareness of financial matters, and it also provides easier access to online financial services. Also, the study reveals that digital finance shows more significant changes for less affluent people and those who live in poorer or more remote areas. Health insurance is one of the forms of insurance not embraced by the Amish to prevent dependency on healthcare provided by health insurers. The article advocates digital finance as one, if not more, of the critical drivers behind household insurance decisions, with the latter being firmed up by the well-conducted tests of the former.

4.4 Future Research Agendas

This section deliberates on the future research agendas mined using content analysis of top two cited publications from selected publication period (2020–2024). The "Limitations" and "Scope for future research" sections of these publications were content analyzed to collect a comprehensive list of future research agendas/questions (see Table 11.2).

5. Conclusion

Conclusively, this study utilized an extensive bibliometric analysis to investigate the scope of research in the insurance literature between 2020 and 2024. By conducting keyword cooccurrence analysis, cocitation analysis, and bibliographic coupling, we have identified important clusters of research topics. These clusters include digital transformation, innovation in insurance operations, behavioral dynamics in insurance markets, economic factors influencing insurance, and risk management strategies. These findings emphasize the complex and diverse character of research in the insurance sector, which involves several disciplines such as economics, finance, technology, and risk management.

Table 11.2. Future Scope of the Research.

Authors	Title	TC	Future Research Agendas
Balcilar et al. (2020)	"Insurance and economic policy uncertainty"	39	(1) What is the impact of economic policy uncertainty on insurance markets in various countries and regions, and what are the underlying factors that cause these differences? (2) What are the long-term impacts of variations in economic policy uncertainty on the stability and profitability of insurance markets, and how do insurance companies adjust their tactics over time? (3) What is the impact of economic policy uncertainty on various sectors of the insurance industry, including property and casualty insurance, life insurance, health insurance, and reinsurance, and what are the consequences specific to each sector?
Hombert et al. (2013)	"Can Unemployment Insurance Spur Entrepreneurial Activity? Evidence from France"	32	(1) What is the impact of the accessibility and extent of unemployment insurance on individuals' choices to start their own businesses in France, and what are the underlying factors that drive this connection?

Table 11.2. *(Continued)*

Authors	Title	TC	Future Research Agendas
			(2) What are the enduring consequences of unemployment insurance on the rate of new business establishment, business longevity, and the broader environment of entrepreneurship in France? (3) What is the effect of various unemployment insurance policies, such as those based on duration of benefits, income level, and eligibility requirements, on individuals' likelihood of starting businesses?
Grima et al. (2021)	"The Perceived Effectiveness of Blockchain for Digital Operational Risk Resilience in the European Union Insurance Market Sector"	92	(1) What are the precise operational risks that insurance businesses in the European Union encounter, and how might blockchain technology mitigate these risks to improve operational resilience? (2) What is the impression of insurance sector stakeholders regarding the efficacy of blockchain technology in reducing digital operational risks, and what are the variables that shape their attitudes and opinions toward adopting blockchain?

(Continued)

Table 11.2. *(Continued)*

Authors	Title	TC	Future Research Agendas
			(3) What are the possible obstacles and restrictions linked to the implementation of blockchain-based solutions for enhancing operational risk resilience in the insurance sector, and how may these hindrances be overcome?
Rawat et al. (2021)	"Application of machine learning and data visualization techniques for decision support in the insurance sector"	66	(1) Which particular decision-making tasks in the insurance industry can be enhanced by utilizing machine learning and data visualization techniques? (2) What is the comparative performance of machine learning algorithms against classical statistical methods in insurance decision support?
Eling et al. (2021)	"The impact of artificial intelligence along the insurance value chain and on the insurability of risks"	35	(1) What is the influence of artificial intelligence on various stages of the insurance value chain? (2) How does artificial intelligence affect the ability to insure different types of risks? (3) What is the impact of artificial intelligence on underwriting, claims processing, and risk assessment in the insurance industry?

Table 11.2. *(Continued)*

Authors	Title	TC	Future Research Agendas
Amponsah et al. (2022)	"Improving the Financial Security of National Health Insurance using Cloud-Based Blockchain Technology Application"	30	(1) What are the ways in which cloud-based blockchain technology might improve the financial security of national health insurance systems? (2) The national health insurance systems face distinct issues, and cloud-based blockchain technology can potentially provide solutions to these challenges. (3) What are the ways in which cloud-based blockchain technology enhances openness and accountability in the operations of national health insurance?
Wu and Li (2023)	"Risk preference, interlinked credit and insurance contract and agricultural innovative technology adoption"	15	(1) What is the impact of risk preferences on farmers' decision to adopt agricultural innovation technologies? (2) What is the correlation between interconnected financing and insurance agreements and the acceptance of agricultural new technologies? (3) What is the relationship between farmers' risk choices and their decisions to use technology, including the influence of interwoven credit and insurance contracts?

(Continued)

Table 11.2. *(Continued)*

Authors	Title	TC	Future Research Agendas
Debener et al. (2023)	"Detecting insurance fraud using supervised and unsupervised machine learning"	7	(1) What is the comparative efficacy of supervised machine learning approaches against traditional methods in detecting insurance fraud? (2) The benefits and constraints of employing unsupervised machine learning for identifying insurance fraud are worth considering. (3) How do supervised and unsupervised machine learning algorithms work together to identify various forms of insurance fraud?
Gatzert and Reichel (2022)	"Sustainable investing in the US and European insurance industry: a text mining analysis"	5	(1) What are the differences between US and European insurance companies in their approaches to sustainable investing, as uncovered through text mining analysis? (2) What are the main themes and patterns in sustainable investment methods used by the insurance business in the US and Europe, as determined through text mining? (3) What is the impact of legal frameworks and market conditions on sustainable investment

Table 11.2. *(Continued)*

Authors	Title	TC	Future Research Agendas
			practices in the insurance sectors of the US and Europe, as indicated by text mining analysis?
Fan et al. (2023)	"Catastrophe insurance and flexible planning for supply chain disruption management: a stochastic simulation case study"	4	(1) How does disaster insurance reduce the impact of supply chain disruptions, as shown in a case study using stochastic simulation? (2) What are the main elements that affect the efficiency of disaster insurance in handling supply chain interruptions, as discovered by stochastic simulation analysis? (3) What is the relationship between the use of adaptable planning strategies and the use of catastrophe insurance in improving the ability of supply chains to withstand and recover from major disruptions, as illustrated in the case study?

Source: Authors' compilation.

On the other hand, citation analysis coming from most cited publications determines other issues that continue to require in-depth treatment. The topics in class that I intend to cover thoroughly include the impacts of emergent technology, such as blockchain and AI, on insurance operations, the impact of economic policy uncertainty on the insurance market, and the assessment of the consequences of behavioral dynamics on insurance decision-making. The areas of study I will mention are functional pursuits for thinkers and practitioners who desire to acquire knowledge and solve demanding issues in the insurance industry.

Therefore, this research is essential in that it improves our understanding of the present state of affairs and other relevant literature necessary for those in academia, policymakers, and the insurance industry. The study uses bibliometric methods to not only reveal the relationships between research themes but also to pinpoint areas that will be the subject of other researchers' inquiry in the future. It allows scholars and insurers to understand and address critical issues concerning insurance relationships.

References

Amponsah, A. A., Adekoya, A. F., & Weyori, B. A. (2022). Improving the financial security of national health insurance using cloud-based blockchain technology application. *International Journal of Information Management Data Insights*, *2*(1), 100081. https://doi.org/10.1016/j.jjimei.2022.100081

Arych, M., & Darcy, W. (2020). General trends and competitiveness of Australian life insurance industry. *Journal of International Studies*, *13*(1), 212–233.

Aslam, F., Hunjra, A. I., Ftiti, Z., Louhichi, W., & Shams, T. (2022). Insurance fraud detection: Evidence from artificial intelligence and machine learning. *Research in International Business and Finance*, *62*, 101744. https://doi.org/10.1016/j.ribaf.2022.101744

Balcilar, M., Gupta, R., Lee, C. C., & Olasehinde-Williams, G. (2020). Insurance and economic policy uncertainty. *Research in International Business and Finance*, *54*, 101253.

Bartol, T., Budimir, G., Dekleva-Smrekar, D., Pusnik, M., & Juznic, P. (2014). Assessment of research fields in Scopus and Web of Science in the view of national research evaluation in Slovenia. *Scientometrics*, *98*, 1491–1504.

Bayar, Y., Dan Gavriletea, M., & Danuletiu, D. C. (2021). Does the insurance sector really matter for economic growth? Evidence from central and Eastern European countries. *Journal of Business Economics and Management*, *22*(3), 695–713. https://doi.org/10.3846/jbem.2021.14287

Belissa, T. K., Lensink, R., & Van Asseldonk, M. (2020). Risk and ambiguity aversion behavior in index-based insurance uptake decisions: Experimental evidence from Ethiopia. *Journal of Economic Behavior & Organization*, *180*, 718–730. https://doi.org/10.1016/j.jebo.2019.07.018

Blondel, V. D., Guillaume, J. L., Lambiotte, R., & Lefebvre, E. (2008). Fast unfolding of communities in large networks. *Journal of Statistical Mechanics: Theory and Experiment*, *2008*(10), P10008.

Broadus, R. N. (1987). Toward a definition of "bibliometrics". *Scientometrics*, *12*, 373–379.

Crocker, K. J., & Zhu, N. (2020). The efficiency of voluntary risk classification in insurance markets. *Journal of Risk & Insurance*, *88*(2), 325–350. https://doi.org/10.1111/jori.12326

Dayour, F., Adongo, C. A., & Kimbu, A. N. (2020). Insurance uptake among small and medium-sized tourism and hospitality enterprises in a resource-scarce environment. *Tourism Management Perspectives*, *34*, 100674. https://doi.org/10.1016/j.tmp.2020.100674

Debener, J., Heinke, V., & Kriebel, J. (2023). Detecting insurance fraud using supervised and unsupervised machine learning. *Journal of Risk & Insurance, 90*(3), 743–768. https://doi.org/10.1111/jori.12427

Donthu, N., Kumar, S., Mukherjee, D., Pandey, N., & Lim, W. M. (2021). How to conduct a bibliometric analysis: An overview and guidelines. *Journal of Business Research, 133*, 285–296.

Dougherty, J. P., Flatnes, J. E., Gallenstein, R. A., Miranda, M. J., & Sam, A. G. (2020). Climate change and index insurance demand: Evidence from a framed field experiment in Tanzania. *Journal of Economic Behavior & Organization, 175*, 155–184. https://doi.org/10.1016/j.jebo.2020.04.016

Eckert, C., & Osterrieder, K. (2020). How digitalization affects insurance companies: Overview and use cases of digital technologies. *Journal for the entire insurance science, 109*(5), 333–360. https://doi.org/10.1007/s12297-020-00475-9

Eling, M., Nuessle, D., & Staubli, J. (2021). The impact of artificial intelligence along the insurance value chain and on the insurability of risks. *The Geneva Papers on Risk and Insurance - Issues and Practice, 47*(2), 205–241. https://doi.org/10.1057/s41288-020-00201-7

Euphasio, J. W., & Carvalho, J. V. (2022). Reinsurance and solvency capital: Mitigating insurance companies' ruin probability. *Contemporary Administration Magazine, 26*(1). https://doi.org/10.1590/1982-7849rac2022200191.en

Fan, Y., Schwartz, F., Voß, S., & Woodruff, D. L. (2023). Catastrophe insurance and flexible planning for supply chain disruption management: A stochastic simulation case study. *International Journal of Production Research, 62*(4), 1108–1125. https://doi.org/10.1080/00207543.2023.2176179

Gatzert, N., & Özdil, O. (2024). The impact of dependencies between climate risks on the asset and liability side of non-life insurers. *European Actuarial Journal, 14*(1), 1–19.

Gatzert, N., & Reichel, P. (2022). Sustainable investing in the US and European insurance industry: A text mining analysis. *The Geneva Papers on Risk and Insurance – Issues and Practice, 49*(1), 26–62. https://doi.org/10.1057/s41288-022-00270-w

Geyer, A., Kremslehner, D., & Muermann, A. (2019). Asymmetric information in automobile insurance: Evidence from driving behavior. *Journal of Risk & Insurance, 87*(4), 969–995. https://doi.org/10.1111/jori.12279

Girardi, G., Hanley, K. W., Nikolova, S., Pelizzon, L., & Sherman, M. G. (2021). Portfolio similarity and asset liquidation in the insurance industry. *Journal of Financial Economics, 142*(1), 69–96. https://doi.org/10.1111/jori.12279

Gottlieb, D., & Mitchell, O. S. (2015). Narrow framing and long-term care insurance. *SSRN Electronic Journal*. https://doi.org/10.2139/ssrn.2580488

Grima, S., Kizilkaya, M., Sood, K., & ErdemDelice, M. (2021). The perceived effectiveness of blockchain for digital operational risk resilience in the European Union insurance market sector. *Journal of Risk and Financial Management, 14*(8), 363. https://doi.org/10.3390/jrfm14080363

Harris, T., Yelowitz, A., & Courtemanche, C. (2020). Did COVID-19 change life insurance offerings? https://doi.org/10.3386/w28172

Harrison, G., Morsink, K., & Schneider, M. (2021). Literacy and the quality of index insurance decisions. *The Geneva Risk and Insurance Review, 47*(1), 66–97. https://doi.org/10.1057/s10713-020-00060-1

Hombert, J., Schoar, A., Sraer, D. A., & Thesmar, D. (2013). Can unemployment insurance spur entrepreneurial activity? Evidence from France. *SSRN Electronic Journal*. https://doi.org/10.2139/ssrn.2329357

Hu, X., Wang, Z., & Liu, J. (2022). The impact of digital finance on household insurance purchases: Evidence from micro data in China. *The Geneva Papers on Risk and Insurance – Issues and Practice*, *47*(3), 538–568. https://doi.org/10.1057/s41288-022-00267-5

India Brand Equity Foundation (IBEF). (2024). *Insurance sector*. https://www.ibef.org/industry/insurance-sector-india

Islam, D. I., Rahman, A., Sarker, M. S., Luo, J., & Liang, H. (2021). Factors affecting farmers' willingness to adopt crop insurance to manage disaster risk: Evidence from Bangladesh. *The International Food and Agribusiness Management Review*, *24*(3), 463–480. https://doi.org/10.22434/ifamr2019.0190

Islam, M. R., Liu, S., Biddle, R., Razzak, I., Wang, X., Tilocca, P., & Xu, G. (2021). Discovering dynamic adverse behavior of policyholders in the life insurance industry. *Technological Forecasting and Social Change*, *163*, 120486. https://doi.org/10.1016/j.techfore.2020.120486

Kautish, P., Khare, A., & Sharma, R. (2021). Health insurance policy renewal: An exploration of reputation, performance, and affect to understand customer inertia. *Journal of Marketing Analytics*, *10*(3), 261–278. https://doi.org/10.1057/s41270-021-00134-7

Koijen, R., & Yogo, M. (2018). The fragility of market risk insurance. https://doi.org/10.3386/w24182

Kremsner, S., Steinicke, A., & Szölgyenyi, M. (2020). A deep neural network algorithm for Semilinear elliptic PDEs with applications in insurance mathematics. *Risks*, *8*(4), 136. https://doi.org/10.3390/risks8040136

Lampe, I., & Würtenberger, D. (2019). Loss aversion and the demand for index insurance. *SSRN Electronic Journal*. https://doi.org/10.2139/ssrn.3406641

Lanfranchi, D., & Grassi, L. (2021). Examining insurance companies' use of technology for innovation. *The Geneva Papers on Risk and Insurance - Issues and Practice*, *47*(3), 520–537. https://doi.org/10.1057/s41288-021-00258-y

Li, H., Bi, G., Yuan, X., & Wang, D. (2020). Trade credit insurance in a capital-constrained supply chain. *International Transactions in Operational Research*, *27*(5), 2340–2369. https://doi.org/10.1111/itor.12766

Moher, D., Liberati, A., Tetzlaff, J., Altman, D. G., & PRISMA Group*, T. (2009). Preferred reporting items for systematic reviews and meta-analyses: the PRISMA statement. *Annals of Internal Medicine*, *151*(4), 264–269.

Mol, J. M., Botzen, W. W., & Blasch, J. E. (2020). Behavioral motivations for self-insurance under different disaster risk insurance schemes. *Journal of Economic Behavior & Organization*, *180*, 967–991. https://doi.org/10.1016/j.jebo.2018.12.007

Naushad, M., Faridi, M. R., & Faisal, S. (2020). Measuring the managerial efficiency of insurance companies in Saudi Arabia: A data envelopment analysis approach. *The Journal of Asian Finance, Economics and Business*, *7*(6), 297–304. https://doi.org/10.13106/jafeb.2020.vol7.no6.297

Nguyen, L., & Worthington, A. C. (2021). *Adverse selection in Australian private health insurance*. Available at SSRN: https://ssrn.com/abstract=3884719 or http://dx.doi.org/10.2139/ssrn.3884719

Palsson, K., Gudmundsson, S., & Shetty, S. (2020). Analysis of the impact of cyber events for cyber insurance. *The Geneva Papers on Risk and Insurance – Issues and Practice*, *45*(4), 564–579. https://doi.org/10.1057/s41288-020-00171-w

Puławska, K. (2021). Financial stability of European insurance companies during the COVID-19 pandemic. *Journal of Risk and Financial Management*, *14*(6), 266. https://doi.org/10.3390/jrfm14060266

Rawat, S., Rawat, A., Kumar, D., & Sabitha, A. S. (2021). Application of machine learning and data visualization techniques for decision support in the insurance sector. *International Journal of Information Management Data Insights*, *1*(2), 100012. https://doi.org/10.1016/j.jjimei.2021.100012

Riasanow, T., Jäntgen, L., Hermes, S., Böhm, M., & Krcmar, H. (2021). Core, intertwined, and ecosystem-specific clusters in platform ecosystems: Analyzing similarities in the digital transformation of the automotive, blockchain, financial, insurance and IIoT industry. *Electronic Markets*, *31*(1), 89–104. https://doi.org/10.1007/s12525-020-00407-6

Small, H. (1973). Co-citation in the scientific literature: A new measure of the relationship between two documents. *Journal of the American Society for information Science*, *24*(4), 265–269.

Volosovych, S., Zelenitsa, I., Kondratenko, D., Szymla, W., & Mamchur, R. (2021). Transformation of insurance technologies in the context of a pandemic. *Insurance Markets and Companies*, *12*(1), 1–13. https://doi.org/10.21511/ins.12(1).2021.01

Wrede, D., Stegen, T., & Graf von der Schulenburg, J. (2020). Affirmative and silent cyber coverage in traditional insurance policies: Qualitative content analysis of selected insurance products from the German insurance market. *The Geneva Papers on Risk and Insurance - Issues and Practice*, *45*(4), 657–689. https://doi.org/10.1057/s41288-020-00183-6

Wu, H., & Li, J. (2023). Risk preference, interlinked credit and insurance contract and agricultural innovative technology adoption. *Journal of Innovation & Knowledge*, *8*(1), 100282. https://doi.org/10.1016/j.jik.2022.100282

Yang, S. A., Bakshi, N., & Chen, C. J. (2021). Trade credit insurance: Operational value and contract choice. *Management Science*, *67*(2), 875–891. https://doi.org/10.1287/mnsc.2019.3571

Zulfiqar, U., Mohy-Ul-Din, S., Abu-Rumman, A., Al-Shraáh, A. E., & Ahmed, I. (2020). Insurance-growth nexus: Aggregation and disaggregation. *The Journal of Asian Finance, Economics and Business*, *7*(12), 665–675. https://doi.org/10.13106/jafeb.2020.vol7.no12.665

Zupic, I., & Čater, T. (2015). Bibliometric methods in management and organization. *Organizational Research Methods*, *18*(3), 429–472.

Chapter 12

Transformative Data Practices in the Insurance Industry: Addressing Benefits, Challenges, Exploring Emerging Trends, and Utilizing Advanced Technologies

Swati Gupta[a], *Navpreet Kaur Sidhu*[a] *and Dixit Kalra*[b]

[a]Chitkara University, India
[b]Chandigarh University, India

Abstract

Purpose: Disruptive technologies are transforming the insurance market, affecting individuals' and organizations' behavior and adaptability. Effective data utilization has become critical to success in the dynamic insurance sector.

Design/Methodology/Approach: The current research utilized electronic Scopus databases to include all pertinent prior studies. Employing cutting-edge technology, highlighting benefits, resolving challenges, identifying emerging trends, and identifying new practices, the study chapter explores how data practices alter the insurance industry.

Findings: The emergence of novel technologies, namely the Internet of Things, mobile devices, blockchains, cryptocurrencies, cloud computing, artificial intelligence, machine learning, and cognitive systems, alter the competitive environment on multiple fronts and at different stages. Insurance companies gain essential insights to enhance their decision-making procedures by addressing data accuracy, integration, and regulatory compliance.

Originality/Value: The overview highlights new developments that are radically changing the evolving domain of the insurance business, including augmented analytics, blockchain, predictive analytics, telematics, and ethical AI. This technology is being used so insurers can improve client happiness, handle risks more effectively, and stay competitive. The insurance industry

Data Alchemy in the Insurance Industry, 183–195

doi:10.1108/978-1-83608-582-920241027

achieves increased efficiency, stimulates innovation, and strategically uses data to strengthen resilience in today's data-centric economy.

Keywords: Data alchemy; Artificial Intelligence; insurance industry; AI-enabled technology; blockchain; Internet of Things

1. Introduction

Artificial Intelligence (AI) has revolutionized consumer services, accelerated previously unheard-of speed and efficiency, and fundamentally changed several sectors (Ananda et al., 2020). These days, AI applications are essential in various industries, such as banking, finance, real estate, logistics, food technology, travel, healthcare, and entertainment. Experts have forecasted that technological innovations, including those in AI, Machine learning (ML), and Big Data, could soon help the insurance industry. Utilizing AI and Big Data-driven technologies holds the potential to save costs, provide novel goods, and provide customers with more individualized and effective services. Investment effectiveness and productivity have increased due to the integration of ML, AI, and financial technology (Ahmed et al., 2022). However, new legal and regulatory issues are brought about by the opportunity that improved data analytics presents for the insurance sector. Significant technical improvements have occurred in the insurance industry, with AI applications—as noted by (Dexe et al., 2021)—playing a pivotal role in enhancing claims processing, pricing methods, and operating procedures. New issues and moral dilemmas are raised by the usage of AI in the insurance industry (Mullins et al., 2021). Younger demographics and administrative and safety personnel working for the government are becoming more aware of AI-driven technology (Kankanamge et al., 2021). Insurers' increased access to customer data might significantly impact the insurance sector. Data collection for risk prediction and pricing has long been a preoccupation of the insurance business, which is data-driven—even before computers were developed. The new advances in Big Data and AI-powered technology tools might bring about previously unheard-of transformation. These technologies facilitate the generation, collection, storage, and processing of enormous volumes of data. They also offer tools for data analysis and learning. Trends that would otherwise be invisible to humans can be identified, and inferences can be made.

AI's development and Ed solution's spread characterize the main factors that contribute to its appropriate use. Now, Machine intelligence (MI) and deep learning algorithms have brought AI systems to a level of complexity that was unthinkable a few years before (Abrardi et al., 2022). However, the new paradigm of modern IT system has not only provided vast amounts of data but also enhanced the computing skills to the limit and so the development and the accuracy of AI applications has become possible (Allam & Dhunny, 2019). Contrary to this, remarkable progress in development of AI has been observed that resulted in rise of different practical applications in a multiple industry. These applications span exercises such as anomaly and pattern detecting, these include: fraud detection, speech recognition, and language generation for a chatbot for instance. Spread of recommendation engines to provide automatic suggestion of products, adoption of image recognition to reinforce public safety (Zhang et al., 2016), and development of automated decision-making systems like robo advice (Faloon & Scherer, 2017) have transformed the insurance industry completely.

AI has been a significant focus for finance, healthcare, manufacturing, and software development for several years (Bughin et al., 2017). According to industry experts, the insurance sector has been less quick to adopt AI compared to other sectors across the globe (Deloitte, 2017). However, there is an expectation that AI will significantly impact the insurance value chain, covering underwriting, claims management, distribution, customer service, and asset management. Hence, insurance executives must comprehend the new technologies fueling this transformation and acknowledge how AI can aid organizations in creating innovative products, extracting valuable insights from emerging data sources, streamlining business operations, and improving customer service.

The pandemic has caused a deceleration in growth across significant sectors in both developed and emerging economies (Akhtaruzzaman et al., 2021). The insurance industry has not been immune to this slowdown. With an increase in the number of claims and the rapid pace of post-COVID-19 recovery, it becomes crucial for the insurance sector to explore the cost–saving benefits of AI applications capable of handling vast amounts of data within this domain. The insurance industry is undergoing a significant transformation driven by the increasing importance of data-driven decision-making. This chapter examines the transformative data practices within the insurance sector, focusing on the benefits, challenges, emerging trends, and the utilization of advanced technologies to drive innovation and efficiency.

2. Benefits That Artificial Intelligence Offers to the Insurance Sector

AI is ready to revolutionize the insurance sector unprecedentedly, benefiting insurers and their clientele. Consumers can anticipate enhanced user experiences and potentially more economical premiums. Insurers stand to streamline operations and potentially introduce AI-driven insurance policies, leading to cost savings. The potential applications of AI are vast, and it is merely a matter of time before these advancements become tangible. In order to remain competitive, the insurance industry must embrace cutting-edge technologies, such as the metaverse, blockchain, ML, robotic process automation, and others (Kahyaoğlu, 2022). Incorporating these latest technologies enhances the efficiency of intricate and laborious insurance procedures. However, integrating these technologies into the existing process is only worthwhile if the adoption of AI in insurance yields tangible benefits (Srivastava, 2023). Let us delve into a few of those via the proposed process displayed in Fig. 12.1.

Fig. 12.1. Proposed Process. *Source:* Author's work.

2.1 Efficient Processing of Claims

One of the significant challenges in the insurance domain is to process insurance claims. It requires agents to meticulously analyze diverse policies and comprehend them in depth to ascertain the appropriate compensation for the customer. AI in insurance automates many such tasks, reducing errors, and expediting claim processing. That is why businesses are increasingly embracing advanced technologies like AI, robotic process automation (RPA), and IoT (Internet of Things) to enhance operational effectiveness. Insurance providers can utilize various IoT devices, such as smart home assistants, fitness trackers, telematics systems, and healthcare wearables, to seamlessly collect vast amounts of data by capitalizing on the growing network connectivity (OECD, 2020). This connectivity helps the insurers maintain a continuous connection with policyholders while obtaining a thorough understanding.

2.2 Evaluating Potential Risks

In olden times we applied the carriers' rules of standard paper works to the applicants, which was a very challenging task. Consequently, they are at high risk of being misjudged once ranked based on the level of their risks and ultimate decision-making is mainly influenced by what they have said as fraudsters never get tired of repeating the same. Therefore, we will mention this issue as well because IoT is growing and now is the matter of better comparing of different solutions with help of high interconnection. Because of that they can deliver more detailed data sets compared with the old ones and those can be full of useful helping information for programmers via ML algorithms. AI integrated with NLP can help insurers to build a verity of sources including nonstructured inputs such as social media and various reports to aid them in the identification of key issues and bolstering their risk evaluation expertise (Owens et al., 2022).

2.3 Identifying and Stopping Fraudulent Activities

The insurance industry has been dominant, the amount of money it has made each year instead of accumulating $1 trillion in premiums. We also realize that when rewards get higher, the risk is also proportionally high. This is why there are numerous cases of fraud related to investing in this industry. Healthcare insurance fraud has an estimate of $40 billion annually and it cost more than $400 as an average for families to get a health insurance with added premiums of another 300 dollars. The move of AI into the insurance sector features a great breakthrough in identification and fraud prevention. The recent development in AI has a capability to recognize suspicious patterns through analyses of the vastly collected datasets and then notify an engineer an instantaneous action on it (Aslam et al., 2022). This function (the capability of insurers) helps doing smooth risk management, minimization of losses, and upholding of the integrity of insurers. AI participation frees insurers of the headache of mitigating fake fraud claims.

2.4 Reporting of Insurance Claims

AI systems can manage autonomously, and the initial notification of loss can be either independent or with minimal human involvement in insurance claims. This includes various tasks such as reporting, routing, triaging, and assigning claims. Chatbots have been crucial in streamlining the claim-reporting process, allowing customers to report incidents conveniently from any location, device, and time (Kumar et al., 2023). AI-powered chatbots efficiently disseminate this information for subsequent processing, making the claim settlement process smooth and effective.

2.5 Handling and Investigating Insurance Claims

AI and ML technologies enabled insurance to gather, sort out, and used data according to business needs, such as claims initiation, approvals, and payments monitoring followed up on revenue tracking (OECD, 2020). By having a blend of applications that are working and meshing in with the technology, it will greatly improve the detection of fraud, which will ultimately reduce the cost and time involved. The AI systems, therefore, work as a medium for insurance companies to carry out their classes of operations, which are now done on a convenient digital platform making the systems and services excellent for the insured customers.

2.6 Enhanced Day-to-Day Operations

AI has caused a paradigm shift in customer service within the insurance sector. The chatbots represent a series of direct methods that initiate processes and seamlessly relay information to subsequent stages without human intervention, ensuring a streamlined, rapid, and error-free process (Nuruzzaman & Hussian, 2020). AI-driven chatbots can suggest complementary products and services based on customer profiles, needs, and past interactions. With the onset of automating repetitive tasks, scalable operations got a boost, enabling human resources to focus on more strategic endeavors.

2.7 Enhanced Estimation of Losses

The evaluation of damages has become notably simpler with the current developments in AI technology, encompassing ML, OCR, and deep learning (Eling et al., 2022). Customers upload an image of the affected item, which enables them to assess the damage's scope swiftly and effectively. These advancements anticipate potential losses and offer invaluable suggestions, especially in the motor insurance industry.

3. Addressing Challenges

Effectively tackling the challenges associated with data alchemy in the insurance sector necessitates a thorough grasp of the distinct barriers insurers encounter when harnessing data to its full potential. By overcoming the following obstacles, insurers can easily unlock the full potential of data alchemy to drive innovation, enhance customer experiences, and stay ahead in an increasingly competitive landscape.

- *Data Quality Assurance:* Insurance firms manage extensive volumes of data, from customer particulars to policy specifics and claims information (Mahanti, 2021). Ensuring this data's accuracy, completeness, and consistency is crucial for reliable analysis and decision-making.

- *Data Integration and Interoperability:* The disparate nature of data sources within insurance organizations often leads to challenges integrating data from various systems and departments. Achieving interoperability and seamless data exchange is essential for understanding risk and opportunity comprehensively (Ahmadi, 2024).
- *Regulatory Compliance and Data Governance:* The insurance sector is subject to stringent regulatory requirements governing data privacy, security, and consumer protection. Adhering to GDPR, HIPAA, and Solvency II regulations requires robust data governance frameworks and compliance mechanisms (Kolding, 2022).
- *Talent Acquisition and Skills Gap:* Building a data-driven culture within insurance organizations necessitates a skilled workforce proficient in data analytics, ML, and other advanced technologies (Khan & Khan, 2023). However, there is a shortage of talent with expertise in these areas, posing a significant challenge for insurers.

Addressing these challenges requires a concerted effort from insurance companies, regulatory bodies, and technology providers to establish robust data governance frameworks, invest in cybersecurity measures, foster a culture of data-driven decision-making, and provide employees with adequate training and development opportunities.

4. Exploring Emerging Trends

The advancements in the insurance industry are so swift that they have caused an upsurge in the fascination of companies to investigate new developments in data manipulation. Data alchemy denotes the transformative method of extracting valuable insights and forecasts from extensive datasets to make the best recommendations (Sharma et al., 2022). Due to the rise of ML algorithms, AI, and advanced analytical methods, insurance firms are delving further into their data stores to reveal concealed patterns, connections, and tendencies to benefit from emerging trends.

- *Predictive Analytics and Machine Learning:* In the past, the advancements made in analytics techniques such as predictive modeling and ML algorithms have been instrumental in revolutionizing underwriting, claims processing process, and risk assessment in the insurance industry (Jones & Sah, 2023). The insurers make more accurate predictions and optimize business outcomes by analyzing historical data patterns and real-time information.
- *Telematics and IoT Integration:* Insurers can collect real-time data on customer behavior, vehicle usage, and property conditions by integrating telematics devices and Internet of Things (IoT) sensors (Kudumula, 2021). This data is invaluable for offering personalized insurance products, managing risks proactively, and enhancing customer engagement, which has made the insurance industry.

- *Blockchain Technology:* Blockchain technology has shown potential for improving transparency, security, and efficiency in insurance operations. Smart contracts powered by blockchain facilitate automated claims processing, fraud detection, and secure data sharing among stakeholders, streamlining processes, and reducing administrative costs (Zhao, 2020). Blockchain allows for secure and transparent storage and sharing of data. Insurance companies are leveraging this technology to revolutionize their operations and incorporating it to record transactions to innovate new business models that facilitate efficient data sharing (Singh et al., 2023). The integration of blockchain into insurance solutions holds promise across various verticals within the insurance sector (Sarrah Pitaliya, 2024).
- *Ethical AI and Responsible Data Usage:* As insurers increasingly rely on AI and ML algorithms for decision-making, ensuring ethical and responsible use of data is paramount (Rajarshi, 2022). Ethical AI frameworks and guidelines help mitigate biases, promote fairness, and uphold consumer trust in algorithmic decision-making processes.

5. Utilizing Advanced Technologies

The insurance industry is growing reliant on advanced technologies to transform its operations and elevate customer satisfaction. When AI, ML, blockchain, and Internet of Things (IoT) devices are efficiently utilized, insurers get streamlined processes, mitigated risks, and improved service delivery (McKinsey, 2010). The insurers scrutinize extensive data sets to refine underwriting decisions, identify fraudulent claims, and customize insurance offerings to meet individual preferences through advanced analytics. It has been a long since real-time data insights from IoT devices like telematics and smart sensors facilitated insurers to provide usage-based policies and proactive services (Gagandeep et al., 2023). Blockchain technology ensures many benefits, such as secure and transparent transactions, expedited claims processing, and reduced administrative overheads (SCOR, 2018). The insurance companies are poised to achieve heightened agility, efficiency, and customer focus as they integrate innovative technologies.

- *Data visualization and Business Intelligence:* (BI) tools offer capabilities for visualizing data and facilitating business insights. Empower insurance professionals to derive actionable insights from complex datasets. Interactive dashboards, visualizations, and reports enable stakeholders to identify trends, assess performance, and make real-time informed decisions. A business intelligence system consolidates data and insights concerning customers, suppliers, competitors, and overall business activities (Rawat et al., 2021). This system enhances strategic and operational planning, providing better control over business indicators and facilitating analysis and optimization of operations. By leveraging this system, businesses can effectively target customers, monitor competitive dynamics, and forecast future trends, thus ensuring successful decision-making and sustainable growth.

- *Cloud Computing and Big Data Analytics:* Leveraging cloud computing infrastructure and big data analytics platforms enables insurance companies to scale their data processing capabilities and extract insights from large volumes of structured and unstructured data. Cloud-based solutions offer flexibility, scalability, and cost-efficiency, driving innovation and agility within organizations (Dahiya et al., 2022).
- *Natural Language Processing (NLP) and Text Analytics:* Natural language processing (NLP) technologies enable insurers to analyze unstructured textual data from customer communications, social media, and other sources (Ly & Wang, 2020). Text analytics tools extract valuable insights, sentiment analysis, and actionable intelligence from unstructured data, enhancing customer service and decision-making processes.

6. Case Studies

Established in 2010, Friendsurance is a licensed insurance broker in Germany, supported by a range of online venture capitalists, including Horizons Ventures, Vantage Fund, e-ventures, the German Start-ups Group, and the ERDP (European et al.). Friendsurance, well-known for being a leader in "social" or "person-to-person" (p2p) insurance, provides auto, household, personal liability, and legal expenditures insurance (Eti et al., 2024). Small groups of policyholders with comparable insurance kinds are formed, either by friends or via the platform. Members can get up to 40% of their premiums back if the group does not make any claims by the end of the year, thanks to a cashback pool funded partly by the group's premiums. The cashback pool is used to resolve claims, which lowers the total amount of accessible cashback. Traditional insurers use partnerships to pay large claims. Peer-to-peer insurance networks encourage group members to behave responsibly, which lowers the number of minor claims and increases membership to increase the pool size (OECD, 2017).

InsPeer is a peer-to-peer (p2p) insurance platform founded in France in 2015. It enables organizations to pool deductibles for future claims. Car, motorbike, and homeowner insurance coverage is offered by InsPeer, which angel investors, Bpifrance, the City of Paris, and Region Ile de France back. Customers might raise deductibles and allocate risks among certain groups to lower rates without changing their insurance contracts. Users organize into tiny groups so members may divide the risk of future claims. Although customers can join several insurance groups, their total responsibility on the site is €1,500, with each participant's liability being restricted to €100 in each group. If there are no claims, InsPeer does not collect fees; if there are, the platform keeps 10% of the insurer's payment. While users can join many insurance groups, their overall liability on the platform is limited to €1,500, with each member's liability being limited to €100 within each group. If a claim is made, InsPeer does not charge fees; if one is, the platform retains 10% of the insurer's payout.

7. Conclusion

The insurance sector is transforming due to changing and developed data practices that allow businesses to take advantage of new possibilities, reduce risks, and provide better customer service. In order to cope with the innovations and competitors, insurers have started using the potential of new technologies like blockchain, IoT, predictive analytics, and ethical AI by tackling issues like data quality, integration, and regulatory compliance. The onset of investing in cutting-edge technology and adopting a data-driven culture help insurance businesses (Eti et al., 2024) to anticipate consumer wants, adjust to changing market dynamics, and prosper in an increasingly digital environment. Using cutting-edge technology, this research study explores transformational data practices in the insurance sector, emphasizing the many advantages, challenges, and rising trends. It is clear from a thorough analysis of the literature and professional opinions that adopting data-driven strategies has transformed business processes, improved client experiences, and spurred innovation in the insurance industry. The rise of Insurtech companies like Friendsurance & InsPeer, the adoption of AI and ML algorithms, the integration of IoT devices for risk monitoring, and the investigation of blockchain for safe data sharing and smart contracts are just a few of the emerging trends that the research has identified as the factors that are influencing the future of data practices in the insurance industry (OECD, 2017).

The main aim is to extract actionable insights from massive volumes of structured and unstructured data and enable insurers to make wise decisions and maintain their competitiveness in a market that is changing quickly; this paper emphasizes the significance of utilizing cutting-edge technologies like big data analytics, predictive modeling, and natural language processing. The insurance business has many opportunities due to the shift toward revolutionary data practices, notwithstanding potential obstacles. Insurers should fully use data to create change, provide better customer service, and prosper in the digital era by embracing innovation, encouraging teamwork, and prioritizing data cybersecurity and ethics.

References

Abrardi, L., Cambini, C., & Rondi, L. (2022). Artificial intelligence, firms and consumer behavior: A survey. *Journal of Economic Surveys*, *36*(4), 969–991.

Ahmadi, S. (2024). A comprehensive study on the integration of big data and AI in the financial industry and its effect on present and future opportunities. *International Journal of Current Science Research and Review*, *7*, 66–74. https://doi.org/10.47191/ijcsrr/V7-i1-07

Ahmed, S., Alshater, M. M., El Ammari, A., & Hammami, H. (2022). Artificial intelligence and machine learning in finance: A bibliometric review. *Research in International Business and Finance*, *61*, 101646.

Akhtaruzzaman, M., Boubaker, S., & Sensoy, A. (2021). Financial contagion during COVID-19 crisis. *Finance Research Letters*. https://doi.org/10.1016/j.frl.2020.101604

Allam, Z., & Dhunny, Z. A. (2019). On big data, artificial intelligence, and smart cities. *Cities*, *89*, 80–91. https://doi.org/10.1016/j.cities.2019.01.032

Ananda, S., Devesh, S., & Al Lawati, A. M. (2020). What factors drive the adoption of digital banking? An empirical study from the perspective of Omani retail banking. *Journal of Financial Services Marketing*, *25*(1–2), 14–24. https://doi.org/10.1057/s41264-020-00072-y

Aslam, F., Hunjra, A. I., Ftiti, Z., Louhichi, W., & Shams, T. (2022). Insurance fraud detection: Evidence from artificial intelligence and machine learning. *Research in International Business and Finance*, *62*, 101744. https://doi.org/10.1016/j.ribaf.2022.101744

Bughin, J., Hazan, E., Ramaswamy, S., Chui, M., Allas, T., Dahlström, P., Henke, N., & Trench, M. (2017). *Artificial intelligence - the next digital frontier?* McKinsey Global Institute. https://www.calpers.ca.gov/docs/board-agendas/201801/full/day1/06-technology-background.pdf

Dahiya, M., Sharma, S., & Grima, S. (2022). Big data analytics application in the Indian insurance sector. https://doi.org/10.1108/978-1-80262-637-720221008

Deloitte. (2017). Artificial intelligence: From mystery to mastery – Unlocking the business value of AI in the insurance industry. https://www2.deloitte.com/de/de/pages/innovation/contents/artificial-intelligence-insurance-industry.html

Dexe, J., Franke, U., & Rad, A. (2021). Transparency and insurance professionals: A Swedish Insurance Practice Attitudes and Future Development study. *The Geneva Papers on Risk and Insurance – Issues and Practice*. https://doi.org/10.1057/s41288-021-00207-9

Eling, M., Nuessle, D., & Staubli, J. (2022). The impact of artificial intelligence on the insurance value chain and the insurability of risks. *The Geneva Papers on Risk and Insurance – Issues and Practice*, *47*, 205–241. https://doi.org/10.1057/s41288-020-00201-7

Eti, S., Dincer, H., Meral, H., Yüksel, S., & Gökalp, Y. (2024). Insurtech in Europe: Identifying the top investment priorities for driving innovation. *Financial Innovation*, *10*. https://doi.org/10.1186/s40854-023-00541-y

Faloon, M., & Scherer, B. (2017). Individualization of robo-advice. *The Journal of Wealth Management*, *20*(1), 30–36. https://doi.org/10.3905/jwm.2017.20.1.030

Gagandeep, Verma, J., & Singh, A. (2023). Analysing the impact of emerging technologies on the existing insurance sector. *The Application of Emerging Technology and Blockchain in the Insurance Industry*, *2023*, 21–28.

Jones, K., & Sah, S. (2023). The implementation of machine learning in the insurance industry with big data analytics. *International Journal of Data Informatics and Intelligent Computing*. *2*(2), 21–38.

Kahyaoğlu, S. B. (Ed.). (2022). *The impact of artificial intelligence on governance, economics, and finance* (Vol. II). Springer Nature.

Kankanamge, N. N., Yigitcanlar, T., & Goonetilleke, A. (2021). Public perceptions on artificial intelligence-driven disaster management: Evidence from Sydney, Melbourne and Brisbane. *Telematics and Informatics*, *65*, 101729. https://doi.org/10.1016/j.tele.2021.101729

Khan, A. A., & Khan, N. A. (2023). *Role of artificial intelligence in life insurance organization: In respect of human resource functions*. https://www.researchgate.net/profile/Noor-Khan-71/publication/373993669_ROLE_OF_ARTIFICIAL_INTELLIGENCE_IN_LIFE_INSURANCE_ORGANIZATION_IN_RESPECT_OF_HUMAN_RESOURCE_FUNCTIONS/links/65081c3d9fdf0c69dfd9160b/ROLE-OF-ARTIFICIAL-INTELLIGENCE-IN-LIFE-INSURANCE-ORGANIZATION-IN-RESPECT-OF-HUMAN-RESOURCE-FUNCTIONS.pdf

Kolding, R. (2022). How AI transforms governance and risk management in insurance. EY Denmark. https://www.ey.com/en_dk/financial-services/how-ai-is-transforming-governance-and-risk-management-in-insurance

Kudumula, C. (2021). Blockchain in insurance industry. *International Journal of Computer Trends and Technology*, *69*(3), 5–9.

Kumar, P., Taneja, S., Özen, E., & Singh, S. (2023). Artificial intelligence and machine learning in insurance: A bibliometric analysis. In *Smart analytics, artificial intelligence, and sustainable performance management in a global digitalised economy* (contemporary studies in economic and financial analysis) (Vol. 110A, pp. 191–202). Emerald Publishing Limited. https://doi.org/10.1108/S1569-37592023000110A010

Ly, A., Uthayasooriyar, B., & Wang, T. (2020). A survey on natural language processing (NLP) and applications in insurance. https://doi.org/10.48550/arXiv.2010.00462

Mahanti, R. (2021). Data governance and compliance. https://doi.org/10.1007/978-981-33-6877-4_5

McKinsey. (2010, March). *The Internet of Things*. www.mckinsey.com/industries/hightech/our-insights/the-internet-of-things

Mullins, N., Forstner, A. J., O'Connell, K. S., Coombes, B., Coleman, J. R. I., Qiao, Z., Als, T. D., Bigdeli, T. B., Børte, S., Bryois, J., Charney, A. W., Drange, O. K., Gandal, M. J., Hagenaars, S. P., Ikeda, M., Kamitaki, N., Kim, M., Krebs, K., Panagiotaropoulou, G., & Andreassen, O. A. (2021). A genome-wide association study of more than 40,000 bipolar disorder cases provides new insights into the underlying biology. *Nature Genetics*, *53*, 817–829. https://doi.org/10.1038/s41588-021-00857-4

Nuruzzaman, M., & Hussain, O. K. (2020). IntelliBot: A dialogue-based chatbot for the insurance industry. *Knowledge-Based Systems*. https://doi.org/10.1016/j.knosys.2020.105810. https://www.sciencedirect.com/science/article/pii/S0950705120301933

OECD. (2017). *Technology and innovation in the insurance sector*. https://www.oecd-ilibrary.org/taxation/oecd-transfer-pricing-guidelines-for-multinational-enterprises-and-tax-administrations-2017_tpg-2017-en

OECD. (2020). *The impact of big data and artificial intelligence (AI) in the insurance sector*. https://search.oecd.org/digital/oecd-digital-economy-outlook-2020-bb167041-en.htm

Owens, E., Sheehan, B., Mullins, M., Cunneen, M., Ressel, J., & Castignani, G. (2022). Explainable Artificial Intelligence (XAI) in insurance. *Risks*, *10*(12), 230. https://doi.org/10.3390/risks10120230

Rajarshi. (2022). *Data ethics in the insurance industry*. https://www.indusnet.co.in/data-ethics-policy-in-the-insurance-industry/

Rawat, S., Rawat, A., Kumar, Dr, & Sabitha, S. (2021). Application of machine learning and data visualization techniques for decision support in the insurance sector. *International Journal of Information Management Data Insights*, *1*, 100012. https://doi.org/10.1016/j.jjimei.2021.100012

Sarrah Pitaliya. (2024). Top 7 Tech trends that will transform the insurance industry in 2024, Radix. https://radixweb.com/blog/insurance-technology-development-trends

SCOR. (2018). *The impact of artificial intelligence on the (re)insurance sector*. SCOR.

Sharma, H., Choudhury, T., & Toe, T. (2022). Machine learning based predictive analytics: A use case in insurance sector. https://doi.org/10.1007/978-3-030-82763-2_14

Singh, A., Sharma, S., Singh, A., & Madaan, G. (2023). *Blockchain: The chain for the changing marketing sphere, blockchain: The chain for the changing marketing sphere*.

Srivastava, S. (2023). AI in insurance – How is artificial intelligence impacting the insurance industry? https://appinventiv.com/blog/ai-in-insurance/

Zhang, Q., Yu, Z., Shi, W., & Zhong, H. (2016). Demo abstract: EVAPS: Edge video analysis for public safety. In *2016 IEEE/ACM Symposium on Edge Computing (SEC)* (pp. 121–122). https://doi.org/10.1109/sec.2016.30

Zhao, L. (2020). The analysis of application, key issues, and the future development trend of blockchain technology in the insurance industry. *American Journal of Industrial and Business Management*, *10*(02), 305–314. https://doi.org/10.4236/ajibm.2020.102019

Chapter 13

Chatbots and Virtual Assistants in Insurance Decision Support

Sonal Purohit[a] *and Rakhi Arora*[b]

[a]Symbiosis Institute of Business Management, India
[b]Chandigarh University, India

Abstract

Purpose: In this chapter, we have theoretically investigated the role of artificial intelligence (AI) supported chatbots and virtual assistants in reshape the decision support systems in insurance industry.
Methodology: For this purpose, we adopted a theoretical approach to investigate the bounded rationality theory, technology acceptance model, and sociotechnical systems theory, and draw insights to comprehend the intersection between AI and insurance ecosystem. These theoretical insights were used to develop a "AI-nudge framework for insurance decision support" that explains the role of AI for nudging the users toward insurance-related informed decision-making.
Findings: It was found that through the user interaction, conversations, sociotechnical system dynamics technology acceptance drivers, the AI can nudge the user toward the use of insurance support systems such as chatbots for informed decision-making. Thus, AI must be integrated to the user interfaces for personalized decision support, ethical considerations, and continuous learning mechanisms. We outlined the future trends and presented the directions for future research in the context of AI-enabled chatbots and virtual assistants for insurance decision support.

Keywords: Artificial intelligence (AI); chatbots; virtual assistants; technologies; decision support; insurance; ethical considerations and implications

Data Alchemy in the Insurance Industry, 197–209

doi:10.1108/978-1-83608-582-920241029

1. Introduction

Insurance industry has witnessed technology advancements that have been crucial to reshaping the industry practices and norms. These advancements have also played a major role in improving the experience of customers. The use of chatbots and virtual assistants in the service-related insurance technologies has modified the way in which customers are engaged with the insurance firms and also the way in which insurance companies provide decision support to the customers (Kumar et al., 2019). Insurance-related decisions are complex and often involve financial security and risk-related considerations along with long-term planning. Since a wide array of insurance products and coverage options are available, it is pertinent to have a decision support system to assist the customers. For this purpose, AI-driven chatbots and virtual assistants have emerged as efficient tools for personalized and tailor made assistance to the customers (Gupta, 2020). Due to these reasons, insurance firms have adopted and integrated the AI-enabled chatbots and virtual assistants to their customer service systems that reflect the evolution of firm–client association as conversational from transactional (Lemon & Verhoef, 2016). Such AI-enabled systems have the efficiency of offering personalized and need-based suggestions to the customers. Through the deployment of AI-enabled chatbots and virtual assistants in insurance services, the possibilities of enhanced customer engagement and satisfaction have been opened.

The AI technology integrates to the sociotechnical systems theory and is based on the natural language processing and machine learning (Orlikowski & Iacono, 2001), and therefore shows the intersection between technology and the social structures within the insurance ecosystem. These conceptual explorations are grounded in decision-support theories. For instance, it is shown in the works of Simon's (1997) on bounded rationality that decisions take by humans have cognitive limitations and their capacity to process the information. These constrains can be mitigated by the AI technologies such as chatbots and virtual assistants as they do not have these limitations. They can thus be used to provide personalized and need based information to the insurance clients (Payne et al., 1993; Tversky & Kahneman, 1996). The technology acceptance model (TAM) proposed by Davis (1989) is also significant in explaining the interaction of users with the AI-enabled systems and their perception toward such systems. TAM has been notably used to explain the adoption of technology and can be used to explain the adoption and use of insurance decision support systems.

Based on this discussion, there are two primary objectives of this chapter. First, to synthesize and critically analyze existing decision support theories within the context of the insurance industry's technological metamorphosis. Second, to illuminate the theoretical underpinnings that inform the adoption, utilization, and impact of chatbots and virtual assistants as instruments of decision support in insurance. Within this theoretical landscape, we propose a comprehensive framework titled "AI-Nudge Framework for Insurance Decision Support." This framework aligns with the essence of our chapter and integrates decision-support theories with the practical application of AI technologies. It positions chatbots and virtual assistants as dynamic catalysts that nudge users toward informed and contextually relevant decisions, thereby optimizing the symbiotic relationship between human intuition and AI-driven assistance. Thus, this chapter offers a foundational base to understand the role and implications of chatbots and virtual assistants in shaping decisions within the insurance domain.

2. Literature Review

The majority of the service sector industries have integrated AI-related technologies such as chatbots and voice assistants into their customer services in order to enhance the experience of customers. In industries such as healthcare, finance, and tourism AI-driven conversational agents have transformed the way in which firm interacts with customers (Hanji et al., 2023; Mehta & Singh, 2022; Jang et al., 2021; Pillai & Sivathanu, 2020; Priya & Sharma, 2023). Still, the applications are not persistent across industries showcasing some commonalities and variations. It is within this broader context that we draw insights applicable to the insurance sector.

AI technologies have slowly emerged as decision support systems. Initially designed to automate routine tasks, AI has evolved to encompass sophisticated functionalities, including natural language processing and machine learning. This evolution reflects a paradigm shift in decision support, propelling it from rule-based systems to adaptive, intelligent interfaces. The emergence of such technologies have showcased how these technologies can impact the interactions with customers and how they can affect their decision-making (Sharma & Sood, 2022). The automation of customer queries, personalized recommendations have been made possible through the deployment of AI-enabled technologies in insurance that have defined the dynamics of customer's engagement with the insurers (Owusu et al., 2023). It has been quite evident in the literature that chatbots and virtual assistants have impacted the conversation between the customer and firm across sectors. However, there is no information on how these technologies affect the adoption of decision support systems in insurance exposing a critical gap. It has been demonstrated in the past that the AI-enabled chatbots and virtual assistants play a vital role in affecting the consumer choices by engaging in a personalized conversation to facilitate decision-making. For instance, Cheng and Jiang (2020) showed the influence of AI-enabled chatbots on consumer experience and purchase-related decisions. Wang et al. (2021) found that AI positively impacts the customer decision-making in areas such as investment and financial planning. Notably, these studies were in the context of e-commerce and financial sectors and despite that these provide valuable insights there is a need to comprehend the applications of AI-enabled chatbots and virtual assistants in insurance industry. This is because the insurance industry is unique with respect to the decision-making, risk assessment, and long-term financial planning. This chapter endeavors to address this gap by synthesizing existing knowledge and offering a focused exploration of AI-driven decision support in the insurance domain.

3. The Landscape of Chatbots and Virtual Assistants in Insurance

The adoption of AI-enabled conversational agents is manifested in the dynamic scenario of insurance. A plethora of leading insurance companies have identified the advantages of implementing the AI-driven technologies and have integrated those to their operations (Gupta, 2020; Riikkinen et al., 2018). These have been implemented in various operational facets such as customer queries handling, recommendation of policies, processing of claims and have therefore become a crucial component of the insurance ecosystem (Zarifis & Cheng, 2023). For instance, the chatbots available on the webpages of these insurance firms can indulge in conversations with the customers and make use of natural language processing to extract information about their needs, preferences, and risk profiles. Based on this information, the chatbot can provide instant quotes for various insurance products, explain coverage details, and suggest policies tailored to the customer's specific requirements (Rajaobelina & Ricard, 2021). As customers explore policy options, they can ask the chatbot questions about coverage terms, conditions, and any specific terms they find confusing. Chatbots respond concisely ensuring that the customers have a thorough understanding of the insurance product. In case of claims, the customers can interact with chatbots for initial guidance. The chatbots explain the claims submission process to the customers and provide real-time updates on the status of the claims (Doultani et al., 2021; Elgargouh et al., 2021; Koetter et al., 2019). Customers seeking to update their policy information can do it through these Chatbots. While the advantages of having integrated chatbots in customer service in insurance seem promising, the challenges are also manifold (Kajwang, 2022). These include concerns over the privacy of data, the presence of bias in the response given by chatbots, and the need for constant training through the datasets. It is crucial to understand these challenges to explicitly understand the scenario and identify areas where research and innovation are required. This backdrop assists in offering a baseline to understand the role of AI as a decision support system for insurance customers.

4. Theoretical Foundations: AI-Nudge Framework

This section discusses the theoretical foundations that support the development of the AI-nudge framework for insurance decision support. These theories elaborate on the complexities of decision-making, AI, and the interplay between human and AI interaction.

4.1 Bounded Rationality Theory

Bounded rationality was proposed by Simon (1997) and serves as a guideline for our framework. This framework sheds light on the limitations of humans' cognitive and decision-making skills. Insurance is a complex product and the decision-making related to insurance involves risk and security concerns. Since AI-enabled chatbots and virtual assistants are not bounded by cognitive limitations, they can act as cognitive extensions and provide suggestions and information that are customized to individual needs.

4.2 Technology Acceptance Theory (TAM)

The TAM model proposed by Davis (1989) serves as another guideline for our framework. TAM focuses on the factors that affect the adoption and behavioral intentions toward a technology by customers. This adoption is based on the user perception and attitudes toward the technology and hence offers insights into the adoption and use of AI-driven decision support systems such as chatbots and virtual assistants. Drawing from TAM we propose perceived ease of use and perceived usefulness of the technology as external variables that shape the attitude of a customer. A positive attitude drives the customers toward the use of AI-driven decision support systems for insurance-related decision-making.

4.3 Sociotechnical System Theories

The sociotechnical system theories (Orlikowski & Iacono, 2001) emphasize the crucial intricacies between technological innovations and social structures. Hence, a fir between the social and technical components is necessary for the success of a system. Taking insights from this theory it can be said that it is not only essential to consider the technical functionalities of the chatbots and virtual assistants but also the social implications and interactions that shape the success of these insurance decision support systems.

We integrate these theories to develop a foundational base of our current study. The insights from these theories provide a dynamic perspective on the adoption, use, and influence of AI-driven conversational agents (chatbots and virtual assistants) in insurance decision support. Bounded rationality theory explains the cognitive limitations of humans for decision-making and guides the exploration of how AI conversational insurance agents can reduce these limitations. TAM offers insights into the factors that affect the adoption and use of these conversational agents. Sociotechnical theories consider the technical and social factors in which these technologies operate and that affect the success of these conversational agents as decision support systems for insurance. The synthesis of these theories helps develop the nudge framework that explains the use and effectiveness of insurance decision support systems.

5. AI-Nudge Framework for Insurance Decision Support

Building upon the theoretical foundations and the existing landscape of AI conversational agents in insurance, the AI-Nudge Framework is designed to elucidate the dynamic interplay between human decision-making, AI technologies, and the unique characteristics of the insurance domain.

5.1 User Interaction

The entry point of an interaction of humans with conversational agents is through the input. The customers input information into the system that is processed by the AI (Koeszegi, 2022) using machine learning and natural language processing to assess the needs, preferences, and queries of the customers. The AI-enabled conversational agent processes the input eliminating the bounded rationality and provides customized information and recommendations to each insurance customer (Mele et al., 2021). Hence, the cognitive limitations to decision-making are eliminated and the decision-support process is initiated. AI conversational agents act as cognitive extensions compensating for the customer's bounded rationality for decision-making.

5.2 AI Conversational Catalyst

By processing the information given by the user and based on the profile of the user, past interactions, and current needs, the AI conversational agents offer personalized recommendations. Thus, by aligning the specific user requirements to the suggestions, the decision support is enhanced by the insurance conversational agent (Carmichael et al., 2022). The conversational agents leverage the natural language processing capabilities to provide clear and understandable information about the terms, conditions, and details of the insurance policy, and therefore transparency is maintained. The virtual assistants facilitate transparent communication, ensuring that customers comprehend the intricacies of insurance offerings. Additionally, the AI system anticipates user needs and offers timely information and suggestions. For instance, the AI may send reminders for policy renewal, and updates based on life changes and critical events thus contributing to proactive decision support (Koetter et al., 2019). Moreover, AI systems constantly learn from user interaction and provide more refined recommendations. The constant learning ensures that the system adapts to the changing customer preferences and industry dynamics. The constant learning also helps to address biases and privacy concerns thus responding to ethical considerations, building trust, and ensuring responsible usage (Leschanowsky et al., 2023). All these factors nudge the customer toward the use of chatbots and virtual assistants as decision support systems for insurance-related decisions.

5.3 Sociotechnical System Dynamics

The effectiveness of AI-driven decision support systems also relies on the sociotechnical ecosystem that encompasses the social structures and organizational dynamics of the insurance industry (Eljaoued et al., 2020; Lee et al., 2022). The effectiveness of chatbots and virtual assistants is influenced by the organizational structure of the insurance company, and the broader regulatory framework impacting the information sharing, privacy, and the expectations of customers of insurance.

5.4 Technology Acceptance

Technology acceptance reflects the perception and engagement of customers with the insurance AI-enabled conversational agents. TAM underscores that the acceptance and use of technology are based on customer perceptions about its usefulness and ease of use. If the customers perceive the decision support system as easy to use or they perceive that it is useful to them then they develop a favorable attitude toward the system and accept it (Baroni et al., 2022). Continuous feedback loops and user-centric design ensure that the technology is intuitive, accessible, and aligns with customer preferences, enhancing acceptance and adoption (Gupta et al., 2022).

The AI-nudge framework draws (Fig. 13.1) from the theories to position AI conversational agents as dynamic catalysts, nudging users toward informed, contextually relevant decisions, and optimizing the symbiotic relationship between human intuition and AI-driven assistance within the unique landscape of insurance decision support.

6. Future Trends and Implications

The field of insurance decision assistance is positioned for revolutionary developments as AI technology continues to grow. Using knowledge from the preceding chapters, this section examines new developments in AI technology for insurance decision support.

6.1 Advanced Natural Language Processing (NLP)

Natural language processing advances are expected to enable virtual assistants to interpret and reply to user questions with even more accuracy and contextual understanding in the future of AI-driven decision assistance in the insurance industry (Dubey et al., 2018; Islam et al., 2022). Improved NLP skills would

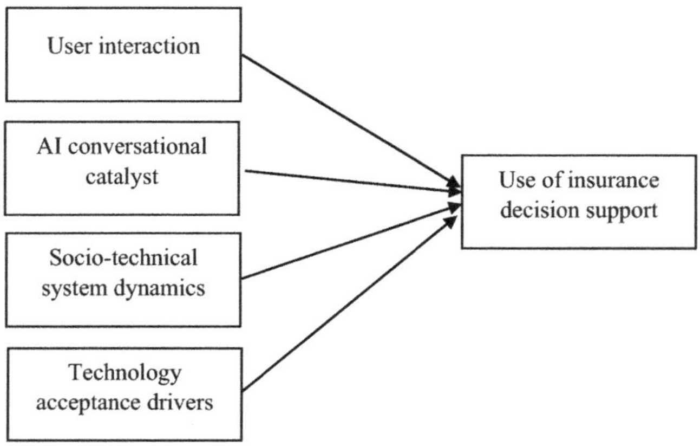

Fig. 13.1. Nudge Framework for Insurance Decision Support.
Source: Created by authors based on literature.

provide more natural and intuitive interactions, resulting in better user–AI conversational agent communication.

6.2 Integration of Predictive Analytics

Predictive analytics integration with AI decision support systems is becoming more and more common. Predictive models are able to foresee client requirements, spot possible dangers, and make proactive suggestions (Jones & Sah, 2023). Risk assessment, claims processing, and customized policy offerings might all be revolutionized by this integration, resulting in more dynamic and data-driven decision-making (Senousy et al., 2018).

6.3 Explainable AI (XAI)

Explainability will probably be given top priority in future AI decision support systems, making sure that user can easily comprehend and see the reasoning behind suggestions made by the AI (Koster et al., 2021; Owens et al., 2023). Explainable AI helps people feel more confident and trustworthy by solving issues with complicated algorithms of "black box" nature (Alfiero et al., 2022; Porrini et al., 2020).

6.4 Human-Centric AI Design

The trend toward human-centric AI design places a strong emphasis on developing systems that give user experience, empathy, and moral considerations first priority. The acceptance and implementation of AI-driven decision support will be greatly influenced by human-centric design concepts, integrating technology with user preferences and values (Pisoni & Díaz-Rodríguez, 2023).

7. Implications for Theory and Practice

7.1 Implications for Theory

The investigation of artificial intelligence in insurance decision support, in conjunction with perspectives derived from theoretical underpinnings and practical considerations, unveils significant ramifications for the theoretical comprehension and pragmatic implementation of decision support systems in the insurance sector. Bounded rationality theory must change to reflect the dynamic nature of AI technology and the mutually reinforcing nature of AI-driven support and human intuition (Natalia, 2022). The complex interplay between AI technology and the social structures inside the insurance ecosystem is clarified by the sociotechnical systems theory (Münch et al., 2022). According to Ciriello et al. (2024), legal frameworks, client expectations, and organizational structures have been affected to a great extent assisted by artificial intelligence. The decision makers get personal information and useful insights of users through artificial intelligence technologies to overcome cognitive biases. The decision-making process has been transformed with the help of AI and resulted rational bias mitigation. The Technology Acceptance Model (TAM) is extensively used by the researchers and becomes relevant to study the perception of users and their interaction with AI decision support systems (Sekgweleo et al., 2017) in future studies.

7.2 Implications for Practice

The integration of chatbots and virtual assistants has led to more conversational customer interaction in using insurance services. AI has a significant impact in improving decision-making and customer satisfaction. Therefore AI assistance should be included strategically in customer interaction by insurance companies and should also provide customized recommendations (Rani, 2021). The insurance advisors should make customer-centric strategy considering their personal information, needs, and objectives using AI technologies. The insurers should also build-up trust with their clients assuring them about data privacy and ethical concerns of AI applications (Loi & Christen, 2021; Mullins et al., 2021). Ethical deployment, transparent algorithm implementation, and user empowerment (Pisoni & Díaz-Rodríguez, 2023; Ho et al., 2020) should be emphasized more in promoting users trust and AI usage. The insurers and practitioners should create a learning set up process for their employees to provide AI-driven decision support to the users by adapting to shifting user preferences, industry dynamics, and regulatory updates.

8. Conclusion

This chapter concludes the revolutionary role of AI in insurance sector focusing on the chatbots and virtual assistants as dynamic decision support catalysts. With the integration of these AI technologies, the customer interaction has become more conversational and able to provide personalized and need-based recommendations. The theoretical frameworks of decision support theories and socio-technical systems are elucidated by relationship between AI developments and the social structures inside the insurance ecosystem. The practical implications of using AI applications are highlighted by decision assistance and ethical considerations. Natural language processing, predictive analytics, and human-centered design are the anticipated future developments in insurance industry. The researchers should further study the ethical implications and user perceptions of AI technologies, as well as the dynamic context of AI acceptance within insurance decision support and the improvement of decision support theories in the AI era. This chapter opens up new avenues for research and innovation at the nexus of artificial intelligence and insurance decision support in addition to the provided basic understanding on the topic.

References

Alfiero, S., Battisti, E., & Hadjielias, E. (2022). Black box technology, usage-based insurance, and prediction of purchase behavior: Evidence from the auto insurance sector. *Technological Forecasting and Social Change*, *183*, 121896.

Baroni, I., Calegari, G. R., Scandolari, D., & Celino, I. (2022). AI-TAM: A model to investigate user acceptance and collaborative intention in human-in-the-loop AI applications. *Human Computation*, *9*(1), 1–21.

Carmichael, L., Poirier, S. M., Coursaris, C. K., Léger, P. M., & Sénécal, S. (2022). Users' information disclosure behaviors during interactions with chatbots: The effect of information disclosure nudges. *Applied Sciences*, *12*(24), 12660.

Cheng, Y., & Jiang, H. (2020). How do AI-driven chatbots impact user experience? Examining gratifications, perceived privacy risk, satisfaction, loyalty, and continued use. *Journal of Broadcasting & Electronic Media*, *64*(4), 592–614.

Ciriello, R. F., Richter, A., & Mathiassen, L. (2024). Emergence of creativity in IS development teams: A socio-technical systems perspective. *International Journal of Information Management*, *74*, 102698.

Davis, F. D. (1989). Perceived usefulness, perceived ease of use, and user acceptance of information technology. *MIS Quarterly*, *13*, 319–340.

Doultani, M., Bhagchandani, J., Lalwani, S., Palsule, M., & Sahoo, A. (2021, May). Smart underwriting-A personalised virtual agent. In *2021 5th International Conference on Intelligent Computing and Control Systems (ICICCS)* (pp. 1762–1767). IEEE.

Dubey, A., Parida, T., Birajdar, A., Prajapati, A. K., & Rane, S. (2018, April). Smart underwriting system: An intelligent decision support system for insurance approval & risk assessment. In *2018 3rd International Conference for Convergence in Technology (I2CT)* (pp. 1–6). IEEE.

Elgargouh, Y., Demraoui, L., Chbihi, R., & Behja, H. (2021, June). Motor claims processing: Digital solutions review and assessment. In *2020 6th IEEE Congress on Information Science and Technology (CiSt)* (pp. 42–47). IEEE.

Eljaoued, W., Yahia, N. B., & Saoud, N. B. B. (2020). A Qualitative-quantitative resilience assessment approach for socio-technical systems. *Procedia Computer Science*, *176*, 2625–2634.

Gupta, R. (2020). Artificial intelligence (AI) in insurance: A futuristic approach. *Shodh Drishti*, *11*(8), 6–10.

Gupta, S., Ghardallou, W., Pandey, D. K., & Sahu, G. P. (2022). Artificial intelligence adoption in the insurance industry: Evidence using the technology–organization–environment framework. *Research in International Business and Finance*, *63*, 101757.

Hanji, S. V., Navalgund, N., Ingalagi, S., Desai, S., & Hanji, S. S. (2023, February). Adoption of AI Chatbots in travel and tourism services. In *International Congress on Information and Communication Technology* (pp. 713–727). Springer Nature Singapore.

Ho, C. W., Ali, J., & Caals, K. (2020). Ensuring trustworthy use of artificial intelligence and big data analytics in health insurance. *Bulletin of the World Health Organization*, *98*(4), 263.

Islam, M. R., Razzak, I., Wang, X., Tilocca, P., & Xu, G. (2022). Natural language interactions enhanced by data visualization to explore insurance claims and manage risk. *Annals of Operations Research*, 1–19. https://doi.org/10.1007/s10479-021-04465-7

Jang, M., Jung, Y., & Kim, S. (2021). Investigating managers' understanding of chatbots in the Korean financial industry. *Computers in Human Behavior, 120*, 106747.

Jones, K. I., & Sah, S. (2023). The implementation of machine learning in the insurance industry with big data analytics. *International Journal of Data Informatics and Intelligent Computing, 2*(2), 21–38.

Kajwang, B. (2022). Insurance Opportunities and challenges in an artificial intelligence society. *European Journal of Technology, 6*(3), 15–25.

Koeszegi, S. T. (2022). Automated decision systems: Why human autonomy is at stake. *Collective Decisions: Theory, Algorithms and Decision Support Systems, 392*, 155–169.

Koetter, F., Blohm, M., Drawehn, J., Kochanowski, M., Goetzer, J., Graziotin, D., & Wagner, S. (2019). Conversational agents for insurance companies: From theory to practice. In *Agents and Artificial Intelligence: 11th International Conference, ICAART 2019, Prague, Czech Republic, February 19–21, 2019, Revised Selected Papers 11* (pp. 338–362). Springer International Publishing.

Koster, O., Kosman, R., & Visser, J. (2021, August). A checklist for explainable AI in the insurance domain. In *International Conference on the Quality of Information and Communications Technology* (pp. 446–456). Springer International Publishing.

Kumar, N., Srivastava, J. D., & Bisht, H. (2019). Artificial intelligence in insurance sector. *Journal of the Gujarat Research Society, 21*(7), 79–91.

Lee, J., Kim, K., Kim, J., & Hwang, J. (2022). The relationship between shared mobility and regulation in South Korea: A system dynamics approach from the socio-technical transitions perspective. *Technovation, 109*, 102327.

Lemon, K. N., & Verhoef, P. C. (2016). Understanding customer experience throughout the customer journey. *Journal of Marketing, 80*(6), 69–96.

Leschanowsky, A., Popp, B., & Peters, N. (2023). Debiasing Strategies for conversational AI: Improving privacy and security decision-making. *Digital Society, 2*(3), 34.

Loi, M., & Christen, M. (2021). Choosing how to discriminate: Navigating ethical trade-offs in fair algorithmic design for the insurance sector. *Philosophy & Technology, 34*, 967–992.

Mehta, D., & Singh, S. (2022, December). Medical insurance virtual assistant: Vaidya. In *2022 5th International Conference on Contemporary Computing and Informatics (IC3I)* (pp. 584–589). IEEE.

Mele, C., Spena, T. R., Kaartemo, V., & Marzullo, M. L. (2021). Smart nudging: How cognitive technologies enable choice architectures for value co-creation. *Journal of Business Research, 129*, 949–960.

Mullins, M., Holland, C. P., & Cunneen, M. (2021). Creating ethics guidelines for artificial intelligence and big data analytics customers: The case of the consumer European insurance market. *Patterns, 2*(10), 100362.

Münch, C., Marx, E., Benz, L., Hartmann, E., & Matzner, M. (2022). Capabilities of digital servitization: Evidence from the socio-technical systems theory. *Technological Forecasting and Social Change, 176*, 121361.

Natalia, I. G. (2022). Assessing the rationality of life insurance behavior amid economic uncertainty. *Top Academic Journal of Economics and Statistics*, *7*(4), 1–11.

Orlikowski, W. J., & Iacono, C. S. (2001). Research commentary: Desperately seeking the "IT" in IT research—a call to theorizing the IT artifact. *Information Systems Research*, *12*(2), 121–134.

Owens, E., Sheehan, B., Mullins, M., Cunneen, M., Ressel, J., & Castignani, G. (2022). Explainable artificial intelligence (xai) in insurance. *Risks*, *10*(12), 230–241.

Owusu, P. K., Nortey, D. N. N., Koffie-Ocloo, D., &Afriyie, G. O. (2023, December). Evaluating customer satisfaction with AI chatbot interactions in the Ghanaian insurance industry: Focusing on Star Assurance Ltd. In *Conference Proceedings* edited by (p. 43). Global trends in IT, Management & Governance in e-World (e-MIG 2023), University of Kwazulu-Natal, South Africa and Open University, Mauritius.

Payne, J. W., Bettman, J. R., & Johnson, E. J. (1993). *The adaptive decision maker*. Cambridge University Press.

Pillai, R., & Sivathanu, B. (2020). Adoption of AI-based chatbots for hospitality and tourism. *International Journal of Contemporary Hospitality Management*, *32*(10), 3199–3226.

Pisoni, G., & Díaz-Rodríguez, N. (2023). Responsible and human centric AI-based insurance advisors. *Information Processing & Management*, *60*(3), 103273.

Porrini, D., Fusco, G., & Magazzino, C. (2020). Black boxes and market efficiency: The effect on premiums in the Italian motor-vehicle insurance market. *European Journal of Law and Economics*, *49*, 455–472.

Priya, B., & Sharma, V. (2023). Exploring users' adoption intentions of intelligent virtual assistants in financial services: An anthropomorphic perspectives and socio-psychological perspectives. *Computers in Human Behavior*, *148*, 107912.

Rajaobelina, L., & Ricard, L. (2021). Classifying potential users of live chat services and chatbots. *Journal of Financial Services Marketing*, *26*, 81–94.

Rani, A. (2021). Multi Criteria Decision Making (MCDM) based preference elicitation framework for life insurance recommendation system. *Turkish Journal of Computer and Mathematics Education (TURCOMAT)*, *12*(2), 1848–1858.

Riikkinen, M., Saarijärvi, H., Sarlin, P., & Lähteenmäki, I. (2018). Using artificial intelligence to create value in insurance. *International Journal of Bank Marketing*, *36*(6), 1145–1168.

Sekgweleo, T., Makovhololo, P., & Iyamu, T. (2017). The connectedness in selecting socio-technical theory to underpin information systems studies. *Journal of Contemporary Management*, *14*(1), 1097–1117.

Senousy, Y. M. B., Mohamed, N. E. K., & Riad, A. E. D. M. (2018). Recent trends in big data analytics towards more enhanced insurance business models. *International Journal of Computer Science and Information Security*, *30111817*, 39–45.

Sharma, V., & Sood, D. (2022). The role of artificial intelligence in the insurance industry of India. In *Big data analytics in the insurance market* (pp. 287–297). Emerald Publishing Limited.

Simon, H. A. (1997). *Models of bounded rationality: Empirically grounded economic reason* (Vol. 3). MIT press.

Tversky, A., & Kahneman, D. (1996). On the reality of cognitive illusions. *Psychological Review*, *103*(3), 582–591.

Wang, Q., Saha, K., Gregori, E., Joyner, D., & Goel, A. (2021, May). Towards mutual theory of mind in human-ai interaction: How language reflects what students perceive about a virtual teaching assistant. In *Proceedings of the 2021 CHI Conference on Human Factors in Computing Systems* (pp. 1–14).

Zarifis, A., & Cheng, X. (2023). AI is transforming insurance with five emerging business models. In *Encyclopedia of data Science and machine learning* (pp. 2086–2100). IGI Global.

Chapter 14

Risk Assessment Models for the Health Insurance Sector

Reepu, Pawan Kumar and Mandeep Singh

Chandigarh University, India

Abstract

Purpose: The article discusses the use of risk assessment models in the health insurance sector, aiming to enhance the quality of care provided to individuals by leveraging technologies such as cloud-based platforms and remote medical sensors.
Methodology: The article reviews various papers on the topic, examining studies ranging from the impact of co-insurance in Vietnam to the architecture of e-health systems. It also discusses different models for connecting body sensors to cloud-based systems, emphasizing the importance of algorithm and shared data models (SDMs) for the health and insurance industries.
Findings: Findings highlight the increasing trend of individuals, families, groups, corporate houses and governments leveraging health insurance policies to mitigate risks, even in areas lacking basic primary health facilities. The article underscores the significance of technologies like data mining and machine learning in adding value to the insurance sector.
Practical Implications: The article presents an architecture for health risk analysis monitoring, consisting of multiple layers to ensure effective risk management.
Originality: The interdisciplinary study of merging designs for healthcare and insurance is depicted as an ongoing process aimed at improving overall care quality. The article explores innovative approaches and platforms, showcasing the originality in addressing challenges within the health insurance sector.

Data Alchemy in the Insurance Industry, 211–219

doi:10.1108/978-1-83608-582-920241032

Keywords: Risk assessment; health insurance; cloud-based technology; remote medical sensors; interdisciplinary study; data mining; machine learning; statistical methods; deep learning; architecture

1. Introduction

Universal healthcare systems, imposed by the government by required savings and price controls, are prevalent in most nations. Furthermore, private insurers offer additional coverage for people. Nevertheless, these insurers are prohibited from limiting basic health benefits or imposing higher premiums on them. By utilizing cloud-based technologies and remote medical sensors, insurers may more efficiently evaluate risks and monitor clients' health behaviors. Additionally, several insurance providers offer initiatives that encourage individuals to adopt healthy habits and work in partnership with wellness facilities. The ongoing interdisciplinary project focuses on integrating healthcare and insurance designs to enhance the overall quality of care for individuals.

2. A Literature Review

Anderson et al. (2012) explicitly examines the consequence of coverage on the usage of medical services among young individuals who become uninsured as an outcome of old out of their parents' protection policies. Nguyen and Connelly (2017) conducted a logical thinking to examine the effects of co-insurance using a quasi-natural experiment referred to as the "QaziNatural" experiment. B. Farahani and Aliee (2019) presents an architectural framework for constructing an e-health system. The authors of the study advocate for a layered strategy in constructing an e-health system, as depicted in the provided architecture diagram. S. Plianbangchang (2018) conducted a systematic assessment on the existing limitations of health systems. The main finding of this study is that a health system should encompass a broad range of criteria, including curative and rehabilitative aspects.

3. An Unified Wellness Insurance Model

Human body sensors are connected to insurance and medical organizations through wired Ethernet cables as shown in Fig. 14.1, which is beneficial for immobilized individuals in hospitals or at home. However, this setup lacks mobility. It can be suitable for patients in high-risk situations who require constant monitoring by a team of physicians remotely connected through the cloud. Remote patient monitoring includes devices like glucose meters and blood pressure monitors, utilizing technology from the 1970s and 1980s when micro-controllers were connected via Ethernet without the need for radio connections.

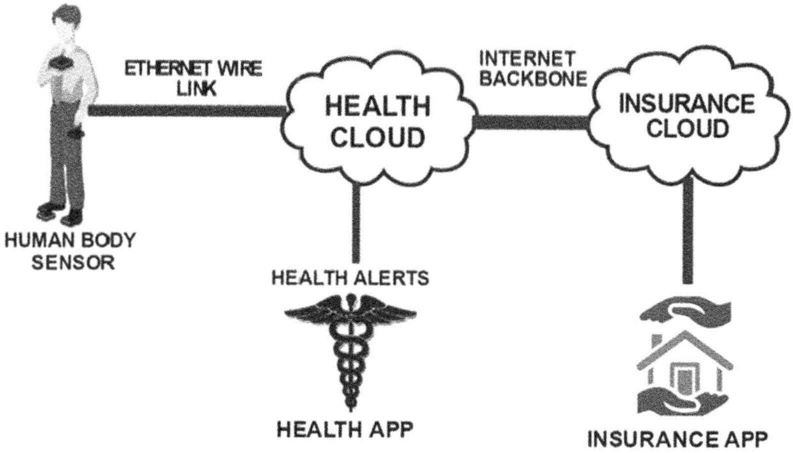

Fig. 14.1. Physical Structure Sensor to Cloud act Over LAN. *Source:* Own.

4. A Physical Structure Sensor to Cloud Act via the Wireless Tie Structure

This text discusses the connection between medical sensors and cellular communication infrastructure as mentioned Fig. 14.2. The goal is to connect wellness and protection clouds, but a connected vesture medical detector is needed. A radio

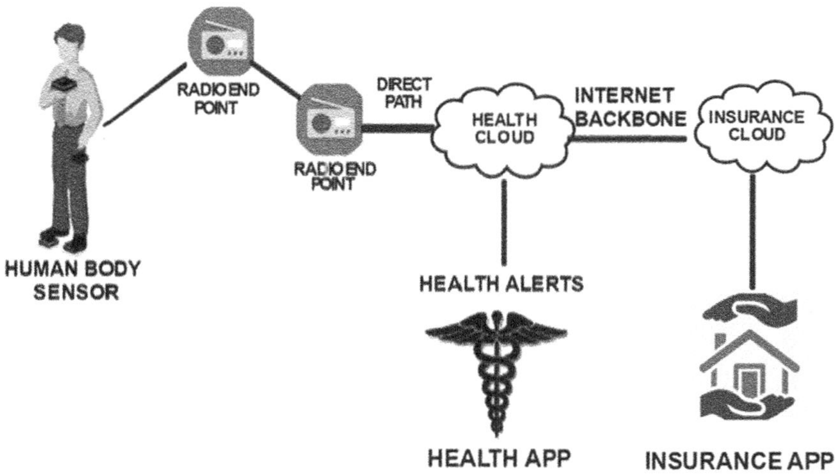

Fig. 14.2. Physical Structure Sensor to Cloud Act via the Wireless Tie Structure. *Source:* Own.

linkup sender is also necessary, which requires a lot of energy. Having a good power source is important for these systems to work well.

5. A Physical Structure Sensor to Long Wireless Linkage Structure

Fig. 14.3 shows wireless body sensors connected radio links. These networks are cost-effective but have limited coverage due to obstacles, making them unsuitable for larger spaces or complex environments. However, they are valuable for monitoring health metrics in real-time and providing critical data to clinicians and individuals for better health outcomes.

Models and platforms in health and insurance rely on algorithms and SDMs. The common risk model uses shared risk indicators for calculations. Progress in fog/edge technology is crucial. Companies can now determine costs more precisely, avoiding unjust premiums for healthy individuals. Computing health hazards is difficult, especially with new diseases emerging (Gomez et al., 2012; Qiu et al., 2017; Ryckaert et al., 2005).

Risk insurance is a way to protect yourself from financial loss due to unexpected events. There are two types of risk insurance: wellness and sickness. Wellness insurance helps you maintain your health by providing incentives for healthy behavior, which reduces the risk of getting sick. Sickness insurance, on the other hand, transfers responsibility for healthcare costs to a third party if you do become ill.

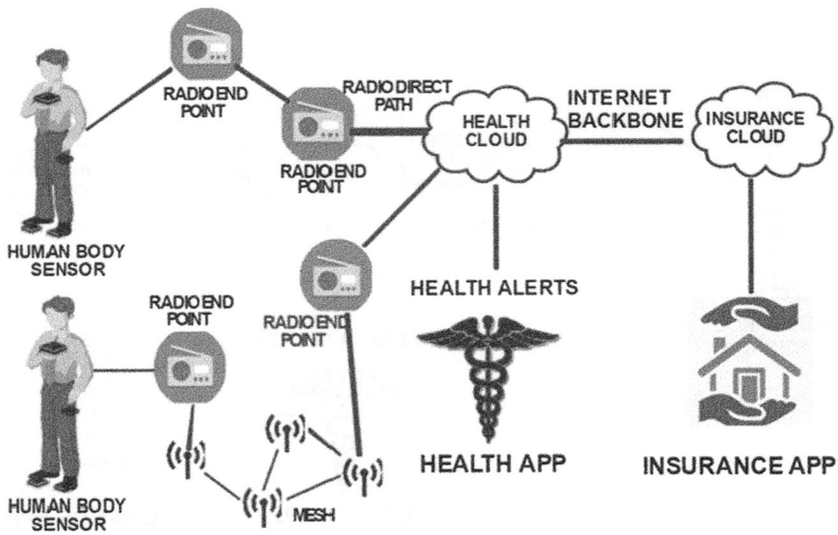

Fig. 14.3. Wireless Communication Bridge Model. *Source:* Own.

Governments and corporations are increasingly using risk insurance as a way to manage potential losses. Health insurance policies are being introduced in areas where basic healthcare facilities may not be available, ensuring that people have access to medical care when they need it.

Innovation in risk insurance relies on new technologies like data mining and machine learning. These tools help enhance the value of policies by creating SDMs between healthcare organizations and insurers. This means that both parties can work together more effectively to reduce risks and improve outcomes for patients.

Overall, risk insurance is an important tool for managing potential financial losses due to unexpected events like illness or injury. By choosing the right type of policy and working with trusted partners who use innovative technology solutions, individuals can ensure that they receive high-quality care while minimizing their exposure to financial risks associated with healthcare expenses.

Applied mathematics methodology is a form of data analysis that utilize various measures such as mean, median, mode, standard deviations, interquartile ranges, and distance formulas to depict and illustrate datasets. As shown in Fig. 14.4, machine learning is the process of instructing machines through observed data to automate tasks in real-world interactions. Active learning entails an iterative approach to acquiring new knowledge by labeling small datasets which leads to labeling larger ones. This is particularly beneficial when skilled labor is scarce or expensive. Deep learning algorithms can be utilized when domain experts are limited or when there is too much data for manual analysis. Transfer learning involves reusing acquired knowledge from similar problems to solve new ones efficiently and speedily. Lastly, a hybrid methodology may entail combining multiple machine learning and statistical methods to produce a stable and effective solution for automated tasks.

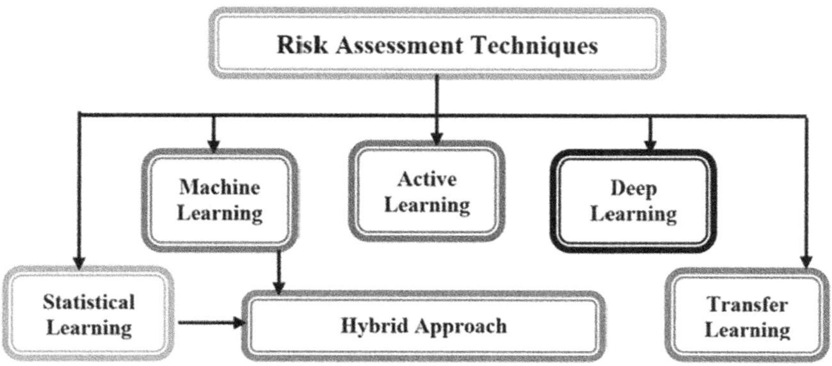

Fig. 14.4. Methods and Approaches for Risk Modeling. *Source:* Own.

The acknowledged discipline belongs to aggregate layers as shown in Fig. 14.5 above. The wearable device authentication process is the first layer of this system, which allows for machine-to-machine validation and user configurable control board. This change connected and radio devices to transaction information and act tasks independent. The second level centering on configuring all detector devices to a popular level for ability, with data being stock in a database incorporate raw data gathered from assorted geolocation detector devices.

In the third layer, health data such as Birth Age, Weight, Height, Visceral Fat, Body Age, Body Mass Index, Blood Pressure, Sugar Fasting, Sugar Post Prandial, Pulse, Waist and other fitness/medical/insurance parameters are stored. This stored data is then linked to insurance companies for analysis.

The fourth layer regard grouping system and communications protocol incidental to the transaction of detector data with the protection industry, which are practical to examine whether the capable is entering a high class of risk in terms of their illness/fitness level.

Overall, this system aims to provide a comprehensive approach to wearable device monitoring by ensuring proper authentication, interoperability between devices, storage of health-related data, analysis of potential risks based on that data, and computation of relevant risk factors using advanced statistical techniques.

6. Machine Learning Modeling

When it comes to machine learning carving for health risk assessment, it is crucial to identify and select relevant features while dropping those that do not affect a person's risk. In the following section, we will delve into the process of selecting risk indicators and applying them to both binary class and multiclass machine learning modeling.

To guarantee quality in device learning, dataset quality is paramount. This quality is determined by position and attribute categories. To select appropriate characteristic, two techniques were used: Pearson correlation to identify attribute association and Medical Relevancy Test to score risk relevance.

In conducting preliminary analysis of the dataset, it was determined that all risk factors have a nonlinear nature. This was validated by moving curved shape just functions using cause and perceptive that none of the comparison followed a linear line graph ($y = mx + c$). Instead, the shape of distribution indicated that they were likely to follow a quadratic curve or higher degree of polynomial.

To derive equations from real-time datasets with missing values or outliers present, missing value treatment and outlier analysis were conducted. Rows with missing or erratic values were eliminated from consideration (Bennasar et al., 2015).

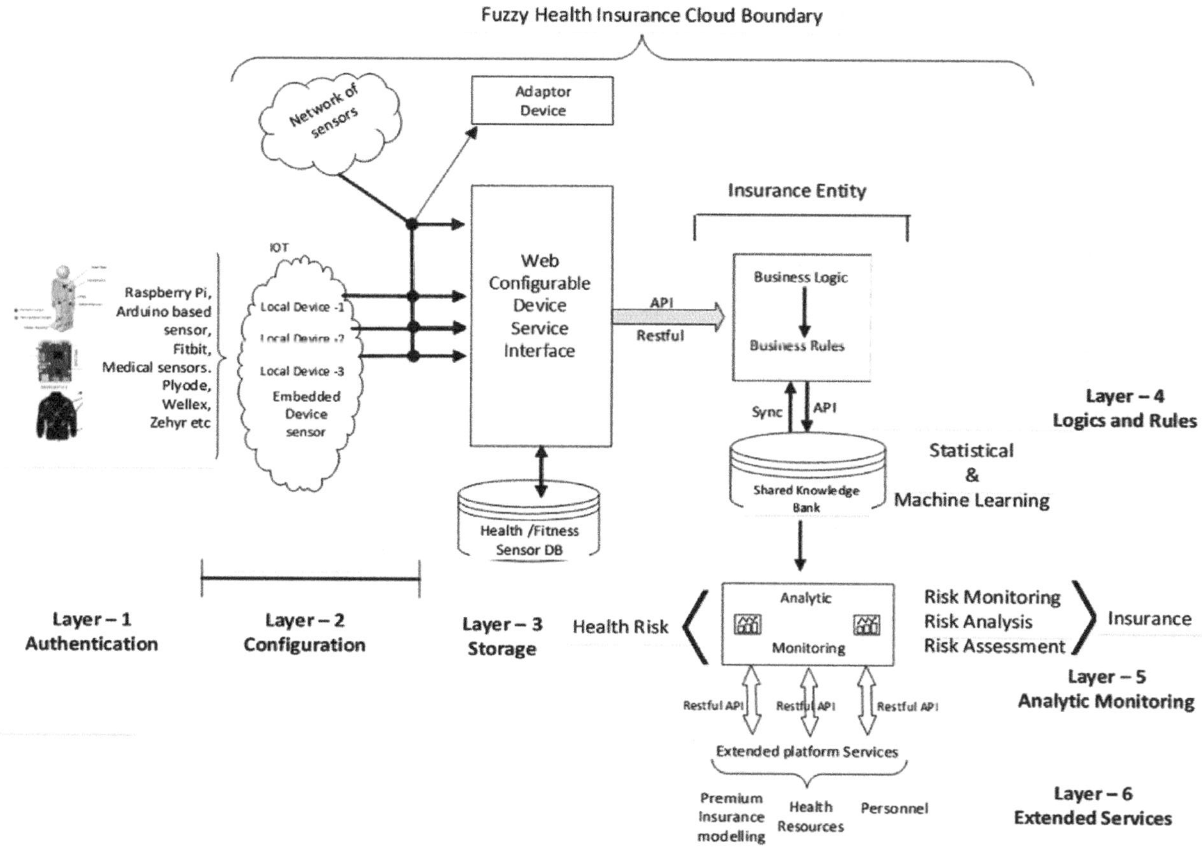

Fig. 14.5. Discipline for Wellness Risk Investigation Observation. *Source:* Own.

7. Discussion

When analyzing data, it is important to understand the correlation between variables. Group A has negative correlation values, indicating that when one variable increases, the other may decrease. This suggests that these variables are inversely related and can be useful in determining cause and effect relationships.

Group C has a correlation value of 0.1–0.5, indicating a strong positive association but not necessarily a cause. It is important to note that inconsistencies may occur in the correlation matrix when it is mathematically impossible to realize a value.

Moving on to Groups D and E, we see higher correlation values between variables. Group D has a correlation value between 0.51 and 0.82, while Group E has a value between 0.83 and 0.89, indicating high dependency between variables. These groups suggest a strong relationship between variables where one variable can be used to predict or explain changes in the other.

It is also important to consider the direction of the relationship when analyzing correlations in data sets. The direction can be found in the correlation matrix, but sometimes it is hard to interpret due to partial correlation where variables have partial influence on each other.

In order to predict risks for insurance purposes, it is necessary to find factors that have shared influence on risks and do equation modeling to understand this shared influence.

However, it is important to keep in mind that in real life situations, the correlation coefficient does not necessarily help find the root cause of risks as it may differ from what experts expect and be unreliable in understanding underlying causes of risk involved.

Despite its limitations, one of the main benefits of using correlations when analyzing data is finding groups of similar factors with strong or weak associations that can be grouped using Pearson's r formula for computation. This information can then be used to make informed decisions based on trends found within these groups of data points.

$$r = \frac{N\sum xy - (\sum x)(\sum y)}{\sqrt{\left[N\sum x^2 - (\sum x)^2\right]\left[N\sum y^2 - (\sum y)^2\right]}}$$

8. Conclusion

The research work described employs machine learning modeling as an advancement over traditional statistical methods. The problem initially framed as a regression or trend-finding issue was transformed into a classification problem. This classification approach was explored at two levels:

First Level (Pairwise Risk Variables):

Pairs of risk variables were considered, including:

Existing machine learning methods were tested using the current dataset. Notably, support vector machines (SVMs) emerged as a frequently used method for automating risk classification.

Second Level (Multiple Risk Variables):

Instead of pairwise combinations, multiple risk parameters were employed:

A well-established machine acquisition algorithmic rule was evaluated. Their hyperparameters were tuned using grid search.

Interestingly, K-Nearest Neighbors (KNN) performed best, but its basic algorithm required modifications.

As a result, a modified KNN 120 algorithm (MKNN) was developed based on this feedback.

This research contributes to the field of health risk assessment, particularly in the context of using SVM for health risk insurance assessment. The outcomes of the SVM experiments are discussed in the subsequent chapter on results and validation.

References

Anderson, M., Dobkin, C., & Gross, T. (2012). The effect of health insurance coverage on the use of medical services. *American Economic Journal: Economic Policy*, *4*(3), 1–27.

Bennasar, M., Hicks, Y., & Setchi, R. (2015). Feature selection using joint mutual information maximisation. *Journal of Expert Systems with Applications*, *12*(22), 1–13.

Farahani, M. B., & Aliee, F. S. (2019). Towards collaborative machine learning driven healthcare internet of things. *Proceedings of the ACM International Conference Series*, *6*(14), 134–140.

Gomez, C., Oller, J., & Paradells, J. (2012). Overview and evaluation of bluetooth low energy: An emerging low-power wireless technology. *Journal of Sensors*, *12*(9), 1734–1753.

Nguyen, C., & Connelly, L. B. (2017). Cost-sharing in health insurance and its impact in a developing country-Evidence from a quasi-natural experiment. *Munich Personal RePEc Archive*, *2*(44), 1–46.

Plianbangchang, S. (2018). Universal health coverage (UHC). *Journal of Health Research*, [Online]. https://www.who.int/news-room/factsheets/detail/universal-health-coverage-(uhc)

Qiu, T., Chen, N., Li, K., Qiao, D., & Fu, Z. (2017). Heterogeneous ad hoc networks: Architectures, advances and challenges. *Journal of Ad Hoc Networks*, *55*(6), 143–152.

Ryckaert, J., Desset, C., Fort, A., Badaroglu, M., Heyn, V. D., Wambacq, P., der Plas, G. V., Donnay, S., Poucke, B. V., & Gyselinckx, B. (2005). Ultra-wide-band transmitter for low-power wireless body area networks: Design and evaluation. *Journal of IEEE transactions on circuits and systems I*, *52*(12), 515–525.

Printed and bound by CPI Group (UK) Ltd, Croydon, CR0 4YY

15/09/2026

14962483-0004